WOODBINE WILLIE

An Anglican Incident.
Being some account of the life and times
of
Geoffrey Anketell Studdert Kennedy
poet, prophet, seeker after truth, 1883-1929

By

WILLIAM PURCELL

The prophet is a fool, the spiritual man is mad
Hosea 9 : 7

MOWBRAY
LONDON & OXFORD

ISBN 0 264 66909 6

This paperback edition published 1983 by A. R. Mowbray & Co. Ltd., Saint Thomas House, Becket St., Oxford OX1 1SJ. (First published 1962 by Hodder & Stoughton Ltd.) Printed offset in Great Britain by Thetford Press Ltd., from the original typesetting.

ACKNOWLEDGEMENTS

Acknowledgement is made to the following publishers for their kind permission to quote from their publications: Chatto and Windus Ltd., Faber and Faber Ltd., J. M. Dent & Sons Ltd., John Murray, A. R. Mowbray & Co., and Wm. Collins & Sons.

PREFACE TO THIS EDITION

Woodbine Willie was the name given by thousands of his contemporaries, to Geoffrey Studdert Kennedy, a legendary padre of the first world war, and a notable proclaimer of Christian truth and social justice throughout the troubled twenties which followed. His fame was destined to rise above the smoke of conflict, like one of those Verey lights once used over the trenches of France and Flanders, and then to decline earthwards, with his early death, into darkness again. But he left a glow which shone for a long time upon the retina of many memories. It was the glow of a Christ like love and understanding of human need, combined with a rare ability to make God a reality in a world in which God often seemed notably absent.

In a strange way, Studdert Kennedy is still around. Many of the circumstances in which he proclaimed his message of God's continuing reality and love, are being reproduced as the Western world moves into recession, and where many of the bright economic promises of yesterday remain unfulfilled. The mass unemployment over which he agonised is with us again. The materialistic outlook of his times is with us again. And, with the coming of the nuclear threat, clouds over our world are darker than ever. He was a marvellous communicator, and people listened gladly to what he had to say, in verse and spoken word, on the continuing love of God and of what that means for human life.

What kind of a person was this man that had the love and regard of so many of his day and age, including William Temple and Dick Sheppard? What was his message? How did he manage so brilliantly to get it across? 'Not enough has been written about this great and good man', was the view expressed by Dick Sheppard of St. Martin's in the Field after Studdert Kennedy's death in 1929. This book was an attempt to remedy that deficiency. This edition will do the same thing for another generation.

May 1982   WILLIAM PURCELL

CONTENTS

FOREWORD

"Nor enough has been written about this great and good man."
Such was the opinion of Geoffrey Studdert Kennedy's contemporary, 'Dick' Sheppard, writing in *The Times* just after his
friend's death in 1929. A few months later, however, in the book
G. A. Studdert Kennedy: By His Friends, seven men who had known
and loved him—they included Sheppard himself, as well as
William Temple—collected together some personal remini-
scences—a symposium which has been of much value to the
making of this book. From then until now, that has been all, and
the memory of one of the most appealing figures of his day and
age has been almost totally lost. This present book represents an
attempt at re-discovery.

The endeavour has certainly proved the accuracy of the opinion
expressed by another of Studdert Kennedy's friends, P. T. R.
Kirk, sometime General Director of the Industrial Christian
Fellowship, that "the story of his life will not be a simple thing to
tell". Chief among the reasons for this has been the fact that
Studdert Kennedy, in his profound humility, was the last person
in the world to consider himself as of sufficient importance to
warrant documentation. The result was that, in terms of personal
memorabilia, he left very little behind. And since his appeal
lay always as much in what he was, as in what he said or did,
personal memories of him, not always easy to obtain at this
distance of time, have been of exceptional importance to the
attempt to form some kind of picture of him.

There have been many, however, who have been generous with
help, and among those I would like particularly to thank: Mrs.
Emily Studdert Kennedy and The Rev. H. G. Studdert Kennedy.

All those others who have also been generous with their time
in assisting, in various ways, this present writer in his inquiries
will perhaps take this brief word as a nonetheless warmly felt
expression of his gratitude.

Perhaps it should be added that, insofar as this present book touches upon the Industrial Christian Fellowship, it does so with reference only to the early years of that still happily continuing body when G.S.K. was connected therewith, and makes no claim to being in any sense a history of it.

This book is the record of a man and his work and as such has not been concerned in any way with his personal and domestic life. This is as his family requested. But it will become clear that the man and his work would not have been possible except at the cost of considerable sacrifice on the part of both Geoffrey Studdert Kennedy and his wife, of their personal and family life. This cost they willingly faced together as part of the price which God demands of those who share a prophet's calling. But perhaps it will not be out of place to express appreciation of Mrs. Studdert Kennedy's unobtrusive share in this "Anglican Incident".

W.P.

CHAPTER I

The Siding at Rouen

TOWARDS the middle of the bitter winter of 1915–16 a very new chaplain arrived in France. Soon afterwards he was to be met, at most hours of the day and night, in a large and noisy shed on the *Rive Gauche* railway siding in the town of Rouen. The shed was a canteen, in which drafts for the front, having come up from Le Havre, could pause awhile before moving on a further stage towards what, in that old war, was likely to be fairly rapid extinction for the majority.

The new chaplain, in his own odd way, was something of a success, foreshadowing the enormous fame which was later to be his. To the Assistant Chaplain General he had mentioned, as qualification for the job of spiritual ministration in the canteen, that he was once "a revolutionary agnostic socialist who used to stand on a tub and talk in public places in the Midlands". It soon became his routine to stand on a box and announce to the crowds of soldiery that he was about to sing: *Mother Machree* for the sons, *Little Grey Home in the West* for the husbands, *The Sunshine of Your Smile* for the lovers. Afterwards he would offer to write home for them, and was to be seen doing so, surrounded by a throng pressing in on him. And, when the time came for them to go, he would be by the train as it pulled out until he was left, heavy with his thoughts, to watch its vanishing tail-light.

He was thirty-two. He had bat-wing ears; his mouth gave the impression of being over large for its surroundings, and the man himself appeared astonished at the fact of his being rigged out in the officer's uniform of the day; Captain's pips at cuff and shoulder, the Maltese cross of a padre in cap and lapels. He wore it untidily. There were occasions later when the untidiness merged into disarray, as when he was discovered wearing immense spurs, one of them upside down.

The new chaplain's name was Geoffrey Anketell Studdert Kennedy, a man destined within a year or so to become known as Woodbine Willie, legendary padre of the first world war. He was also fated to rise in reputation, like a Verey light, above the smoke of it; to hang in the sky, a portent and a prophecy, for ten years afterwards, and then to decline earthwards into darkness again. But he left a glow, and it will be that glow which will concern us in this story, because it is very precious. It is the glow of Christ-like love and understanding combined with an immense ability to make God understood in a world in which, as a person, as a power, as a presence to make Everyman open his soul as a daisy to the sun, he appears sometimes to be dead.

There have not been many since who have had that power to do something vital to ordinary life so that,

> When the strife is fierce, the warfare long,
> Steals on the ear the distant triumph song,
> And hearts are brave again and arms are strong.

But Studdert Kennedy can do this still. 'He, being dead, yet speaketh.' And it is important now, thirty years and more after his death, to try and hear what he had to say, and to mark how he said it, and perhaps above all, what manner of person he was, because he made God live in the hearts of the indifferent to a degree to which very few in this century have attained. How was it done? How did Studdert Kennedy 'communicate'—get across? This is an important question. Anyone who contemplates the impact, or lack of it, which the things of the spirit make upon the life of the present must, if he be at all concerned, own to certain misgivings. Is it really getting across, the good news of God which the Church exists to proclaim? Is it getting across, that is to say, on a sufficient scale to make any noticeable difference to things as they are? Or is that process remorselessly continuing to which C. F. G. Masterman nearly half a century ago spoke of in *The Condition of England*. "The work of civilisation steadily advances. The vision of a universe beyond or behind the material steadily fades." The fortress of indifference in which the majority live continues to remain impressively unaffected by the various assaults made upon it by the christian forces outside: the great lowered portcullis of indifference does not budge an inch upwards. And to the millions of folk—for this fortress is a very vast place—dwelling far within, such minor affairs outside their walls are far beyond sight and sound.

What force lowered the gate, shutting out from the lives of so many the feeling that God mattered? Largely, perhaps, it is the fact that he has *seemed* to matter less as the largely unconscious faith of generations in a beneficent power behind all life has been shaken by a whole succession of earth-tremors during the last forty years. There has been a transition, as H. G. Wells put it, "from that blind confidence in Providence, that implicit confidence in the good intentions of the natural order of things, no matter what our mistakes or misdeeds, characterising the human mind in the nineteenth century, to that startled realisation of the need for men to combine against the cold indifference, the pitiless justice of nature, which is the modern attitude".[1]

But occasionally a voice speaks which pierces this indifference. Such a voice was, and is, Studdert Kennedy's. There has not been one quite like it since. And his story, with its pathos and its grandeur, and its subsequent oblivion, is worth the telling just because of what it has to record of the strivings of one dedicated soul to get through to the heart and mind of Everyman that God is not dead; but living still.

It is still possible to encounter men and women who knew him in the flesh, and who felt that the experience, in some indefinable way, had enlarged their understanding of Christ. Indeed, he was the means by which some came to an understanding of Christ at all. So the fruits of his life are to be found in the subsequent effects upon theirs, rather than in any progress towards fame and fortune in his. He started no movement, reached no position of distinction. His is not a success story, as the world reckons such.

It was after the first war when he was chief missioner for the Industrial Christian Fellowship, that he was at his most potent as an influence. One who listened to him in those years, and who

[1] H. G. Wells: *An Experiment in Autobiography.*

later became, among other things, a high official in the Ministry of Labour, found herself decisively affected by him. It was at a meeting in Liverpool, before an audience, in the winter of post-war discontent, markedly indisposed to listen to anyone. As Studdert Kennedy rose to speak he was observed to be unrolling a galley proof from one of his books then in press. The book was *The Word and the Work*. He began to read from it in the Irish brogue which came from his ancestry and irritated some who loved him not. But that evening in Liverpool, as in so many hundreds of other evenings when he was sick to the soul with weariness and wondering maybe whether, after all, the struggle really did avail nothing, he captured the mind of at least one listener. Here was a man, she discovered, who preached a new social gospel which somehow made sense of the tragedy of men and women, with a suffering God at the heart of it. And that discovery, in that life, has gone on bearing its fruits ever since. Such instances could be multiplied many times.

From out of the obscurity in which time has hidden this singularly gifted christian soldier there are other glimpses to be had, too. There is an old church in the heart of the City of London, St. Edmund, King and Martyr, of which he was Rector from 1922 to 1929, holding the benefice concurrently with his immense labour as I.C.F. missioner. A third Studdert Kennedy, as different from Woodbine Willie of popular reputation as from the public figure of the campaign platform was to be encountered there. At St. Edmunds' he was to be found as a spiritual counsellor of deep insights to whom all sorts and conditions of men resorted. A portrait of him hangs in the vestry there to this day. Looking from it to the little garden beyond the window, one seems to see him still, walking in his cassock after service, talking to many friends, the Sunday streets outside and the empty office windows looking down. What sort of a priest was he? Here is one memory:

"I want to mention an incident which is very precious to me, and which shows the wonderful understanding he had. I went to the Rector for my first Confession, and among all the sins which I had to confess there was one which made me squirm. But it had to be done, of course. He saw how I felt, and as I finished he said with infinite tenderness: 'Yes, my dear, that's my great temptation, too!' "[1]

One is reminded somehow of the similar pastoral touch which made a famous contemporary, Dick Sheppard, so well beloved. A kneeling communicant in Canterbury Cathedral was moved one morning when the Dean, as Sheppard at that time was, paused to greet her by name as he came to her with the sacred elements. Studdert Kennedy would have understood that gesture.

The painting of him in the vestry of St. Edmund's brings out one feature of his physical appearance which was remarkable— the expression of the eyes. They were very large, very brown; but also, for some reason or other—and we shall be looking for that reason often in this narrative—quite extraordinarily sad. Many people have sad eyes in this world, and with reason. But here, it seems, were eyes reflecting deep within themselves a sadness more profound, more elemental than anything arising from the mere slings and arrows of outrageous fortune. Here were eyes, in fact, whose sadness seemed to be of an other worldly dimension, as though the possessor of them had found God himself in tears.

Maybe he had. As we shall see, the concept of a God who suffers here and now, daily and hourly because it is the divine will to be involved forever with the sins and follies of mankind, was central to Studdert Kennedy's thought. He battled his way—and a hard way it was—to what for him was that great truth. Thereafter he proclaimed it with all the strength that was in him.

> Father, if he, the Christ, were thy Revealer,
> Truly the first begotten of the Lord,
> Then must thou be a sufferer and healer,
> Pierced to the heart by the sorrow of the sword.
>
> Then must it mean, not only that thy sorrow
> Smote thee that once upon the lonely tree,
> But that today, tonight, and on the morrow,
> Still it will come, O gallant God, to thee.

[1] *G. A. Studdert Kennedy: By His Friends,* Hodder & Stoughton.

This is a vision which does not date. It is as relevant to our day as to his, as meaningful to a nuclear age as to that of the Flanders fields and their aftermath in the day before yesterday. But it is a vision of a kind not often granted to anyone now, certainly not allied with the power to express it which this man possessed. Those eyes of his and the sadness in them are important to the picture. Not the least of the interest in talking to many who knew him, has been the fact that they have tended to mention the almost unearthly sadness in him as something which they themselves alone noticed, as though a personal message had come through to them from what they had somehow, if only for a moment, seen therein.

Yet he was a merry man, as chockful of mischief and laughter as a clown. Could it be that the simile is curiously exact, as though in Studdert Kennedy the fun were as near to tears as it often seems to be behind the grinning mask, the outlandish make-up, of the figure in the circus ring? But if Woodbine Willie was a clown, then he was certainly God's clown, and a very able and gifted one at that.

He was exceedingly absent-minded. It is said that in the course of his travels, which were many in the days of his missioning, he left behind him a trail of pyjamas and toothbrushes. P. T. R. Kirk, sometime General Director of the Industrial Christian Fellowship, records how it was usually necessary to remind him by telegram of the destination at which he was next due, and how, not infrequently, he became lost *en route*, falling into reverie, perhaps, by a bookstall as his train pulled out, or simply going to the wrong place altogether.

So, then, we may see him, while it was yet the railway age, and when people still sent telegrams to each other, one of them, maybe, in his pocket as a reminder, deep in some book as his interminable trains clattered through the culverts and the tunnels and the cuttings of England's by no means green and pleasant land. Meetings in Manchester, in Newcastle, in Leeds, in Birmingham, in Liverpool; in a street in the Potteries, in a rowdy hall up a South Wales valley during the coal strike, in the street again. Truly it is touching, like visiting an old battlefield, to wander backwards in time towards the scenes of anyone's past endeavours, including our own: touching because time makes everything seem to matter so little. The heartaches and the strivings — even the objectives — of a former day become overgrown with time as the strong-points for which man once died in droves in some forgotten conflict become covered in bramble. But how did the heartaches and strivings seem to those who experienced them? How did the Studdert Kennedy of the campaignings of the twenties appear to those who shared some of them with him? Here is the answer of one of them: a fellow-worker of those years with the I.C.F., George Bromby;

"Two impressions of Kennedy remain always with me, the first when as a returned ex-soldier and unemployed I looked in vain to the Church for help and guidance. I was taking part in the leadership of the unemployed, and Communists were exploiting the situation, but the Church seemed almost painfully silent, until I got in touch with the I.C.F. Soon I met Studdert Kennedy and was deeply impressed by his love for people. He blazed with righteous indignation at the waste and degradation of human life. It was this more than ever which led me to throw in my lot with the I.C.F.

"The other occasion was some years later when I was put up at Queen's College, Birmingham, during the Copec Conference. The party consisted of William Temple, Charles Gore, Hewlett Johnson, Studdert Kennedy and others. Night after night we sat up talking and talking. One evening the topic was the limit to which the human brain could be stretched. Hewlett Johnson said he had learned a new language every ten years and had begun to read the literature on that race and country in the original. I remember looking at S.K. With his deep passionate eyes he was looking up bewildered and saying: 'I don't know I can go that far, or want to. I just *feel* the truth.'

"During the Potteries Crusade, most of the Crusaders had been infected with sore throats. That night when we went to the pitch there were only two of the team, F. E. Mercer and myself with anything left of a voice. Mercer started to speak in Tunstall Square and lasted for about ten minutes. Then I was put up, and told that Kennedy would take over. That was about 7.45, and I got into my stride, and talked and talked, but still no Kennedy could be seen. I was just told to keep going, and frankly don't know even to this day what I talked about. There was a large crowd waiting for 'Woodbine' but not as eagerly as I was. Then about 8.45 I saw Kennedy at the back of the crowd, nodding agreement and apparently not anxious to butt in. By that time I had taken off my collar and tie and even my coat, and my throat seemed twice its normal size. I turned and croaked to F. E. Mercer, 'Woodbine's out there' and at last he was brought on to the platform. My last recollection was of some people trying to force me to put my coat on. The next I knew was the following morning when S.K. sat by my bedside, the tears rolling down his cheeks. He was really in pain because he felt he had let us down. He said, 'You were doing fine and I didn't want to interrupt your message.' There was the humility of Kennedy. The crowds had come to hear him. But he preferred to stand on one side and not get in a youngster's way.

"He had an amazing memory. Often during missions and crusades he would be asked to talk many times a day. Indeed, we all felt, too many times, and we would beg him to say just a few words. But he would reply, 'I can't, they must have the lot; it's easier to put on the whole record than try to improvise.' And it would come out all in one piece. Whilst he had mannerisms, which some people unkindly said was play-acting, we all knew it was not so. He did not care for applause; he just wanted to get over the truth to a largely apostate generation.

"The Kennedy we loved deep down was in Retreat. To these days I remember his penetrating teaching on the 23rd Psalm. He cut away all our vain hopes of complacency and made us one with him in his passion for souls and his concern for the Church, that instrument of redemptive power and action.

"He could not be trusted with money. If he had it he would give it away to the first one who asked. There was one occasion when he came back without his overcoat. When asked where it was he looked up with a wonderful smile and said, 'I saw a man who was old and cold, and I gave it to him.'

"I recall another occasion when we were travelling on a tram in a certain town. We used to swear those trams had square wheels. The noise and clatter were deafening. I looked round and S.K. was miles away. When we left the tram, he said, 'I was thinking of the love of God, and the beauty of holiness.'

"To us who had the unique advantage to work with Studdert Kennedy, we always remember to thank God that the joy was ours, and whilst it may be true his methods were not everyone's, it still remains abundantly clear that in his particular period of history, he did a great work to open the eyes of men to see the Living God."

And then again there was the Studdert Kennedy as he was seen in the pulpit: "His little figure in the red cassock of a royal chaplain, the blue hood of Trinity College, Dublin, the scarf and ribbons, those big, brown eyes with their far-away look, and that irresistible smile which was so quick to come."[1]

He was never at any time in danger of being that horrible thing, the fashionable preacher. For some, he was not nearly conventional enough, or restrained enough. It could be off-putting to some worthy people, for instance, to hear, as one of them did, Kennedy remark from the pulpit: "There comes a toime, in ivery man's loife, when he must wonder what the *hell* it is all about." Nor did he share with the fashionable preacher the doubtful advantage of speaking always to numerous or easy gatherings. As a speaker, he took the hard way: the street corner knew him as often as the pulpit: and he could be discovered often enough, in some chill lunch-hour service in a provincial city, standing in the pulpit of some down-town church, addressing a handful of people.

Once again like his contemporary, Dick Sheppard, of St. Martin in the Fields, he suffered much from asthma: the terrible nervous asthma of the one who lives perpetually stretched on the rack of his sensibilities. That these two men, whose lives ran parallel for some years, and who in many respects were of the same genre, should have suffered, both acutely, the same malady, is an odd thing. In the end, it killed both of them. And each, in

[1] *Ibid.*

his winding way towards that inevitable end, suffered the tortures of self-doubt which seem to be among the numerous thorns in the flesh to afflict the hypersensitive. As with Sheppard, so with Studdert Kennedy, the private life behind the scenes knew more griefs and heartaches than were evident to the eye of the beholder. One of the many trials of the self-giver, of the man whose life is spent in the utterly exhausting business of giving of encouragement, sympathy, and leadership, is that he seems so rarely to receive some of it in return. He bears other's burdens; but few lend a hand with his. It would appear to be the destiny of such to fill the hungry with good things; but themselves to be sent empty away. So the Studdert Kennedy of the platform and the pulpit was often dramatically different from the Studdert Kennedy to be seen in the vestry afterwards.

"One of the last scenes will not soon be forgotten, when, at the close of a mission he sat, still in his robes, in the clergy vestry, almost in a state of collapse, his body shaken with sobs. He was fighting for breath in one of his attacks of asthma, and trying to blurt out apologies for not doing more for the parish, making, as he said, 'such a mess of it'."[1]

He was in every way a most humble man. Greatly loved, much honoured as he was, a conviction of his own failure lay always heavily upon him. And here may be recorded a memory of him which throws some light upon this important fact.

"A candidate for ordination went to him to ask what were the essential qualifications for a priest. The reply was that he thought a clergyman ought to be three things — a prophet, a pastor and a priest. The enquirer was a little nonplussed at such an apparently innocent and orthodox reply, and proceeded: 'I can understand what you mean by the first two. By prophet I take you to mean one who proclaims the truth as far as he sees it; by pastor I take you to mean one who cares for and feeds the souls of his flock; but what do you mean by priest? Do you mean one who dispenses the sacraments?' Kennedy replied, 'Yes, but more than that. I mean one who bears upon himself the burden of the sins and sorrows of his people. But I don't want you to misunderstand

[1] *Ibid.*

me. Don't think for a moment I conform to that ideal. My ministry, such as it is, might be regarded as a success; but all I'm conscious of is continual faillure'."[1]

This feeling persisted through the years and remained to the end. In 1919, when he had achieved an enormous fame as a chaplain, he was asked if he felt he had really made much impression. His reply was that "he thought he could point to at any rate not less than fifty people who during the past six months appeared to have been illuminated, and whose lives had been changed in consequence". Ten years later, after what William Temple described as "a wonderful decade of prophecy", it was the same.

Possibly he was a failure. As the story of his times solidifies into history, so that its prominent features may be made out, it becomes apparent that he is not among them. The Woodbine Willie legend was fatal to the full recognition of the real Studdert Kennedy. The mountebank obscured the thinker. True, he died in 1929, a most untimely death. He should have died hereafter. But even by then, in terms of the influence he had exercised, he was an important figure. The present concern of the Church with the spiritual challenges of industrial society owes much to his hard thinking and missionary energy. There again, in that field, he is overshadowed—as who is not—by the greater figure of William Temple. Yet it is some measure of Studdert Kennedy's quality that Temple himself profoundly admired him.

Above all, he had the ear of his day and age. The common people heard him gladly, as they once did another. They heard him, moreover, in a time when there were more of them more dangerously discontented than there have been since. It should not be forgotten that Studdert Kennedy was talking on street corners about the love of God when there were plenty of people about ready to deal roughly with anyone bringing such a message. The background to the larger part of his ministry was, first, that of men dying in the mud of appalling battlefields and then, secondly, of the survivors rotting in dole queues. Those were the days of what many saw as a great betrayal. Those were the days

[1] *Ibid.*

when hard thinking and hard talking were called for from those who sought to justify the ways of God to men. Kennedy did both.

To wander backwards in time to the Church of those days is to come upon ghosts. The gentle spirit of Sheppard can be met in the porch of St. Martin; the glasses of Temple can be seen glinting at yet another conference; the jutting beard of Bishop Gore advances belligerently over Lambeth Bridge upon an ageing Archbishop in the palace at the other end of it; the black cassock of Father Jellicoe flits among the slums of St. Pancras; the voice of Evelyn Underhill comes very quietly, from the chapel of a retreat, and the handsome features of Cosmo Gordon Lang ponder in the study at Bishopsthorpe over the infinitely gradual progress of the Revised Prayer Book through Convocation and Assembly. And always, behind it all, like the back-projection of a film, is the sound and vision of parish life; a single bell calling to early Communion in some down-town church on a Sunday morning, lit windows at evensong in a country church with bicycles askew by the porch, the water-clear music of Merbecke at a Eucharist, solid people singing psalms in the suburbs, and the phone ringing in the vicarage.

Somehow, Studdert Kennedy does not seem to have a place in the picture. Neither fame in the affairs of Church and State, nor the quieter satisfactions of a pastoral ministry were his. What gives shape to any life is surely the gradual attainment of an objective, whatever it may be. Neither can be found in his. He is associated with the name of no celebrated church: he cannot be identified with any particular cause, save that of the Kingdom of God. The King honoured him by making him one of his chaplains: the King of Kings would seem to have favoured him even more highly by allowing him to suffer much in his service. He was an itinerant missioner for the last ten years of his life, he died of 'flu in a strange bed, and he has been very largely forgotten.

Perhaps that is as it should be. There is august precedent for being rejected by the world and then crucified by it. But certainly such a story stands in considerable, even refreshing contrast to the lives of not a few eminent divines, in which worth is met with acclamation, and where the subject dies at last, full of years and honours, having met with wisdom or, if all else fails, at any rate with fortitude, the issues of his particular day. And sometimes there are memoranda prepared for the biographer when the time should come.

For the most part such biographies, always interesting, are at the same time edifying, as the spectacle of virtue in action usually is. And yet somehow there seems something lacking. What can it possibly be?

Stubbornly, the feeling persists of something missing, even among all this excellence. Can it be that the missing quality is, quite simply, nothing other than 'the mark of the nails'; the evidence that the disciple has followed sufficiently closely in the steps of the Master as to be involved, in some mysterious way, in his sufferings and his failure?

This mark of the nails, this mysterious stigmata, is something which the ordinary man recognises and respects as authentic. Thousands recognised it in Woodbine Willie. He was one of the rare people of whom it is possible to feel that they are personally bruised for our iniquities and wounded for our transgressions. We have to witness the torture which our world inflicts upon them before we can have our eyes opened to what sort of a world it is.

Such is one of the special functions of the prophet in any age. And Studdert Kennedy, forgotten as he may be, was one of them.

"His Voice," J. K. Mozley said at the Requiem in Grosvenor Chapel in April 1929, "was the authentic voice of a prophet. . . . The prophet speaks because he must: his bones consume within him and he cannot keep silence though he would."

But he has left little of himself behind. His written work is small in volume, and the difficulty which always presents itself in portraying a man who was large of heart as well as of brain is particularly evident in his case. People loved him for what he was even more than they esteemed him for what he said, or wrote, or did. And personality leaves no record, only memories. William Temple, writing of the man and his message, stated this difficulty with his usual clarity:

"No man can be fully appreciated by those who do not know

him personally: but some can be appreciated at their full worth as orators, or thinkers, or even perhaps as prophets, by those who only know them through their writings and speeches. Geoffrey Studdert Kennedy was not one of these. His personality and his message were so completely bound up in one another that each required the other for its full interpretation. No doubt there were many who from his books or (still more) from his speeches received a very vivid personal impression. And the admiration felt for him by thousands who never met him was deeply coloured by personal affection. Yet it remains true that his speaking and writing struck home with still greater force upon those who had the high privilege of his friendship."[1]

That we cannot have. But at least we can follow him through the changes and chances of his life, from the gaslit vicarage of a poor parish in Leeds where it started, to the bedroom of another where it ended forty-six years later. Between those two quiet places there is much to be seen, much to be heard, some laughter, many tears, as is the way of things in Vanity Fair.

And meanwhile we can leave him awhile longer among soldiers of an old war in the canteen by the railway siding at Rouen while we trace back the routes and the connections which had brought him to that place at that time.

[1] *Ibid.*

CHAPTER II

The House in Leeds

THERE was a vicarage in a poor district of Leeds, in the eighties of the last century, the garden of which was encompassed by a workhouse, a board school, a brick quarry, and a pub known as the Cemetery Tavern. The area was dirty, a region of courts gas-lit, doubtful by night. There were those, indeed, who claimed Quarry Hill, Leeds, to be one of the worst slums in the North. There, suitably enough, the story of Geoffrey Anketell Studdert Kennedy began.

But now the house has vanished. So has most of the district, as once it was, which is no doubt just as well, slum clearance having made spaces where once the courts clustered. So also have gone almost all of the family into which, in the vicarage, on June 27th, 1883, Geoffrey was born. But the church of St. Mary's still stands, that church, with which, for many years, the lives of the Studdert Kennedy's were bound up. So it is there, then, preferably in the silence of some week-day afternoon, when the voices of the past come through into the quiet, that a beginning can best be found.

It is not in the least impressive, this church. It could be any one of the many like it up and down the land whose blackened towers, seen from the train across factory roofs and pluming smoke, make melancholy additions to the industrial landscape.

In this church, in a side chapel, behind a curtain, there is a tablet, one of four in a building bare as a hangar. It has this to say:

This Chapel dedicated to the Holy Child
was fitted and furnished for divine service
by the congregation and friends of St. Mary's Church
to the glory of God and in affectionate memory of Joan
wife of the Reverend William Studdert Kennedy,

Vicar of this parish. A good example to us all during
thirty years as wife, mother, and friend.

A.D. 1913

This is the woman who lay in childbed over at the now
vanished vicarage on the 7th day of June, 1883. For her, it was a
familiar experience. There had been six babies before this one,
and there were to be two more. For her husband, also, such
occasions were by no means novel, since there had been five
children of his first marriage.

William Studdert Kennedy, second son of the Very Reverend
R. M. Kennedy, Dean of Clonfert and Anne Studdert of County
Clare, was an Irishman.

Fifty-eight at this seventh baby's birth, he had begun his ministry as curate of Ballymena. He became Rector of St. Doulough's,
Malahide, Dublin, and there stayed for fourteen years. After that,
like so many of his kind, he crossed the Irish Sea and for a further
fourteen years was Vicar of Shires Head, Garstang, in Lancashire.
And then, in 1876, he was instituted to St. Mary's, Quarry Hill,
Leeds, brick kiln, Cemetery Tavern, Workhouse and all. He
remained there thirty-seven years, until his death in 1914.

By his first wife, a Miss Russell of Malahide, there had been
Mabel, Norah, Eve, Francis and John Russell Kennedy, later to be
head of the Far Eastern Section of the Associated Press in Tokyo.

And then that blow fell upon the bearded rector which was so
familiar a feature of the Victorian scene. His wife died. The
widower, perplexed as to the future of his young family, after a
suitable interval sought a second. He found her in an eighteen-
year-old girl, Joan Anketell of County Clare. She was his partner
for forty-one years, an understanding person whose energies and
interests, not surprisingly, found more than enough to absorb
them in bringing up so large a family. And if for her, such pre-
occupations were enough, the daily round of a parson's life in a
working-class parish was amply sufficient for her husband. He
never achieved distinction of any kind: unless the ability to labour
faithfully in a humble sphere not only without receiving applause,
but equally without desiring it, may be said to be a distinction in

itself. The church of St. Mary's was large, far larger than any congregation it ever attracted in his long day. But those who came were faithful, and there was an air of homeliness and intimacy about the services. That love for the poor which burned in his famous son Geoffrey in after years had its beginnings in the affectionate relationships with them among which, in his father's parish, he grew up. It came to be Geoffrey's opinion that, though his father was never an evangelist on a great scale, those whom he had evangelised were christians for life. Venerable, kindly; such was William Studdert Kennedy. He has left few pictures of himself. But his children long remembered his voice extinguishing, as it was often called upon to do, some excited family debate with, "Now you're talking nonsense, and I suppose you know it." And once, prophetically, he laid his hand upon Geoffrey's head to say, when that young man was maintaining, in a torrent of words, one of the fantastic propositions in which he delighted: "His brain works so hard his head gets hot." So the Vicar of Quarry Hill was a quiet man, not easily separated from, nor often found out of, his parish. He could be persuaded to a concert in Leeds, of which there were many in that musical city, only if his wife were singing, which she often did. But for the most part to stay in his parish, to support any Liberal in politics, and the nationalism of John Redmond, represented the limit of his ambitions. He had, however, one aversion, and that was for doctors. He maintained, with the confidence of one whose own health was perfect, that "they made people sick by making them sick-minded". Christian Science came in time to claim the allegiance of several of the family, so that the Church of their baptism knew them no more, and that of Mrs Eddy claimed them for its own. Indeed, there was a time when it almost claimed Geoffrey himself, in which case the Church of England would have lost a prophet and that of Christ Scientist gained, maybe, another practitioner. But how far this development was due, ultimately and unconsciously, to the aversion of the vicar to doctors it is impossible to know. But the fact of it may be allowed to be significant.

Yet all this was very far in the future when the new baby

arrived on that June day of 1883. What sort of a child was he? Often, when people who knew in childhood one who later achieved some prominence, are asked to rummage among their recollections for glimpses of him, they tend to produce pictures unconsciously touched up by later events.

So it is with some of the memories of Geoffrey. When a storm shrieked over Leeds one night in his second year, it brought down a chimney in the vicarage at Quarry Hill. The debris fell by the cot; but when the child was brought out of the wreckage he was observed to be still smiling broadly. When he was seven the asthma which shadowed him through life struck for the first time and it was remembered how, as the boy lay wheezing, his very large, hurt brown eyes seemed to become more noticeable than ever. And a little later the braying laughter of the same child, as he stood with others round a nigger minstrel show, so grated upon one of the performers that he turned to him with the remark: "My lad, you have a horrid laugh." Thus the man of the years to come was seen, or thought to have been seen, in the child. That combination of the gallant, the pathetic and the ridiculous many found, in after times, to be not the least among the many oddities of the man which so strangely touched the heart.

There were other characteristics which early emerged in him. One was absent-mindedness. His excuse was usually that 'he was thinking of something different', as on the occasion when, sent to order two pounds of strawberries and a stone of potatoes, he caused to be delivered two stones of strawberries and one pound of potatoes. Such, at any rate, was for long a family tradition, just as a family memory was of the dismay of the boy when he discovered, as often happened, the inconvenience his forgetting had occasioned. But the cause of this dreamy detachment was plain enough. He was a reader, as insatiable as unselective. Any print seemed to fascinate him, and the man who in later years could become in a train so lost in a book as to forget even his whereabouts and the nature of his journey was foreshadowed in the boy to whom reading was from the first a passion. The matter is of importance. He was often judged in later times to be a shallow thinker who made up by showmanship what he lacked in depth. That was never true. The showmanship may well have existed. Indeed, it was the means by which his message was communicated. But the message was there. That he was a voice, and of other things nothing, could never with any justice be said of him, even though it was in fact often said.

He was educated at a private school, run by a Mr. Knightley, at Leeds Grammar School, and, above all, at Trinity College, Dublin. But the sequence in which these things happened was unusual. Geoffrey went to T.C.D. before he went to school, thus following his three elder brothers, Robert, William and Hugh, the only difference being that none of that three ever attended a school at all, but were coached at home by the indefatigable Mr. Knightley. Since of the three William later became a Canon of Newcastle and Hugh Foreign Editor of *The Christian Science Monitor*, it would seem that the system could work quite well. It was, nonetheless, an odd one which puzzled not a few observers of the Kennedy family. The key to an understanding of it is that it was then possible to obtain a degree from Trinity College, Dublin, without keeping every term in residence. Much of the time between examinations could be spent *in absentia*, and in Geoffrey's case was. The route of his educational progress, therefore, shows him zig-zagging across the Irish Sea, between the ages of fifteen and eighteen, from a main base in the classical sixth at Leeds. It is not surprising that he struck most of his contemporaries there as somewhat different, and certainly more mature than the generality. Whether he would have done better to make his way to Oxbridge, as some of his friends thought he should have done, and as he himself, like so many others, sometimes regretted not doing, is a question which ignores the circumstances. The father's income was small. It was cheap to be able to send a boy to Dublin where there were relatives in plenty to give him lodging. And clearly it also seemed proper, to William Studdert Kennedy, that an Irishman should send his sons to that ancient foundation where he had been himself.

Geoffrey was happy at Leeds Grammar School. And it says a

good deal for the civilised nature of the place that his almost theatrical Irishness caused little friction. No one could mistake that upper lip: and if they did the accent would have put them right. That was something he always tended to overdo. A fellow student at the Ripon Clergy School in after years exclaimed, "I wish Kennedy wouldn't speak like a Dublin jarvie to show he's an Irishman!" But Kennedy did, and in times to come many thousands of people, including captains and kings of his day and age, heard him doing so, not always with approval.

There was a boy about this time, in the late nineties, with Geoffrey at the Grammar School, whose name was J. K. Mozley. Thus chance brought Geoffrey's way a mind whose ideas came considerably to affect the development of his.

Mozley was one of the many subsequently distinguished men who came to have affection for Geoffrey. President of the Union during his time at Cambridge, later Fellow of Pembroke, head of Leeds Clergy School, and finally Canon and Chancellor of St. Paul's, Mozley became one of the prominent figures in the theological world of his generation. In 1926 he published a book *The Impassibility of God*. The book was concerned with a matter at the heart of all religion—whether God is personally concerned, divinely involved, in the sufferings of mankind, or whether he is 'impassible', beyond the reach of feeling. If that were true, then the multitudes who, in an infinity of private griefs, had taken their sorrows to him down the ages, would have done so in vain.

Such a statement of the question admittedly does violence to the subtleties involved. But there, for him, was the essence of the matter. The great, all important and continuing question was whether God cared. And behind that lay yet a further one: if he cared, how did he show it? It would not be too much to say that the search for the answers to these questions, and for a language in which they could be simply and directly communicated to everyman remained always a major preoccupation of Geoffrey's. There were those, indeed, who came to feel that he over-emphasised the whole matter, stressing too much a sorrowing God forever involved in human suffering. But such a preoccupation surely arose from the very nature of the man himself intensely loving, intensely compassionate, always fearfully open to the impact of the sorrows of others. The Jesus who wept was, for that very reason, the Jesus who, to Geoffrey, seemed the nearest to the human condition. There was also another reason for the pre-eminence of the issue for him, and that came from the nature of the period of history through which he was destined to live, a period of unexampled horror and cruelty followed by a decade of terrible disillusion. Does God care? The question boiled in the mind of Studdert Kennedy when the mass-slaughter of the first world war gave to it a terrible urgency. How could these things be, and the concept of God as love be even spoken of without cant?

> Hast Thou no tears to shed upon our sorrow?
> Art Thou a staring splendour like the sun?

This he asked in those days of mud and blood. Millions wanted an answer. He gave them one. We shall see, in due course, what the answer was, and how he gave it. The point here is that the answer, as well as the question, came into his mind directly through this early friendship with Mozley. Frequent were the times when, in the vicarage at Quarry Hill, they would 'hear the chimes at midnight' as they debated, as young men will, the mysteries of life. Mozley worked his way to a theologian's answer; Studdert Kennedy found his along the more painful path of the prophet and the poet.

"Leeds Grammar School." Mozley wrote, "meant a great deal to Geoffrey ... It would not be true to say that he made many close friends; but it was always natural to him to like and admire people, just as I think it has always been impossible for anyone who has come to know him at all well not to like and admire him. To his school contemporaries he was always a bit of a wild Irishman; but I think those of us who know him best realised something of the intellectual ability which lay behind his oddities. And from quite an early stage in my friendship with him I was struck with the firmness of his character. This impressed itself greatly upon me."[1]

Another boy at Leeds recalled an occasion when the effect of the year Geoffrey had spent at T.C.D. before going to the Grammar School showed itself clearly. "In the 6th at Leeds we were running through the *Apology* and Kennedy was translating. There are some rather long sentences in Socrates' speeches which, if not broken up, seem rather involved. Kennedy, without taking any liberties with the Greek, rolled out sentence after sentence of perfect English. The master, the excellence of whose degree was not at that time equalled by practical good sense, said: 'That's a very good translation, Kennedy. Are you using a crib?' I was sitting next to Kennedy and I feared an explosion. It was interesting to see the look of fury on his face, and to hear his indignant protest."[2]

The same man went on to say: "In temperament he was certainly older than most of us, and I think his harmonising influence was of great value. His voice always struck me as very melodious. On one occasion, at a debate on Capital Punishment, which he strongly opposed, he made an exquisite bull: 'You are sending him to hell for a crime he has never committed'; but the charm of his voice kept us all silent." This was not always the case. "If those Kennedys are elected members", said the secretary of the School Debating Society, "I shall resign." Geoffrey apparently he could stand; but another one of the same tribe—in the shape of his young brother, then also at the Grammar School, would be too much.

When Mozley compiled his short memoir of Geoffrey, he rightly gave prominence to the boy's connections with this Debating Society. For Geoffrey became one of the most remarkable speakers of his day: remarkable, that is, in the exact meaning of the word; causing remark, even astonishment; at times indignation, even repulsion, but always remark. He could never be ignored, as the words poured from him and the eyes glowed and the Irish voice went on. It is true that he became dangerously

Ibid.

[2] *Ibid.*

32

adept at playing upon crowds as on an instrument, as on the occasion of a great meeting in Edinburgh when, having raised his audience to a height of emotion he chilled them into instant silence as, with trembling contempt and quivering outstretched finger he shouted to them "Hypocrites!" The incident made an enormous impression. Such a power could be sinister, and not uncommonly has been. But Geoffrey, while possessing the power, offered it to his Master, and so redeemed it. It remains true, however, that no understanding of him is possible, and no story of him worth the telling, without the constant realisation that a good deal of his fascination lay in his powers as a speaker. On a platform, at a street corner, even in a pulpit, he could be orator or demagogue at will, according to what he sensed the demands of the situation to be. Roger Lloyd, historian of *The Church of England in the Twentieth Century,* once heard him doing that very thing. "Years ago, in Manchester, I had to arrange a big meeting in the Houldsworth Hall for the Industrial Christian Fellowship. The speakers were William Temple and Studdert Kennedy, and the theme was Social Equality. Temple arrived at the last minute, having somehow contrived to lose the letter which gave him the theme, so he asked what it was he had to talk about, and we told him. He explained how it was that he was entirely unprepared (which was not usual with him) and said that he would do his best. He then proceeded to talk for fifty minutes, holding that large audience spellbound. I think it was possibly the most brilliant thing I ever heard him do, and I heard him do plenty.

"Well, then it was poor Studdert Kennedy's turn. I must say that my heart rather bled for him, especially as he was very far from well. However, he rose to the occasion, and talked for forty minutes or so and, though it was not of the same class as Temple's, it was far from being unworthy to follow it. I think the point is that he didn't, on that occasion, use a single slang expression, or tell any funny stories. But what he said, and the way he said it, was exactly in the same classic tradition as Temple's had been.

"I am quite sure that Kennedy was one of those people who absorbed and reacted to atmosphere, and he gave you what he had entirely in the manner in which he sensed the audience or congregation were rather expecting to hear it. Sometimes, in church, he could be quite outrageous. At other times, in a hall, when that kind of example had just been set him, he could speak the most lovely prose."

The very same man could speak very quietly in ways that touched the heart, and enlarged the understanding. And now, alas, all is vanished away, except for some few of his words on paper, of that many coloured speech. But—and this is worth repeating—he who would recall Geoffery as he was must remember that much of his impact was in fact made thus through the spoken word. That, unfortunately, withers like a plucked flower with the years, so that those coming later upon its dried remains wonder that men and women, once upon a time, were so moved by it.

So Geoffrey in the Debating Society at Leeds Grammar School, was much in the picture. The school magazine is the evidence that, on February 24th, 1900, he "made a poetical speech on the Boer War which had little or no connection with the subject of the debate." There was another occasion when, having undertaken to propose a motion that arbitration should be substituted for war, he found himself converted at the last moment to the opposite viewpoint.

So the years passed, at Leeds Grammar School. Yet, important as the place was to Geoffrey, it occupied only half, perhaps less, of his life. A stronger influence was his home; the crowded, affectionate life of the Irish family in the vicarage. It is time to look now more closely at it, and we may as well begin with a photograph, six inches by nine, smelling of camphor. There are fifteen people in the picture, surrounded by the ferns and tasselled curtains of some studio in Leeds. All wear the sad expression common to photographs of the period. The causes of this melancholy have been disputed; some attributing it to bad diet, some to overcrowding, some seeing in it reflected the alleged repressions of Victorian society. In the case of the Kennedys in this picture, however, the cause was more probably sadness at having to keep still and keep quiet while the plate was exposed.

William Studdert Kennedy, in the picture, is frock-coated;

dark beard streaked with grey. His wife wears the white cap affected by ladies at the time, the effect of which was to make them appear considerably older than they were. The solemn child on her lap, maybe the youngest, cannot be much more than three. Neither parent, strangely enough, looks in the least Irish. The big noses and cheekbones appear more Scottish than anything else, which may be indicative of the fact that both the Studderts and the Kennedys were originally among the many settlers in Ireland who came in from Scotland. But Irishness looked out of the faces around them unmistakably.

A young man at the back, as bearded as his father, could be that John Russell who became head of the Far Eastern Section of the Associated Press in Tokyo. A girl on the far left in the back row, who seems to match him in age, could be one of the four daughters of the vicar's earlier marriage.

The small boy in sailor-suit sitting on the photographer's stool in the front row, head back against his father's knee, will be Geoffrey. Suitably enough, he is almost in the centre of the group. On the right, as close in picture as they always were in life, are the two eldest, the sisters Rachel and Kathleen. Neither married; both became Christian Science practitioners, living in Harrogate for many years, dying, the one a year after the other, in the early thirties. A solemn boy near them is Robert. William, born 1878, also was ordained. His life and ministry were both long; he died in 1948, aged seventy, Rector of All Saints, Gosforth-on-Tyne, and Canon of Newcastle.

Also in the picture is Hugh Anketell, born 1879, with whom the movement of so many of his brothers and sisters towards Christian Science began. He was ordained, and went as Curate to Rugby parish church, where Geoffrey later was to follow him. But then came a change. Whether his own ill-health was the prime cause of Hugh's turning towards the teachings of Mrs. Eddy seems very probable. What is certain is that his action had marked and lasting effect upon the family in Quarry Hill vicarage.

One can but guess at the agonising reappraisals, the enormous debates, which must have gone on within the family when his decision became known. However, he resigned his orders, crossed the Atlantic, became a United States citizen, and joined the staff of the *Christian Science Monitor*. He became its foreign news editor, and so remained, for many years.

Nor was that all. There appeared in 1947, four years after Hugh's death, his last book; *Mrs. Eddy: Her Life, Her Work, Her Place in History*. It was the result of much labour, a full-length biography of the founder of the Christian Science movement.

Here, then, was a man of very considerable abilities in whom one may perhaps see foreshadowed some of the qualities so strongly developed in his younger and more famous brother, fervour, literary powers — even maybe a certain degree of instability.

Maurice, the next son in order of birth, looks out of the picture from a position next to Geoffrey, on the floor, about his father's knee. Maurice was not ordained; he spent his life in business. But, like his two sisters Rachel and Kathleen, he followed his brother Hugh into the Church of Christ Scientist, and so remained to the end of his days. So also did Cecil, born in 1884, in due course to be ordained and to resign his orders, like his elder brother Hugh. Cecil, a product of Trinity College, Dublin and Leeds Clergy School, became a Christian Scientist while acting as his ageing father's curate of Quarry Hill. Later, Cecil married, went to Canada, became a teacher in Victoria, Vancouver and, inevitably, a Christian Science practitioner. Gerald, not in the picture, but later to be born, spent most of his life in India, after being assistant in the mission which Trinity College Dublin maintained in Belfast. From there, he passed to the Dublin and University Mission in India; and thence, over a period of many years, to various positions on the sub-continent, including the headmastership of Bishop Westcott's School for Anglo-Indian boys in Ranchi.

Thus did the family, posed in unity in the camphor-smelling photograph, disintegrate with the years. Yet while they were together, they were united. The vicarage at Quarry Hill, about the turn of the century, impressed more than one observer with its peculiar atmosphere of merriment and eccentricity.

Now the quality—or lack of it—of the family life of vicarage or rectory very rarely, it may be noted, escapes observation. It is lived in the public eye to a degree never approached by the celibate secrecy of the presbytery or the purely congregational concerns of the manse. The Anglican parson's family is there for all to see, and to criticise, and a fearful and wonderful curiosity often attends its every movement. Thus the domestic affairs of the Brontës in Haworth no doubt brightened the life of that perhaps rather sombre parish for some years. Nor is this devouring interest necessarily confined to the homes of the lesser clergy. It can extend to the Archiepiscopal palace itself. The fact that Mrs Cranmer had a beard appears to have affected posterity powerfully. It follows that any vicarage family which is remembered for the kindliness and charm of its life may safely be assumed to have in truth possessed those qualities in no uncommon measure. The family at Quarry Hill indubitably did.

These were the years when J. K. Mozley—he who debated so often with Geoffrey the impassibility of God—was as boy and young man in and out of the place. He wrote, "I cannot but wonder whether my appearances were not more frequent than was altogether reasonable, but if anyone at the vicarage thought so, it made not the slightest difference to the atmosphere of ungrudging friendliness into which the front door gave entry. The front door was indeed a symbol of the whole house. It may have allowed of being locked at nights, though how far such a practice prevailed is doubtful. The idea that it could have had its use in keeping people out as well as in letting them in would, I am sure, have caused universal merriment. A characteristic manner of entry for myself, or one of the boys, was to pull the bell and walk in, having first called 'shop'. The family was very large, with a considerable measure of diversity among its members, but the deep harmony which prevailed among them was a wonderful thing to experience. It was a home well-calculated to draw out the affectionate side of Geoffrey's nature. There was plenty of laughter and of a special brand of what we called 'organised humour' in which Geoffrey and his brother were experts while, when it was necessary, order was restored by the intervention of the venerable Vicar, with whose kindliness of heart there went a capacity for an occasional caustic remark."[1]

The wit was very often at Geoffrey's expense. As he grew up those traits of absent-mindedness and what his brother Maurice called a certain 'wild carelessness' became more noticeable. So did the passion for indiscriminate reading which led now to the habit of indiscriminate talking. The same brother Maurice said: "He did not confine himself merely to absorbing ideas: he used his information, and gave it out generously to all and sundry—always and ever wanting to share his mental gains like everything else he had . . . So exhaustively did he cover any topic that it was frequently said jokingly that if ever he came to preach sermons (a happening which then seemed incredible) he would cover the whole field of debatable theology in one."

That was the field, in the main, of the midnight talks with Mozley which were so important to Geoffrey's development. Not a few men have found that the argument and discussion with companions of differing backgrounds at their university turned out in the end to be at least as valuable and usually more memorable than anything else the place had to offer. Geoffrey, being mainly an external student at T.C.D., missed this enriching experience. But he did have in Mozley a stimulating intellectual companion. We may see them, therefore, both nineteen in the summer of 1902, in the vicarage at Quarry Hill, the rest of the household asleep, silence over the gas-lit streets, debating questions which seemed to them of such enormous concern. It was not only the question of whether God cared. They were concerned also, as thinking men certainly for the last forty years have been, by the 'higher criticism', that scrutiny of the Scriptures which subjected them to the same standards of critical judgement as any other body of writings. Then also there were, in another field altogether, the writings of the disturbing Mr. Blatchford, that socialist pioneer whose *God and My Neighbour* was causing not a few christians to feel novel prickings of a social conscience.

[1] *Ibid.*

And, as usual, in any age at any time, there was a crisis in the Church.

So the two young men had plenty to occupy them in their nocturnal explorations of the nature of things, while tens of thousands of their generation occupied themselves with growing up, fortunately unaware that within fifteen years large numbers of them would be dead.

The Chaplain who, in that oncoming war, was to appear now and then wearing spurs upside down, already, at home in Leeds as a youth, tended to be peculiar in his dress. It was part of a quite unaffected carelessness. "Being ready to give or lend any thing in the world that was his," his brother Maurice wrote, "it seemed natural to him to credit others with the same generous impulses. He would borrow freely from any of our wardrobes without the necessity of asking. Proudly arrayed for some special occasion, he would encounter first one and then another of us, and be met with the remark: 'Yes, that's a nice tie of mine: I always rather liked it', or 'Well do I remember buying that waistcoat. It used to suit me very well', and so on. To all of which he would reply with a huge good-natured smile, and perhaps an apologetic murmur that we could have anything of his; and very well we knew it. The only trouble was that, so complete was his disregard for the preservation of clothes, anything that was his would have been far too disreputable to borrow."[1]

But there was another side to this sort of whimsy. The same brother wrote: "One thing that impressed itself constantly upon me in regard to him at every stage of his life was his gentle, forgiving, loving nature. He would blaze with indignation at anything treacherous or unkind, any injustice done to another; but always took with a patient, sad forgiveness, any unkindness or injustice shown to himself. Some of us who had known this generous forgiveness have upon occasion, like Peter, 'wept bitterly' . . ."[2]

At the end of 1902 Geoffrey left school to take the T.C.D. third year examinations. He gained a Junior Moderatorship and

[1] *Ibid.*
[2] *Ibid.*

Silver Medal in Classics. Mozley had already himself left school in the summer of the same year to go to Cambridge, so that the two friends were henceforth during term time separated. But the friendship continued, as it did to the end of Geoffrey's life. So it is with some of Mozley's memories of those final student years that the record of this period ends. There was tennis in summer on the sooty, shrubbery-surrounded court at the vicarage; there was wild fun at Christmas when the Leeds and District Christmas Gift and Yuletide Present Procuring Company Ltd. sprang into existence, as it did every year, leading to all the boys of the family at home going shopping together. This practice could have its moments, as on the occasion when one of the company, waiting outside a shop for the rest, was moved on by the police. There was the annual custom, also sacred to Christmas, of Mozley himself reading a thriller aloud to the whole family. And in summer there were, for the two friends, those Edwardian expeditions, between dust-powdered hedges, which seem, in their innocence and simplicity, to belong to an age at once as dead and remote as the moon. And then at the close of the academic year of 1904 Geoffrey completed his degree at Trinity College, Dublin, after a final furious burst of work. He was twenty-one. It was time for him to go out into the world.

He turned to teaching, as so many have done in years of waiting for life to show its hand. Yet to imply indecision is to over-dramatise the situation as it was then for him. The fact is there never seems to have been any time in his life when he wondered, anxiously pondering the question, whether he should or should not be ordained, like his brothers, his father; his father's father. The point is worth dwelling on. The feeling dies hard that any religious experience, especially any one involving a major decision, must be accompanied by emotion. And since the decision to become a priest is one which affects the totality of a man's life it has often been felt that the moment of decision must be accompanied by a correspondingly acute emotional experience. In other words, a man must not only be called; but must hear it, loud and clear, as Isaiah heard the voice in the temple.

Yet such is far from being always the case, and he who examines the matter, if on a lower level than that of the prophets and saints, will find that an emotional decision has not necessarily been a preliminary to a life devoted to the sacred ministry. There is a striking difference, to take one instance alone, between the approach to ordination of two men who occupied the archiepiscopal See of York before going on to Canterbury during Geoffrey's lifetime. In the case of Cosmo Gordon Lang, there was indeed an element of emotion. True, there had been a period of hesitation for the young Fellow of All Souls on the eve, it seemed, of a brilliant legal career. But the moment came when doubts ceased, and the light broke through to show the path. "How well I remember the scene," he noted a long time afterwards, writing of evensong in Cuddesdon Parish Church; "I sat alone in the little seat immediately below where the pulpit used to be. The service passed, and the sermon. I only remember a curious feeling: 'when is the answer to be given to me?' That it was coming, that it was inevitable, I could not doubt ... The sermon closed; the hymn was given out. It was *Lead, Kindly Light*. I knew the answer had come. The long debate was over, the grip had tightened ..."[1] However, as events turned out, the brilliant career which had seemed to lie before Mr. Lang was not wholly sacrificed. On the contrary, it was exchanged for another one: and the throne of St. Augustine replaced, in the fullness of time, what might have been the Woolsack.

It was far otherwise in the case of William Temple, Lang's successor at York. Here there was a battle of the mind. "I have been determined to be ordained longer than I can remember," he wrote, "and I had very likely got quite used to the idea before really knowing what it meant."[2] The doubts and the hesitations, both of the gravest character, came later. Both were overcome; but nowhere in the whole story is there the smallest trace of emotional as opposed to intellectual experience as a deciding factor.

Somewhere between these two august extremes lies the case of Geoffrey himself, the humble working parson. Though deeply emotional by nature, and indeed often criticised in later years for

---

[1] *Cosmo Gordon Lang:* J. G. Lockhart. Hodder & Stoughton.
[2] *William Temple:* F. A. Iremonger. O.U.P.

being too much so, there is none of it traceable in connection with this major decision. Nor, for that matter, is there any sign of the classic pattern of intellectual doubt followed by acceptance, or any suggestion of that sequence of events which for a very long time has formed the classic pattern of conversion: hostility, encounter; surrender. All his battles came later; but they arose from the effort to serve Christ rather than from doubts as to whether he were in fact the way, the truth and the life. Thus a great archbishop, and an Irish parson who made, as few have managed to do, ordinary people feel the love of God, both set out upon their life's work without any of the emotion which is often held to be a necessary part of the process. Those, and they are many, who on the one hand suspect religion as being a matter of the feelings only, as well as those who reject any manifestation of it which is not, may perhaps find here matter of some interest.

. . . . .

The Grammar School whose staff Geoffrey joined in the January of 1905 was at Calday Grange, in Cheshire. He was there two and a half years, happily teaching general subjects, outwardly content enough, yet inwardly stirring with the pressure of new ideas. Mozley at this period found the extravagance of some of them disturbing. That element of instability which others remarked in later times he noticed now. He found him immersed in, among other things, "an ethic of Tolstoyian character which made him doubt whether the Gospel ever allowed a man to look for personal pleasure". That one single phrase has much to tell about Geoffrey himself, and of the age through which he was living. It makes plain that instinct to reflect the prevailing moods of his day and age which was so characteristic of him. Thus the same man whom Roger Lloyd years later observed catching the mood of a meeting set by William Temple, and then successfully falling into line with it, is here doing precisely the same thing in response to the prevailing wind of ideas which happened to be blowing when he was a young schoolmaster in Lancashire at the beginning of the century. It was a curiously inconstant wind, blowing in a variety of directions: but at any rate blowing; now towards a Fabian socialism, now towards a new religion, now towards a dimly comprehended concept of some Nietszchian superman. Not that its direction mattered: provided only that it blew away from the past and smelt excitingly of modernity the earnest Edwardian pondering, in cane-bottomed chair, was content.

Thus Geoffrey's "new ethic of a Tolstoyian character" falls perfectly into place in the mood of that time. Wells, in a passage in *Ann Veronica,* has the enthusiastic Miss Miniver using the very word:

"The women are taking it up," said Miss Miniver, "The women and the common people, all pressing forward, all roused . . . You must let me take you to things – to meetings and things, to conferences and talks. I must take you everywhere. I must take you to the Suffrage people, and the Tolstoyians—"[1]

The same enthusiast, a wild light in her eye, fingers bursting through her gloves, in an earlier passage of the book, memorably describes that new age: " 'Everything,' Miss Miniver said, was 'working up': everything was 'coming on' – the Higher Thought, the Simple Life, Socialism, Humanitarianism: it was all the same really. Hitherto in the world's history there had been precursors of this progress at great intervals, voices that had spoken and seared; but now it was all coming on together in a rush. She mentioned, with familiar respect, Christ and Buddha and Shelley and Nietszche and Plato. Pioneers all of them. Such names shone brightly in the darkness, with black spaces of unilluminated emptiness about them, as stars shine in the night. But now it was different: now it was dawn, the real dawn."[2]

It was absurd, of course; looked back upon, it was even tragic; because it was not a dawn, but a twilight. Yet it was stimulating, an exciting time for earnest people to be living in, and Geoffrey was one of them. Nor was an ethic of a Tolstoyian character his only enthusiasm. Mozley found him immersed also in the consequences of Freud and Havelock Ellis and what was

[1] H. G. Wells: *Ann Veronica.*

[2] *Ibid.*

known as the New Psychology, especially those aspects of the matter which were concerned with sexual behaviour. It is difficult to avoid the impression that Mozley found his friend's researches into such a subject peculiar and at the same time praiseworthy, as though it were a courageous act for a man to immerse himself in subjects which were on the whole, for the most advanced of Edwardians, still a fair way beyond the pale even of conversation. It was an interest, however, which persisted with Geoffrey, and emerged in later times, in his books, *The Warrior, the Woman and the Christ* and *I Pronounce Them*.

In any event, the time was one for experiment. Already a very large gap in outlook and ideas had appeared between people of William Studdert Kennedy's generation and that of his children. Maybe this tempo of the times, with its emphasis on change in a new century, had some connection with the turning to Christian Science of so many of the family. It was certainly true that the period abounded in new creeds as a cactus-house with peculiar shapes. Theosophy and Mrs. Besant were to be encountered; reincarnation was discussed as a matter of some moment; and the grisly hand of spiritualism was watched by some with breathless interest as it groped at the veil held to shroud the Beyond. Everything, to those who thought at all, and were young enough, seemed in a state of flux, and this spirit of the times bore with particular force upon the whole field of belief. To quote *Ann Veronica* again:

"Old-fashioned people . . . knew right from wrong: they had a clearcut, religious faith that seemed to explain everything, and give a rule for everything. We haven't. I haven't, anyhow . . . I suppose I believe in God . . . never really thought about him. I suppose my creed is, 'I believe rather indistinctly in God the Father Almighty, substratum of the evolutionary process, and in a vein of vague sentimentality that doesn't give a datum for anything at all.' "

Such were some of the ideas frothily afloat on the surface of some lives at that time. They seemed important; but the sad hindsight of history reveals them as trivial compared to the sombre undetected fact that the pace of the whole fateful stream which bore them along was quickening as it approached the Niagara of the catastrophe which was to come. That catastrophe, of course, engulfed them all, including Geoffrey, and those who survived to surface again in the post-war whirlpool at the foot of it were different people, in a different world. That is part of Geoffrey's story, too, as we shall see.

Meanwhile, for him, in his early twenties, the years of teaching at Calday Grange were happy enough, a period of vigorous, disordered reading, an extension into adult life of the habit of childhood. Each new idea as it came along possessed his attention wholly, with the result that he tended to be taken with a series of notions as they came along. He was an enthusiast, then, as always. And whether the current enthusiasm were for a commentary on Isaiah, or for some work on varieties of sexual behaviour made little difference to the zest with which he would talk of it. And all the time his essential quality shone through. "What impressed me," Mozley wrote, "was this sense of what the Christian Gospel demanded of him personally. His readiness to face facts as he saw them was now, as always, a striking characteristic of his nature." The same good friend wished that Geoffrey could have opportunity for more sustained theological training and thinking. And then, in the October of 1907, the opportunity came. Geoffrey abandoned schoolmastering to enter the Ripon Clergy College.

CHAPTER III

The Lodging at Rugby

THE founder of this Ripon Clergy College was a remarkable man, Bishop Boyd Carpenter. The mind dwells with astonished admiration at his prodigious energy, his abounding gifts. Even to read the record of the eminences he attained is to catch some echo of the opulent years: Canon of Windsor, Clerk to the Closet to Edward VII, friend of the Empress Frederick, confidant of the Kaiser. He was an ardent advocate of good causes. The Children's Act and Old Age Pensions engaged his energies. He had written many books, including a thriller called *The Last Man in London* under the *nom de plume* of Delaval Boyd. He had enjoyed other titles in his time, however. His first vicar had called him 'The Extinguisher'; the public at large, by the time Geoffrey encountered him, were calling him 'the silver-tongued Bishop of Ripon'.

That is the point, in this tale, at any rate. Boyd Carpenter was the greatest popular preacher of his long day; an orator of the first order, gifted with a beautiful voice. It was therefore natural for this prelate to take especial interest in the preaching abilities, if any, of the young men in the College hard by his palace. He therefore gathered them together from time to time, in his library, to receive instruction and to demonstrate whatever skill they had. One of those who benefited by such tuition was a certain W. H. Elliot, destined many years later to become a religious broadcaster of genius.

But when it came to Geoffrey's turn, as in due course happened, the Chrysostom of his day found his attention unusually engaged. Here was something different; here was something, in this Irish voice, this intensity, of real power. One thing, however, was clear: the man was unique, could be fitted into no mould. As regards instruction in the art of preaching Studdert Kennedy, in fact, was best left alone to develop in his own way. The verdict was a percipient one.

Boyd Carpenter was not the only person at Ripon to note the unusual qualities of the newcomer. A fellow-student, A. T. Woodman-Dowding, who was himself later Vice-Principal of the College, remembered how he and Geoffrey, having been sent, as the custom was for Ripon men, to take service in a neighbouring mission church, Geoffrey seemed able to forget himself, the place, and the clock; and to make the congregation of tired children and women on a hot afternoon do the same, as both were jointly carried away. "The spectacle of the preacher," Woodman-Dowding wrote, "entirely lost in his subject, is not forgotten. The broken and throbbing voice, which betrayed his Irish ancestry, still sounds on the inner ear." The same observer found Geoffrey nonetheless withdrawn from the crowd, as if either unaware that the crowd was there, or too much preoccupied with his own inner life to become involved with it. And then, suddenly, his attention would be engaged, maybe by some overheard remark, so that he would begin to talk, and go on, and on, and on— There is a foreshadowing here of an incident many years later, when Geoffrey met William Temple for the first time. The occasion was a dinner-party in Worcester. When Geoffrey arrived he was silent, and continued so as the meal progressed. The impression made was not pleasing. It was only when something in the conversation going on around him caught his ear that his own attention was, as it were, ignited. Thereafter he held the stage, while his fellow-guest listened with growing fascination. Shrewdly, Woodman-Dowding, recalling the Ripon days, applied to Geoffrey what was once said of Newman in the Oriel Common Room: "When his mouth was shut, it looked as if it would never open: when it was opened it seemed as if it would never close."

Geoffrey was at Ripon Clergy College from October 1907 to the June of the following year, a very short time by modern standards in such matters. But, brief as the period was, it proved important to him. For that matter, the time a man spends at a theological college generally is important, for better or for worse, since the people he meets there, and in particular those who teach him, are likely to make an abiding impression. In the case of Geoffrey himself it was the Vice Principal at Ripon, H. D. A. Major, later Principal of the College when it became Ripon Hall, Oxford, who influenced him markedly. Major's lectures on the Philosophy of Religion, Geoffrey used to say, were of critical importance in forming his ideas. He was fortunate, too, in another respect. Ripon, as such places go, was relatively easy in its regimen, so that the oppressive seminary-like atmosphere to be found in some theological colleges, had not there to be endured. Had it been so, Geoffrey, like any other man of nonconforming mind, might well have been less happy and less helped than he was.

The endeavour to see him there in the early nineteen hundreds involves trying to form some kind of picture of what in fact a theological college, so called, was like. The short answer may well be that it was like nothing else at all, being unique, after the manner of so many English institutions, which emerge and develop rather than are created with any clearly defined form in view. Certainly the theological college was not intended to be a seminary, since the English have a deeply-rooted historical antipathy to the very word, though some, it is true, were in their early days, suspected of being such. Nor did they emerge as ministerial training colleges after the manner of the institutions of that nature maintained by the Free Churches, and usually staffed, very sensibly, by the best men to be found. Nor were they uniform in nature: most were created to serve the needs of a particular diocese; some reflected those party divisions which were among the less desirable by-products of the nineteenth-century. But these were the extremes: the great majority of theological colleges, deeply characteristic of the Church they served, kept to the middle way, and pursued it quietly. Ripon was one such.

These colleges did, as they continue to do, a very important work unobtrusively. Usually small, housing perhaps fifty men under a staff of three or four, often near a Cathedral. Sometimes upon the edges of a university, they lacked – again as they still do – any of the mystique which seems to attach itself to the seminary. It is probably much in character that the Anglican theological college should appear as romantic as a cold bath and that its characteristic sound should be, as often as not, laughter coming from its junior common room.

Even so, it is not to be underrated. Sometimes, men of rare devotion have given their lives to teaching in such places, often creating, out of the most unlikely human material, good men and true to serve God in their day and generation. There was, for instance, the saintly B. K. Cunningham, of Bishop's Hostel, Farnham and Westcott House, Cambridge, whose work, the historian Roger Lloyd considered, "did more than any other single act to keep up a high standard in the ordination candidates during the years 1900 to 1940". And there have been, as no doubt there will be, other such who leave no memorial, but something of whose labours are to be seen whenever in after times one of their men touches a heart with the love of God, or brings comfort and hope when both are needed.

Such, at least, is the ideal. The reality can be very different, and not the least of the interests in observing the theological college phase of a clerical life lies in noting how the subject reacted to its very real tensions. Archbishop Garbett of York, for one, discovered his time at Cuddeson something of a trial to be endured rather than enjoyed. But such trials are valuable, since to be subjected, for a considerable stretch of time, to the test of daily intimate association with some who may be found difficult, is in itself a fair preparation for a life which will, as any priest's is bound to do, always contain much of the very same thing. In the case of Geoffrey, the surprising thing about the account of him at Ripon is the phrase, used by his contemporary Woodman Dowding, that he was "a quiet-seeming man". If that were the case it can mean only that at Ripon he was subdued for the first and the last time in his life. Or it may be that he was preoccupied with those inner concerns, those private searchings of the soul for which the theological college gives, for all its inadequacies, rich opportunity.

Certainly, a man kneeling in the chapel of his theological college in those years could expect hard times in a bleak house.

The temper of the age, and the working conditions of the clergy, were both difficult. For that matter, they always are. But as regards the former there were particular circumstances beginning to operate which were bound sooner or later to add to the already not inconsiderable difficulties of the parson's job.

.   .   .   .

In the seventh year of the reign of Edward the Seventh, Herbert Henry Asquith being Prime Minister; David Lloyd George, Chancellor of the Exchequer; Winston Spencer Churchill, Secretary of State for Home Affairs; in the Archiepiscopate of Randall Davidson, any man who went out with the word of God into all the regions round about could expect to encounter certain difficulties. There would be difficulties in persuading intelligent people to take him seriously, or working people not to regard him as a fraud. And though between the two, in that wide class-area which included the comfortable and the conformist, he could expect support, its fragile nature was shown in the fact that within twenty years a good deal of it had melted away. The prospect before him, in short, was unpromising; he stood within sight of the beginning of a very wide spiritual desert in which the faith of many was to be tested, and that of not a few to die. A man who was ordained at twenty-four in 1908 could expect, for the next thirty years, to exercise his ministry in a very lean time indeed.

If he were very perceptive he might have sensed at times earth tremors beneath his feet. Geoffrey in his seeking for a gospel of Tolstoyan simplicity was only reflecting in himself, as a young schoolmaster before he went to Ripon, a restlessness felt by a few. The majority were intent upon quite other matters.

One was the conviction, held by some of the best minds of the day, that modern man had somehow outgrown the need for God. Miss Miniver was not the only one to maintain that the new wine of fresh ideas could not by any means be contained within the old bottles of a traditional faith. That faith was in fact often seen as one of the main obstacles in the way of triumphant modernism. Thus Professor Bury, a notable historian of the time, held, after a careful examination of the record of history, "that at last the victory of liberty had been won, and its enemy, Christianity, stricken with a mortal disease". To such thinkers the craggy concepts of Sin and Judgment, of Incarnation and Redemption, basic to the religion they rejected, seemed ana-chronisms at once gloomy and absurd. There was no longer any need for them. "The higher man of today," Oliver Lodge wrote — that same Oliver Lodge who turned to Spiritualism after the memorial to his war-killed son had gone up on the wall of a Birmingham Church — "is not worrying about his sins at all. As for Original or Birth-Sin, or other notions of that kind, that sits lightly on him. As a matter of fact, it is non-existent, and no one but a monk could have invented it."[1]

Not that idealism was dead, by any means. There was a great deal about, and a striking amount of it was concerned with the relationships between capital and labour, which were in fact becoming immensely embittered. It was also concerned with a visionary and quite unrealistic view of Christianity as but one of the faiths which could, in the course of time, be synthetised with others. These, being equally useful and true, needed only to be rationalised to provide inspiration fitting to the ever onward and upward climb of triumphant man. For man was triumphant; there was no doubt about that at all. His vast material civilisation was there for all to see. As Kipling's ships' engineer McAndrew, meditating upon his marine engines, had put it:

> We're creepin' on wi' each new rig — less weight and larger
> power;
> There'll be the loco boiler next, and thirty miles an hour!

Yet contemporary press and literature, and especially such social surveys as that of the Rowntrees in York, often showed a markedly seamy side to that confident age. And apart from such obvious sources there are still to be found, among the lumber of our grandparents, maybe, others which mirror the age with touching clarity — touching because so many of its conclusions

[1] Quoted by Lloyd *The Church of England in the Twentieth Century*. Longmans.

and almost all of its aspirations, turned out to be, respectively, wrong and unreal. There was a publication for instance, called *Bibby's Annual*. Published by a wealthy Liverpool oil-cake manufacturer each year from 1906 to 1922 as an expression of a personal idealism, its fading copies present now a collection of some of the main notions, held by men of goodwill, of those tragic years.

The first was the feeling that traditional Christianity had had its day. "The preacher," said *Bibby's Annual* for 1909, "who can cast his memory back over thirty years will observe a striking change in the mental attitude of his congregations today. There is not the same intellectual submission . . . many feel themselves to be adrift, with no anchorage anywhere." Even so, Christ remains; but he is changed indeed:

"The Great Master, Whom we venture with all due reverence to describe as our Elder Brother, had without doubt reached that stage of evolutionary progress where it is seen that individual, social, national and international progress can only be achieved through the unfolding of the higher potentialities of our nature . . . He was concerned with making better men."

And the better man was on the way. The last number ever to appear of *Bibby's Annual* opened with the statement "Man is a God in the making. Latent within him are all the attributes of divinity. There is no virtue he cannot evolve. There is no degradation from which he cannot arise".

This self-sufficiency, an idea based upon a foundation, solid as brass, of great wealth, represented a second serious difficulty for religion, since it is hard to interest the self-satisfied in the need for repentance. It is difficult, as was long ago pointed out, for the rich man to enter the Kingdom of Heaven. The pursuit of money as the main end in life makes it equally so. And the pursuit of it in those Edwardian and early Georgian times was conducted, by those who had any chance of getting any, with remarkable devotion.

Mr. Bibby gently reflected this, also. By 1915 he is quoting Lloyd George: "We have been too comfortable, too indulgent, many perhaps too selfish . . ." But by then, of course, it was rather late in the day to discover the fact.

Even so, though the materialism of the age was a depressing fact, it did not seem, by the time Geoffrey came to be ordained, to have begun adversely to affect church attendance. On the contrary, Edwardian churches were fuller, and their social acceptability greater, than for many a long year afterwards. But there was certainly something wrong with the social foundations upon which all this outward conformity rested. The Edwardian Church scene was as much dominated by material prosperity and the ideas arising therefrom as the American church scene is now, and paid bitterly for it in time to come.

Not surprisingly, all this went hand in hand with a class-structure of society which added greatly to the difficulties of the christian ministry by being divisive and hatred-breeding in its effects. This was especially so when the Church was felt, often not without reason, to be largely identified with the possessing classes.

The whole picture can be seen most clearly in Masterman's *The Condition of England*. There is made clear, among other things, that social pyramid which carried upon its apex the upper classes, hard, glittering, irresponsible. Beneath them came the middle classes, the white-collared denizens of the new suburbia stretching for miles around the great cities, containing within their myriad houses every possible gradation of class, and all conscious of it. One thing alone united these to those above them — the fear of those below, of "an uprising of the uneducated, suddenly breaking into their houses; their clumsy feet on the mantelpiece, their clumsy hands seizing and destroying all beautiful and pleasant things. So they lie awake at night, listening fearfully to the tramp of the rising host; the revolt of the slave against his master."[1]

Mr. Bibby, too, was very concerned about this host. All was not well with them. The theme of strikes and unemployment figures much in the pages of his *Annual* as the years go by.

Such, then, was the prospect, and such was the world, stretching, not very invitingly before the prospective clergyman of 1908. And unless its enormous social injustices, its cruel class-divisions

[1] C. F. G. Masterman: *The Condition of England.*

and its political ferments are borne in mind, the story of Geoffrey, now to begin a life-long struggle in the midst of them, loses much of its meaning.

In the summer of 1908, in the Cathedral at Worcester, he was ordained deacon, and went thence to Rugby Parish Church, where his brother had been before him.

.   .   .   .

The new curate dropped upon the parish like a bomb, making a small crater in its collective memory the outlines of which can even still faintly be made out. The lodging where Geoffrey had his bed-sitting room has gone: Sun Court, the slum area in which, before he had been there long, the children used to follow him as though he were the Pied Piper in a cassock, has vanished away. But the memory of the extraordinary character who came upon them persisted in Rugby for a long time afterwards.

In one thing at this time, Geoffrey was extremely fortunate—the character of the then Rector of Rugby, A. V. Baillie. The kind of man whom any curate encounters as his first vicar is likely to have a vital influence upon his future. Geoffrey could have encountered a disciplinarian, such as Cyril Foster Garbett who, as vicar of Portsea, used to regiment his curates with military precision; as though the Kingdom of Heaven could be brought in, if not by force, at any rate by numbers. Equally, he could have been sent to some placid man content enough to leave all well alone, including his curates, provided the same consideration was extended to himself. He might have encountered a crank, which would have been quite fatal, since he was one himself.

There can be little doubt about that. It is quite clear that the new curate struck many as being wild, undisciplined; in many ways foolish. It is also true that he continued to be so for a very long time afterwards, perhaps to the end of his life. But that the wise humanity of the Rector of Rugby provided a steadying influence when it was critically needed is clear.

A. V. Baillie, godson of Queen Victoria, a nephew of Dean Stanley, and subsequently for many years Dean of Windsor, belong unmistakably to the officer class of the Anglican ministry.

That there should be an officer class in such a body may be regrettable; even reprehensible. But it was a fact. The public school and Oxbridge bishops, when Geoffrey went as curate to Rugby, vastly outnumbered those, if any, with any other background.

Obviously, such a system, where preferment was often closely related to a man's family background could lead to serious spiritual dangers. The squire and his relations could be held to rate, even in the sight of God, that priority of esteem which their social position gained for them in the sight of man. The layman in a country parish who told his bishop in the eighteen fifties that he did not take communion, because 'that was for the gentry' was but expressing a feeling widespread at any rate in country districts. And though the system could lead to occasional bitternesses, when under-privileged merit felt itself overlooked, yet on the whole it worked surprisingly well.

It was working extremely well when Geoffrey arrived there to join a staff of curates which, during Baillie's rectorship eventually reached the number of nine. It was an interesting time to arrive in Rugby, since the whole place was going through a phase of radical change. Indeed, the situation in Rugby in those days merits a closer look, since it illustrates clearly an abiding truth about the English social scene – that behind an outward face of the ordinary lurks an inner life – usually understood only by the natives and guarded by them as an esoteric secret – of the most extraordinary complexity.

Thus to the outward view the Rugby upon which Geoffrey descended was a plain-faced town of uninspiring aspect. In the middle of it stood Rugby School. Nearby was the parish church, completed in the nineties. Opposite the church was the market square; on the outskirts was the great railway centre. And, springing from this, the factories of heavy industry were making their appearance. The result was a variegated community in which the social classes could be discerned as clearly as the layers in a cake.

At the top came the professional classes; beneath them the

established tradesmen, then the railwaymen. All these were held together by mutual esteem. The outsiders, rudely breaking in upon a long established pattern, were the industrial workers. There were also further complications. The old market town of Tom Brown's Schooldays, pre-railway, and long pre-industrial, was a centre for hunting and, of all things, polo, so that there were still men to be found in it who could say, as one groom did shortly after Baillie's arrival: "Very nice gentleman, the new Rector—a good rider, with fine hands."

There were also certain old ladies of Rugby who, because of the peculiar nature of their origins, supplied yet another touch of individuality. There had been a time when admittance to the school had been a right for the sons of local residents, a fact which over the years had brought many gentry to the town. So the sons had been schooled, and gone off their several ways. Then the parents had died. Those left behind were often the daughters—ladies, by the early nineteen-hundreds, of formidable dignity, great piety, and long memories. It was thus quite possible for a clergyman on the staff of Rugby parish church to encounter, within the bounds of the parish, variations of personality ranging from an Irish squire such as Captain Beatty, R.N., in his house opposite the church, father of the famous Admiral to be; an elderly lady who could remember being confirmed with Matthew Arnold during the headship of his father; sundry masters of the school, various doctors and solicitors, numerous tradesmen and businessmen, innumerable children, and a not inconsiderable section of the very poor. And the chances were that most of them, in the Rugby of those days, would be connected with the church.

Furthermore, the admirable man who was Geoffrey Studdert Kennedy's first rector had found, upon his arrival, sections marching and counter-marching upon each other in a number of private wars. In other words, there were factions within the large parish. Some were 'high', and some were 'low'; some for Apollos, some for Paul, according to the predilections of the priest who had chanced, under the previous rector, to be in charge. That, in its turn, was another complication. There had been but two rectors in seventy-five years, John Moultre and John Murray. Both were men of character, and the former something of a saint, after the quiet Anglican style, which means he was intensely venerated in his immediate locality and virtually unknown anywhere else. This was the man who died of smallpox, after a ministry of fifty years, while visiting a child parishioner in the epidemic of 1874. He was very greatly beloved, though he could be sharp when he wished, as when, an earnest evangelical lady saying she had sat under his ministry for many years and gained no good from it, he looked at her quietly for an appreciable time before saying, "I perceive it, Madam." His successor, Murray, a stern Tractarian high-churchman, much feared in the town, with an untidy beard and a habit of drinking cold tea throughout the day, used in the latter days of his ministry to astonish visitors already impressed by his own antiquity by taking them along to see his mother, still briskly surviving.

These were great men. It was true that towards the end of Murray's reign, when his grip had relaxed, the factions aforesaid had arisen in the parish. But between them they had built up the work and prestige of St. Andrew's, Rugby, until, by the time Baillie came, and Geoffrey arrived as one of his curates, it was among the more notable parish churches of the country. The opinion this shrewd rector formed of his curate is interesting.

"K. was one of the strangest characters I ever knew. An Irishman, with brains, he had infinite charm, complete devotion to his work, and a fine sense of humour. But mentally he was incredibly undisciplined. At least once a week he dashed into my room with some new idea. They were sometimes quite preposterous; but they were always held by him with burning earnestness. If one argued with him gravely about them, he was quite clever enough to have defended his position with success, when the result would only have been to harden his beliefs. But his new idea always had a humorous side due to its very exaggeration, and an appeal to that brought him down on his feet again.

"In his earlier days he preached a sermon in the heat of the moment in which I felt he had gone more than a little too far. After church I took him for a walk in the Rectory garden and, with apparent gravity, I said, 'You know, I think you exaggerated when you said there had been no one between yourself and St. Paul who had understood the Gospel'. At once he burst into a shout of uproarious laughter. He had learnt his lesson. I always told him he must not come to me with more than one heresy a week, as after that it became a bore."[1]

This was leadership of genius. It is difficult to think of any other kind of guidance, so patient, humorous and wise, which could more effectively, or at all, have held Geoffrey on even an approximately even keel. And since the result was to preserve him for the Church as a burning and a shining light it is possible to feel some little gratitude, even at this distance of time.

Christian Science, which had already claimed his brother Hugh while curate in this very same parish of Rugby, very nearly did the same to Geoffrey himself at this time. He was greatly attracted, and the movement towards it within the family which his brother Hugh had begun, was an additional factor. However, it did not happen, and there was enough variety in the parish life at Rugby to claim all his attention. He was considerably eccentric, especially as regards money and clothing.

"K. had no sort of discipline about small things," Baillie recorded, "what he had in his pocket he gave away, until his landlady took charge of his money and rationed him with it. It was the same with his clothes. He gave them all away and walked about almost in rags, wearing a cassock to conceal the fact."[1] Baillie does not record, however, that the landlady in question, a good soul by the name of Miss Moore, having in pity bought him an overcoat, was not unnaturally incensed when he immediately gave it away. The overcoat was not replaced. Quixotic generosity, however appealing, is not always easy to live with. It can sometimes be a pose, though with Geoffrey it seems, by the test of continuance, to have been natural enough. The extreme open-handedness continued throughout his life, so did the sartorial eccentricity. Twenty years after these early days in Rugby, when he was a national figure, there was an

[1] A. V. Baillie: *My First Eighty Years*.

[2] *Ibid.*

occasion when he set off for an important occasion in Westminster Abbey wearing football shorts under the scarlet robes of a royal chaplain. Even then it was necessary for him to return hurriedly to the vicarage of Christ Church, Westminster, where he was then staying, because he had forgotten his teeth.

Baillie is clear, however, on one important fact—that the new curate, all oddities notwithstanding, was a remarkable man. "His complete sincerity," he wrote, "his passionate belief and astonishing eloquence made him a great power for good in my Rugby parish. We had one small district that was practically a slum, and K. gravitated there, getting me to buy a derelict Nonconformist Chapel as the centre for his work. His work was very useful. One of his activities was to wander in and out of the pubs and talk to the men. His personality made it easy, and the men would welcome him even in the worst and lowest places."[1]

Here, already, then, in Rugby, the twin characteristics which distinguished his life to the end were already visible: the eloquence and the deep love of the poor. As to the first, it was not long before masters of Rugby School formed the habit of going to hear him whenever they knew he was to be in the pulpit. Herbert, sometime Bishop of Blackburn and Norwich, who was a fellow-curate at Rugby, recalled of that preaching:

"There must be few men of whom it is true, as it was of him, that from the moment of his ordination he was really miserable if he were not allowed to preach at least twice a Sunday. There was so much he wanted to say, so many thoughts bobbing up in his mind, that silence was a severe discipline. As to the matter and manner of his preaching, clear impressions will remain for all who heard him. A sermon on the Holy Communion, tracing the universal power of that sacred bread and wine, through all ages and amongst all sort of people, which the listener suddenly realised to be a sermon entirely in blank verse; or again a Good Friday sermon on the meaning of the Atonement which made a somewhat complacent congregation think as it had seldom thought before: or the simple mission addresses to his own special

[1] *Ibid.*

congregation of tramps and lodging-house inmates – these were indications of his mind that those who heard him will not forget."[1]

And as to the second characteristic here to be seen emerging, that love of the poor, the word 'gravitated' used by Baillie is significant. Geoffrey gravitated towards the slum area of the parish as a compass swings to the north because it was a built-in disposition of his to do so. It was part of the man. He was genuinely at home amid the smell of poverty, the doss-house mutterings, and the pitiful anxieties of want. Some people – and they have included some of the most high-principled possessors of the social conscience – have entered this shadow world of burst boots and pieces of food wrapped in newspaper out of a sense of duty. Geoffrey belonged to the much smaller number of those who go there, not because they think they ought to, so much as because they really want to. He was glad when they said unto him that he had to go into the house of the poor. That was where he belonged.

"I can see again," Herbert wrote, "that small slim figure strolling into the unattractive pub where his beloved lodging-house tramps were to be found, and standing up to the bar in his cassock to sing 'Nazareth', while half his audience 'felt within a power unfelt before'. They loved him – loved him for his great laugh, the smile that transformed his face, the Irish brogue, but most of all because of his love for them. He was entirely at home in the dirtiest of kitchens, and would sit for hours smoking and talking, or watching by a sick-bed, forgetting, in all probability some important engagement elsewhere. This was sometimes a source of trouble: he was known on more than one occasion to start off to take a funeral at the cemetery and then, dropping in on someone on the way, to forget all about it."[2]

There was another fellow-curate of Geoffrey's at Rugby, Selwyn Bean, later Archdeacon of Manchester, who was personally involved in some of the consequences of this forgetfulness.

"In those days, Rugby with its five churches, the Hospital Chapel and the Workhouse Chapel, meant careful planning and

[1] *G. A. Studdert Kennedy: By His Friends.*

[2] *Ibid.*

60

organisation. If this was to be properly carried out it was necessary for each member of the staff to be at the right place at the right time. K. found this one of the most difficult tasks to carry out. Each curate in turn was responsible for a week's duty. This meant that the man on duty was responsible, among other things, for funerals for which no special arrangements had been made. My lodgings were quite close to the cemetery, and I well remember one week, in which K. was on duty, I was sent for early on Tuesday afternoon, before I set out visiting, to take a funeral which was waiting at the cemetery gate. I rushed round to the cemetery, robed, and took the funeral. Exactly the same thing happened on the following Friday and I was a little disconcerted when I hurried to the cemetery to hear one of the onlookers say that is the second funeral I had forgotten that week! I felt it was only fair to mention it at the staff meeting on the Monday morning. K. was very penitent and said that he would try very hard not to forget a funeral again. In those days death certificates were printed on blue paper and the parish clerk would put the day and time of the funeral on the death certificate and leave it at the lodgings of the curate who was on duty. Some weeks later, I met K. in the Market Place of Rugby and he had stuck in his buttonhole what looked like a blue spill of paper. I jokingly asked him if he had joined the blue riband brigade. His reply was typical – 'No, I have got a funeral this afternoon and I'm trying to remember it.'

"Within a stone's-throw of the parish church there was a small slum area, which disappeared years ago. But in 1910, it consisted of three or four very rough lodging-houses and a number of houses and cottages which were hardly fit for human occupation. On the edge of this area, stood the Parish Hall. The Rector put K. in charge of this district. Here every Sunday evening he held a mission service, and the way in which he gathered his congregation from lodging-houses and slums was indeed remarkable. There was something irresistible about K. and they loved him. I always remember one old woman in that district who, when she was dying, sent for K, and after he had said some prayers said, 'Now sing me the *Mountains of Mourne*', and K. with his wonderful voice sang as she passed away.

61

"During his short time at Rugby, he already showed signs of that amazing gift for preaching, which made him so well known in later years. But it is true to say that his style, and indeed his matter, did not appeal to some of the ladies who formed the weekday Evensong congregation at Holy Trinity. It was the custom at the beginning of the year for one of the curates to preach at the Choral Evensong on each Saints Day. I well remember on one occasion when I was taking the service on the Feast of St. Simon and St. Jude. K. startled and almost horrified his congregation by the opening words of his sermon in which he stated the Epistle of St. Jude is the most repulsive document in the New Testament. One of the maiden ladies of the congregation wrote to the Rector afterwards and complained. On another occasion in the same Church of Holy Trinity, in which many of the stained glass windows had been placed in memory of the friends and relations of members of the congregation. K. during the course of the sermon on the reality of religion somewhat distressed many people by saying there were times when he would like to take a great sledge-hammer, smash every stained glass window in this church and go out and celebrate the Lord's Supper in the fields with a cup and platter."[1]

But if Geoffrey was good for Rugby it is equally true that Rugby was good for him. One of the ways in which the eminently sensible Baillie sought to heal the divisions in the parish was to refuse to make an issue out of any one of them. Thus, whether his various churches were 'high' or 'low' did not seem to Baillie to be a main concern. What he did insist upon was that all should live and work together as members of one body.

The staffing of these various centres he affected on an equally common-sense basis. "I put my men to work," he said, "in the church where they would find themselves in harmony with the general atmosphere." Acting upon this principle, he sent Geoffrey to Holy Trinity, a church which was rather 'high'. The label thus affixed to him never altered. Even so, the point is not an important one. Geoffrey, at no time very interested in such matters, was at all times inclined to be violently impatient with those who were,

[1] Privately communicated.

driving through the trivia of church life, as an admirer once said of him during the war years, "like a tank through barbed wire." But he was very interested indeed, as one to whom beauty in all forms was the elixir of life, in the beauty of worship. He was very particular in such matters, and the forgetful carelessness which afflicted both himself and his friends in other departments of life stopped well short of the actual conduct of worship, in which he was most particular.

So Baillie attached his new curate to Holy Trinity, Rugby, and from there his work among the poor branched out. It also invaded the lodging which he had with the long-suffering Miss Moore, she who bought him the overcoat. The house, in a street leading from the Market Place to the main gate of Rugby School, was full of narrow passages. Most of its rooms were small; but there was one of some size. This was soon converted into a playroom for the children of Sun Street nearby, most of them barefooted, after the habit of the day. Sun Street, in fact—perhaps so called because it was usually in shadow—was the scene of Geoffrey's most typical work in Rugby. For the small children chiefly of this region he invented the Babies' Service, where the congregation on a Sunday afternoon would be composed entirely of such, with Geoffrey in the middle of them, telling stories, having them sing verses, helping them light birthday candles. There are not many men, as opposed to women, of whom such a story could be told without a certain queasiness. Yet no one seems to have found any of it odd in Geoffrey. No doubt the Babies' Service was crude sentiment. But he was a crudely sentimental person, which is a valuable asset when working among the Sun Streets of this world. Moreover, Geoffrey's sentimentality, as represented especially in some of his war poems, was of a characteristically proletarian variety, where 'you' tends to rhyme with 'thru' and all emotions are a little larger than life, like the porcelain flowers under a glass dome on a sooty Edwardian grave labelled 'Mum'. A slum priest who could quite naturally revel in this sort of thing himself would by that fact be well on the way towards the hearts of his people. With Geoffrey, this innate sentimentality was as magnetic to simple folk whether their slum happened to be Sun Court, Rugby; a trench in the France of the first world war, or a dole queue afterwards. The same disposition enabled him, a little later, when he had a parish in Worcester, to make such a thing of funerals, where it was not uncommon for all concerned, including the officiant, to be bathed in tears.

Yet with Geoffrey this sentimentality did not, as it so often does, go with simplicity. He was no fool. The masters from Rugby School did not go to hear him because he talked nonsense, but because what he said had power. Nonetheless, his marked sentimentality and intellectual ability made a curious combination. Perhaps the verdict of his fellow-curate Herbert approaches as close as possible to an explanation of it:

". . . He was entirely unacademic. Not only was his mind out of tune with a purely scholastic atmosphere; but it was impossible for him to disassociate his thought of God from his love for men. For him the setting and the stage of religion was this world, and his own intense humaneness kept his intellectual side harnessed, if not subordinate, to his pastoral work."[1]

He was happy at Rugby, though he was certainly not treated with undue indulgence. Another of Baillie's admirable customs was to welcome his curates to his house on Sunday evenings and to command them, in a body, to his study on Monday mornings, when the duties of the week would be discussed and allocated. The body so assembled contained a high proportion of able men; Herbert and Askwith were future bishops of Norwich and Gloucester; Julian Bickersteth a future headmaster of a famous Australian school and Canon of Canterbury. These among others were not the kind of men likely to accept the dogmatisms of an excitable junior without reply. So there were frequent disputations among the young men in each others' rooms, often, as Herbert remembered, with Geoffrey walking up and down the carpet, violently destroying all arguments brought against his current viewpoint, then as suddenly, and with a wide smile, admitting he was wrong. So he was kept in order, given due scope to follow his own various bents, and

[1] *G. A. Studdert Kennedy: By His Friends.*

surrounded by friendship. That indeed was the environment which his particular kind of personality, at once singularly warm-hearted yet liable to hurt, needed beyond all else.

It continued four years, during which, after a two years diaconate, he was ordained priest. It might have been prolonged considerably. The Edwardian curate not of officer class often stayed as he was for a very long time. As it happened, however, events were taking place back in his father's parish at Quarry Hill, Leeds, which seemed to Geoffrey to call for his return to the place of his birth.

All was not well there. By 1912 William Studdert Kennedy had been Vicar of St. Mary's, Quarry Hill, thirty-five years, and was eighty-seven himself, a survivor from a vanishing world. Even by the time of his arrival at Quarry Hill in the eighties the great old parish church of Leeds nearby—'t'owd church', as it was known—had far overshadowed its humbler neighbour, and as time passed this became more marked. Even in Geoffrey's boyhood, St. Mary's could hardly have been called flourishing. But now, with the new century, had come other influences to change noticeably the whole character of the area. The clothing trade of Leeds had brought in many German Jews, a large number of whom had settled in the parish, and the old vicar could but note sadly the replacement of the Leeds folk he had lived among for so many years by these newcomers. So St. Mary's by 1912 was a run-down church, and its vicar was a very old widower.

There then came another event, like one of the ill-tidings in the Book of Job, to trouble his old age. Cecil, younger brother to Geoffrey, was the next to go the whole way with the Church of Christ Scientist, ultimately becoming a Christian Science practitioner in Victoria, Vancouver. But the immediate issue, in the year 1912, was that he was curate to his father at St. Mary's, Quarry Hill. The climax—the tensions leading up to which can but be guessed at after this length of time—came with his resignation, of curacy and orders together. That was the point at which Geoffrey left Rugby to return to Leeds.

He went to be curate in the place of his brother. Rather curiously, however, there arose some difficulty with authority, which apparently did not approve, except on the condition that Geoffrey should regard himself as on the staff of the neighbouring Parish Church. There, as one of twelve other curates, he would be under the surveillance of the Vicar of Leeds, Dr. Bickersteth. It would be easy to make too much of this minor matter, the true reasons behind which are in any event long past discovery. But it would seem to suggest a certain amount of caution at this stage on the part of those responsible for Geoffrey, especially when viewed alongside the fact of his two years diaconate in Rugby, instead of the usual one. Yet whatever the reason for it, the arrangement worked well enough and for the next two years, until the death of his father in 1914, he was in Leeds.

CHAPTER IV

The Vicarage in Worcester

Two years before Geoffrey returned to Leeds, a curate of the Parish Church in that city, on his way back from evening duty at the Infirmary, noticed an unusual density of crowd around one of the three statues in the square opposite the station. The place was an open-air forum at any time, and the three effigies, sooty and pigeon-whitened, of Peel, Wellington and Victoria offered ready-made platforms upon their steps. From one such vantage-point, the young man noted, a speaker of considerable skill was delivering an attack upon religion in general. The curate, having heard enough to convince himself of the formidable nature of the onslaught, resolved to report the matter forthwith to his vicar; Bickersteth.

Investigation following, it became clear that the attack was well organised. Not only local speakers, but also more expert propagandists, sent from London for the purpose, were engaged in a planned campaign, and were attracting much attention. The cloth-capped audience often extended far around the square. Counter-measures were resolved upon. Two or three times a week henceforth, christian spokesmen were to be heard in the square, often contending from the plinth of one statue while their adversary held forth from another.

It must have required considerable courage on the part of the men whom the Vicar of Leeds sent as advance guard to secure a pitch and attract attention. That achieved, they would drop out of the picture, like the first stages of a rocket of a later day, and the main speaker take over. These were sometimes men of distinction; Michael Sadler, at that time Vice-Chancellor of Leeds University, W. H. Bragg, then Cavendish Professor of Physics, and a future President of the British Association, and W. H. Draper, later to be Master of the Temple. But of them all, the one who caught and held most effectively the crowd in Victoria Square was Geoffrey himself. Bickersteth—he was father to one who had been a fellow-curate of Geoffrey's at Rugby—put him on to this work soon after his arrival. The effect was immediate. And since the whole episode was of importance to Geoffrey's future work, Bickersteth's memory of it is worth recalling.

"I can recollect none who more instantly caught the attention of the crowd of upturned faces, lit up by the glare of the electric light ... Wherever I sent him to speak probably nothing gave him greater pleasure, as he and a crowd were born to react on each other. If they thought he was only a pup because of his short tail, alluding to his short coat, they also knew he could bark, and if need be bite ... I can hear and see him now, speaking in short sharp sentences, sometimes with a good story, always with a good argument, soon leaning forward in the attitude of a John Knox as he warmed to his subject ... Undoubtedly the experience there gained revealed Geoffrey's gift for open-air work."[1]

He never ceased to exercise that exhausting gift for the rest of his life. He was orating on street corners in the lean twenties. He was holding forth, if not always in the open air, at any rate in canteens and hutments in the France of the first war. Even his audiences gave the curious impression of remaining always basically the same: critical, yet essentially friendly once their hearts were warmed. So the cloth caps in Victoria Square in 1912 and 1913 merge into khaki caps of Kitchener's armies, then into the steel helmets of the Somme and afterwards. And later still the picture mixes again back to the cloth cap, but this time of the twenties and the dole-queues. And all the time there is this Irish parson talking to them, pleading with them, making them laugh. True, that kind of audience seems, at some point down the road of time, to have vanished from the scene, like a phantom army over a cliff. Maybe its disappearance is part of the vanishing from the scene of the whole genus working man, in those days, as for time immemorial before, clearly identifiable by

[1] *Ibid.*

his costume and speech. And, as with the man, so with his woman: not only her speech, but equally her clothing separated Liza Doolittle from the rest of society. Here, clearly labelled, were the members of that great grey army of the working class of which, as Masterman showed in his essay, the higher strata of society were so afraid lest it break out, like some Caliban, easily to overpower Prospero, for all his culture, and to carry off Miranda to a fate worse than death. It is very important, all through Geoffrey's story, to have this vast army of the under-privileged in mind. Some of his main ideas sprung from the fact of its existence, just as his famous dialect poems of the war period presupposed, at that time rightly, whole battalions of men speaking like Alfred Doolittle:

> I've drunk and I've swore,
> And the girl next door
> Is a' breakin' 'er 'eart thro' me—

And here now in Victoria Square, Leeds, were crowds of this very sort of men listening with relish to anti-religious propaganda. That also was much in character. It formed part of the normal atmosphere of many a town parson's life at that time. But it was a depressing atmosphere, for all that. Not only was the Church—and in particular, far beyond all others, the established Church—felt to be possessed by the possessing classes, but also an obstacle, like some ancient boulder athwart a stream, to the onward flow of social justice. In consequence, most left-wing political thought was automatically anti-religious, in spite of the fact that not a few trades union leaders, like Ernest Bevin, owed much to chapel backgrounds. Nor was that all. The speakers against whom Geoffrey contended in Victoria Square were well organised. Two or three well-financed societies of rationalists and free-thinkers existed, each one with its weekly newspaper, of which by far the most effective was Robert Blatchford's *Clarion*. This weekly, very ably edited, exercised a great influence. "It was to be found in every working men's club or mechanic's institute, and in a vast number of working class houses. The secular spirit was growing, and was on the march. It was implicit in the materialistic

and competitive ethics of international and industrial relationships. About this social disorder, and its awful results for human
lives, thinking workers complained that the Church had all too
little to say . . ."[1]

Maybe that was true. Certainly, Geoffrey's life work, notably
in the decade after the war, was devoted to saying what it was
alleged the Church had so far failed to say in that regard. And yet
one wonders whether the charge was altogether accurate. It is
surprising, to say the least of it, that all the social activities of the
Church for a hundred years since the Industrial Revolution
should have resulted a century later in the public image of that
same Church as a body indifferent to such concerns. To have
pioneered popular education and to have sent generations of
clergy to selfless lives in the stinking slums of the nineteenth
century were some few among the honours which the Church
could claim, and they were not minor ones. Yet the critics seemed
scarcely to have heard of these things.

Yet the evidence was often clear enough. Leeds Parish Church,
upon the staff of which Geoffrey now found himself, was a case
in point. Among its vicars had been a certain Walter Farquhar
Hook, Vicar of Leeds from 1837 to 1859. To him was due the fact
that the parish church by Geoffrey's time was one of the most
notable in the country, occupying a position of honour in the life
of the city. Like the parish church at Rugby, though on a much
greater scale, it had adapted itself to the pressures of an expansion-
ist epoch. Also like Rugby, it had been enabled to do so by the
outstanding quality of its ministry in critical times.

That leadership was Hook's. How he brought order and
dignity to the worship of the church, how he rebuilt a place in
which, at his first coming, churchwardens arriving for a meeting
were in the habit of piling hats and coats on the altar, how he
affected profoundly the whole thinking of the Church as to its
proper place in the scheme of things for generations to come,
and that before Keble and the Tractarians had begun their work,
belongs to another tale than this. But what is relevant is his
social work. Leeds, when he arrived, was a hell-hole.

[1] Roger Lloyd: *The Church of England in the Twentieth Century.*

"Labour was a mere commodity, to be bought in the cheapest market and to be dispensed with the moment it was no longer needed . . . To shelter these people, row upon row of flimsy, back to back houses were run up. There was one room up and one room down. Four or five privies supplied the sanitation for all the street. Yet these places, poor as they were, seemed palaces compared with the holes in which those of the working class who could not get them were forced to herd themselves. Brothels abounded."[1]

There were thirteen of them, it may be added, hard by Hook's own church. Nor was that all.

"Into these foul streets, already supercharged with dirt, disease and every misery, the Irish famine of 1846 discharged thousands of gaunt and starving wretches, wild-eyed and in rags . . . Where they could they packed into cellars and attics, and if this was impossible they knocked up shanties in the already abominable streets. With no sanitation and no water supply, only one result could follow. It came — first typhus fever and then cholera."[2]

A few weeks later, one of Hook's curates, on funeral duty, found twenty-three bodies awaiting burial in a great pit, in which corpses already lay six deep.

Such were some of the fantastic conditions with which Hook had to contend. Not surprisingly, they were accompanied by bitter anti-clericalism. The river of that indifference and hostility which some encountered for the first time in uniform in the first war, and which Geoffrey and the Industrial Christian Fellowship were encountering in the twenties may well have risen far backwards in time in such wildernesses of the industrial scene as the Leeds of the forties of the preceding century — and there were many such. When Hook first went to Leeds there was scarcely a single working man in his parish who would do other than scowl at him. Nor was this hostility directed only at the established Church. Thomas Cooper the Chartist was a Methodist local preacher until his conscience moved him to give it up, since he could no longer square it with the duty of preaching

[1] C. J. Stranks: *Dean Hook.*

[2] *Ibid.*

71

eternal damnation to the starving. It was around the same time, too, in Leeds, that "one Sunday morning, as the bells rang for church, a 'poor, wretched man' brought out his Bible and Prayer Book and publicly burned them in the yard near St. Peter's Church.'[1] The terrible grief and disillusion implicit in the act come still through the record of it. Yet within twenty years a Leeds labourer brought back from a country walk a bunch of flowers for Hook, saying, "Do take them, for I like your teaching." Another man pressed him to have his photograph printed and sold cheaply so that the people could hang it in their homes.

And why? Because by that time the poor of Leeds had seen the 'tender, tender heart', as one of his curates described it, of this great man so often moved for them, privately in many acts of charity, publicly in political action. "I would rather ten thousand times be in a scrape with the good hearted than on the highest pinnacle with the merely right-headed," he once proclaimed, and the battles he fought bore it out: popular education; the Ten Hour Bill, to limit the intolerably long working day of women and children in factories, were among them. The dispensary opened in his parish employed three doctors, in its day. That day had been over long before Geoffrey went to Leeds Parish Church. But it had been succeeded by a golden age. Since Hook, there had been seven vicars of Leeds: all were men of distinction, and the parish with its vast congregations, its honoured place in civic life, its vigorous men's societies and lad's clubs, so characteristic of the parish life of the period, all so soon to become war casualties, testified to the triumphant manner in which, where there had been men such as Hook to match the early Victorian hour, the Church had been enabled to meet a challenge unparalleled in its history. The statement that it had neglected the people, selfishly hanging on to its privileges the while, was not nearly so true as the critics in Victoria Square maintained. When Hook went to Leeds in 1837 the vicar of a neighbouring parish stated that in thirty years he had never seen a young man come to the altar. Within a few years there were five hundred communicants on Easter Day in the parish church itself.

[1] *Ibid.*

Such, then, was some of the background to Geoffrey's two years at Leeds. His position was a curious one; at once on the staff of the parish church and not fully of it, since his first loyalty was to his father in the vicarage at Quarry Hill. There at St. Mary's, run down as the place was, Geoffrey's coming brought a rapid change for the better. Even to that unlikely area he began to attract even from a distance, so that people began to make their way to hear him as the masters at Rugby School had once done.

Sometimes, too, he went further afield. He was beginning to be heard of. Thus in November 1913, when a mission was to be held in Barrow-in-Furness and last-minute difficulties over a missioner had arisen, someone recalled hearing of an extraordinary young curate working with his aged father in a slum parish in Leeds. Not without doubts, he was sent for. The doubts were deepened by his appearance. He arrived in glossy black clothes and an astonishing, a truly remarkable silk hat from which it was difficult to avert the eye. Clearly very young, very Irish and very shy, he was not inspiring. But all doubts vanished when he gave his first address. One who was there, and recalled the occasion many years later, remembered the startling impact of the torrent of words, in manner and meaning so unusual, upon those who heard it. And then, as suddenly as he had arrived, he left, having to produce a play, he shyly explained, back in his father's parish. The man who thus encountered him, a fellow-missioner at Barrow, scarcely ever met him again. But as the years passed, and he heard of the fame of the little Irishman, he was not surprised.[1]

Even so, it was probably a good thing that he had the steadying influence and the good fellowship of the parish church at Leeds behind him at this stage. There is a glimpse of an anglican era vanished forever in the picture of Friday lunch-times in Leeds Vicarage in these years, when no less than a full dozen of curates – for such was the size of the staff in those opulent days—gathered for their weekly meeting, followed by lunch and billiards. Geoffrey would be with them, and often afterwards he would stay to discuss with Bickersteth his own particular problems at

[1] *Church Times.* March 15th, 1929.

St. Mary's. It would have surprised that good man, as it would indeed have astounded anybody, to know that within seven years at the most the large-eyed, Irish curate anxiously discussing the affairs of the neighbouring parish with him would be a national figure.

Meanwhile, there was another aspect of Church life with which he was involved as eloquent of a vanished day as the dozen curates. This was the Lads' Club. It was the great day of such bodies, albeit the evening of it. There was not much time left before many of the boys who had formed their membership were to become names on war-memorials, to be accorded, once a year, the passing tribute of a poppy-wreath and the quavering last-post of a local bugler. Even those who survived were to come back with very little disposition indeed, as regards what once had been their Church, to take up where they had left off. But in nineteen twelve and thirteen Lads' Clubs still flourished. In a sense, they were yet another part of the working class problem as it was seen at the time.

"The vast majority of these clubs existed to serve the young working lad . . . His position in society and in the Church was often heart-rending. To be a Christian, even to be a good citizen, took some doing in a back street in Portsmouth or Birmingham. Taken from school when his new adult powers of body were coming upon him and bewildering him, and then flung upon the labour market into the nearest factory, it was no wonder he often drifted into vacancy of mind, flabbiness of body, and desperate, noisy unhappiness of soul."[1]

The problem, it may be observed, still exists. Only the poverty is missing. Meanwhile, Geoffrey found himself as much at home in such work as he did later on encountering a similar kind of society in canteens in France.

So the years passed at Leeds. Looking back on them from the remoteness of 1919, Geoffrey in a letter to Bickersteth recalled them as especially happy, thereby conforming to a sad little mannerism very noticeable in the memoirs of the twenties. It was as if, in the eyes of the survivors of the war, the years im-

[1] Roger Lloyd: *The Church of England in the Twentieth Century.*

mediately preceding it were suffused in a golden light, the glory and the freshness of a dream. So the French came to remember the summer of 1914 itself as one of exceptional splendour; the trees never so heavy, the fields never so rich. (Years later the British were to feel exactly the same about the summer of 1940.) Personal memories, too, seem similarly affected; so that the holidays of those final years are invested with a colour which, one suspects, existed only in the eye of recollection. Thus J. K. Mozley, he with whom Geoffrey had in former times so often heard the chimes at midnight, recorded the vacations of 1912 and 1913, which he took with Geoffrey and the latter's brother, Gerald, as expeditions of enormous gusto and enjoyment, when they tramped about the Lake District and Geoffrey's umbrella, which for inexplicable reasons he had taken on the ascent, blew out on the precipices of Great End.

It was about this time that Geoffrey wrote Mozley a letter which gives some indication of the quality of his mind. Mozley had been asked to lecture on Wells, and wrote to Geoffrey for his views. The result was a perceptive study of that writer. It is worth noting as yet another instance of how mistaken those many were who saw, as Geoffrey rose to fame in the years now fast approaching, as one incapable of balanced judgment.

"What is wrong with Wells is that he does not ask what is right. He is essentially a Greek to whom the Gospel will always be foolishness. He is a very typical product of evolutionary philosophy ... Dimly on the horizon of his thought there moves the shadowy spectre of sin, at present the only forms in which he knows it are stupidity, the monopoly of the rich, and ignorance, the monopoly of the poor. These are to be overcome by education and universal Good Will ... His analyses of character are always defective, in that he allows no place for a moral nature. Sanity, courage, humility, simplicity: he has all these in the intellectual sphere; of their Christian counterparts he knows nothing."

The words stand yet as a sound judgment, not only of Wells, but equally of that whole cast of mind which, finding as it did so many literary expressions in the twenty years after the war, did such immeasurable harm to the social thinking of at least two generations.

In his private life there now came to Geoffrey a development of the utmost importance. He fell in love, and became engaged to be married. Emily Catlow he had known for some time as a friend of the family. A dark, rather reserved girl living with an aunt in Leeds, she for her part at first endeavoured to control a passion in him which was characteristically violent. He would have, she told him, to wait. But it was not to be. The climax came during a summer camp at Scarborough of a parish Lads' Club which Geoffrey had accompanied. Miss Catlow was on holiday also, and the two young people soon found each other. There was an evening when they both sang at a Camp Concert of the club. Geoffrey proposed to her. A little later Geoffrey Anketell Studdert Kennedy was married to Emily Catlow, on St. Mark's Day, 1914, in St. Mary's, Quarry Hill, by J. K. Mozley.

The death of Geoffrey's father, followed shortly afterwards by his own departure from Leeds, provided the opportunity for the marriage.

William Studdert Kennedy, Vicar of St. Mary's, Quarry Hill, for thirty-seven years, died in the early months of 1914, aged eighty-eight, in the same place, in the same house, where the large family by his second wife had been brought up. She herself had pre-deceased him by a year. It was the end of the house in Leeds as far as the Studdert Kennedys were concerned. And for Geoffrey himself it was the end of a phase in his life. The whole point of his returning to the place had gone with the death of his father. Considerable efforts, culminating in a deputation of St. Mary's people to the Vicar of Leeds, were made to keep him there. It was felt that he should succeed his father. But authority decided otherwise, as it always wisely does in such matters, and the curate was offered employment in the neighbourhood. But that also was not to be, since Bickersteth at this same time received a letter from a friend who was Archdeacon of Worcester containing the suggestion that, as the living of the small down-town church of St. Paul's, Worcester, was vacant, the man who had already made a name for himself in the diocese during his curacy at Rugby, should go there. Other offers came at the same time. But the reason why Geoffrey chose Worcester was typical. He said to his wife, "St. Paul's has the smallest income and the poorest people—go and look at the house, and if you think you can manage it I will accept."

He was instituted to the living on the unpropitious date of June 9th, 1914.

.   .   .   .

St. Paul's, Worcester, belonged, just as St. Mary's, Quarry Hill, had done, to the category of a minor town parish—a church of the little streets put there after the streets had appeared. Often enough, the parochial boundaries of such a place were the creation of administrative fiat rather than the result of a natural process, as in a country parish. There, with the village around it, the church sat naturally enough at the heart of things, an integral part of the community. Even to the outer eye, it seemed to belong. But that could rarely be said of the back street churches which came into existence in such numbers during the nineteenth century. There, where a parochial boundary of one might end at a gasworks as arbitrarily as that of another might extend as far as a shunting yard or a canal, the sense of parochial community had to be created. Sometimes it never was, so that some of these urban churches from the moment of their consecration supported a kind of sick half-life, not infrequently breaking the heart of the clergyman responsible for it, and continuing so to do even unto the present day. Too often, they were ill-founded and inadequately equipped from the start. One critic of the system they represented, Edgar Gibson, Vicar of Leeds, writing towards the end of the century, complained that the bishops had produced new parishes furnished with the cheapest possible churches with the slick fertility of a conjuror delivering rabbits out of a top-hat. In the St. Pancras area of London four ancient parishes had given birth to thirty new ones. The inevitable result was the gradual sinking into a state of contented dejection of many vicars of these new parishes, who were simply left alone in an impossible position to do an impossible job."[1]

[1] *Ibid.*

Such was the sombre background to not a few of those down-town churches. And it is perhaps one measure of their lack of impact upon the imagination that they, their clergy and their people, never seem to have achieved any literary reflection of note. Few have bothered to write about the town parson; many have delighted to do so of country rectory and cathedral close. The reason may seem to be that the true life of the kind of church born to blush unseen behind gasworks or brewery is often to outward seeming as unglamorous as those institutions themselves.

Yet the truth in the inward parts is very different. That church is rare indeed, however grimy, ill-found, depressing, which in fact has not touched some lives at least with the beauty of holiness. And some have evoked a staggering degree of inarticulate loyalty and devotion from those who have worshipped in them for a lifetime. It was true of St. Paul's, Worcester, that the district was poor. But the church itself was rich in one respect: in the foundations laid by its saintly first vicar, a certain Canon Douglas. Here, in fact, when Geoffrey went there, was a living organism very much alive with the tradition which Douglas had bequeathed to it, and which his successors had faithfully maintained. Like the mission church at Rugby, to which Geoffrey had been attached, St. Paul's was regarded as 'high', which meant in fact that Douglas had been an heir of the Tractarians and had striven to make of St. Paul's — into which church and parish, incidentally, he and his wife had put not only their lives, but also their personal fortune — a worthy mirror to reflect the reverence, the devotion, the modest ceremonial of the 'Church revival', as it was sometimes curiously called, of the nineteenth century. In the days of Douglas himself the mode of worship and the sacramental emphasis of the whole were forerunners of what came to be the normal practice of a later day, so that surpliced choir and a visible reverence for the altar, upon which phenomena the curious and the critical had once not uncommonly gone to gaze, had become, long before Geoffrey's time, accepted things.

So St. Paul's was 'high', more so than, for instance, the Cathedral pursuing the even tenor of its way at a little distance across the city, watching the Severn flow by, and the white figures of cricketers moving upon the county ground beyond the river in that summer of 1914.

Such a setting as St. Paul's suited Geoffrey admirably. He valued the ritual he found there. It was drama: it was beauty, and that always meant enormously much to him. But such things were secondary.

It was all summed in his saying, as once he did, that he would rather, as a matter of personal choice, celebrate the Holy Communion on an upturned packing-case, than amidst the most elaborate ceremonial. Even so, he respected and used ceremonial when it was there.

It was there at St. Paul's, and he used it effectively, in his modest corner of Worcester, as great parish priests of a like kind in an earlier day had done. A colleague of his at Worcester compared him, in fact, to some of the notable clergy of the catholic revival of the previous century.

"He was in the true line of succession of Stanton and Dolling and Wainwright", Hunt, his curate, wrote, "diligent, self-giving, and utterly faithful to the Church system and worship. He loved the daily services and made the most of all the Church offices. He made the baptismal service real for parents and sponsors, and often quoted his poetry to them. His poem 'Christopher' was used on such an occasion . . ."[1]

This is the first appearance of the famous 'poetry', of which in the course of his life Geoffrey wrote a good deal as the emotion of the moment gave cause. It was always the basis of his reputation. Indeed, within three years of these days at St. Paul's, Worcester, his Rough Rhymes were selling in edition after edition. For that matter, the appeal of his verse has been maintained and shows no sign of fading. A fourteenth edition of his collected verse appeared in 1947. And three of his poems have even achieved the special distinction of becoming hymns, if rarely sung ones. Awake, awake to Love and work, Close by the heedless worker's side, and When through the whirl of wheels, and engines humming.

What would be worth knowing is the effect upon some

[1] G. A. Studdert Kennedy: By His Friends.

baptismal party in those far-off days of having read to them by
the author the following:

> Bear thou the Christ,
> My little son,
> He will not burden thee,
> That Holy One,
> For, by a mystery,
> Who bearest him he bears,
> Eternally,
> Up to the radiant heights,
> Where Angels be . . .

Perhaps it is as good an indication as any of the odd power of
this man that he would make such an action not only acceptable
but memorable.

This personal magnetism—and there seems no alternative to
the well-worn phrase to describe it—was very noticeable, and
during the years to come was to be experienced by many people
indeed. It had already made itself felt at Rugby, when the masters
of the school had heard him as gladly, and been drawn to him as
strangely, as the outcasts in the lodging-houses. And now here at
Worcester the same process began again. In his first letter in the
inevitable parish magazine he had written the trite words: "my
study is a place where anyone can come and talk and be sure of a
hearty welcome . . . I do want to be a friend to everyone . . ."
Ninety-nine out of a hundred earnest young clergymen might
have expressed such sentiments without either expecting or
receiving any particular response. But this one was different.
Within a short time the wife of the new Vicar of St. Paul's had to
restrict the numbers of those who wanted what lay behind the
'hearty welcome' and the 'talk'. What they wanted, of course, was
to unburden themselves of some of that heavy weight of sins and
doubts and secret things which some of the most outwardly
normal carry invisibly about with them throughout life. So
burdened men and women, like mediaeval cripples hobbling to
a new shrine, will always tend to respond to such apparently

quite inexplicable magnetism as Geoffrey's by seeking him out eagerly, if sometimes furtively, as Nicodemus did Christ by night, and then unloading upon him some of the weight which afflicts them. And always, naturally, there will be among them the cranks, the neurotics, the frauds. The possessor of such magnetism, of which popularity is the counterfeit, or bastard form, is surely much to be pitied, since it is often enough to bear one's own sorrows without having added the infinite weight of so many others. When, years later, Geoffrey told the ordinand who questioned him on the matter that a priest was "one who bore upon himself the sins and sorrows of his people" he certainly knew by that time, from infinite experience, what he was talking about.

This same uncanny power of drawing people was to be seen in operation, when he had been at Worcester only a little while, after the Sunday evening service at St. Paul's. The sedate order of evensong, which flows quietly like a stream in the flat English midlands, which becomes dear only as it becomes familiar, and can be markedly uninspiring to the newcomer, does not generally seem designed to be a high, dramatic occasion. Indeed, it was never intended as such, being rather a choir office for the close of day which the invention of gas lighting, for the first time brought into the evening hours. Herein lay the original of the social *cachet* for long attached to mattins. The better sort, having leisure to do so, tended to keep their particular rendezvous with Almighty God in the morning. Evensong was for the servants, in such areas where they were to be found, and for the servantless, who by that time might be assumed to have the chores of the day behind them. So it was the humbler sort, domestics and tired mums and dads, who came at evening when the sun was set to the familiar words, "Lighten our darkness we beseech Thee, O Lord . . .", and listen with respect to the sermon. So broad a generalisation obviously cannot be wholly accurate; but it does represent a pattern of social behaviour which was strong when Geoffrey went to St. Paul's in Worcester.

There, evensong soon ceased to be a service and became an experience. "The service," Hunt wrote, "was alive with passion

and earnestness. He preached (generally without text or introduction) plunging into his subject at once, and all eyes were
riveted on him. He turned the lights out so that people should
not be disturbed by the dress or manners of others about them.
The effect of this preaching was terrific." After the service came
the supplicants, awaiting him in numbers, often each requiring a
long and troubled interview: people burdened in conscience,
in sexual and domestic difficulty; alcoholics, drug-addicts, and
the lonely and the desperate. Such a phenomenon had not been
seen in Worcester before, and it is some revelation of the under-
side of life, even in a Cathedral town in 1914, that it could be
seen at all. Yet Geoffrey at St. Paul's somehow seemed to have
the power of drawing private anxieties from their various sorrowful obscurities. But it was a costly business: the price to be paid
in personal strain was enormous, and continued to bear upon
him more or less unremittingly from this time until his death
fifteen years later. Once a physician identifies himself with the
sufferings of his patients, he is treading a dangerous path. Even
the confessional is said to require a certain clinical detachment,
and the psychiatrist needs to be the observer and by no means the
sharer, of the troubles of those who seek him out. All such
relationships between suffering and its treatment are a world
away, and exist upon a different plane altogether, from what
happens when suffering chances to meet, not treatment, but a
love which appears, for some mysterious reason, to need to
share its burden. That kind of love, that kind of understanding,
Geoffrey had. The trouble is that the world's griefs in the end
make a cross so heavy that the bearer of it eventually has to
fall under the weight of it. He is in fact doomed as soon as
he shoulders the thing. So Geoffrey in Worcester, when the
sick in soul came to lay their burdens upon him, had already
begun his *via dolorosa,* and hard and long was to be the
way of it.

Meanwhile, the quixotic generosities which had annoyed his
landlady when he was a curate at Rugby continued at Worcester.
The difference was that now he had a wife, and there were times
when she found her position required considerable forbearance.

There was the occasion, for instance, when he carried a whole bed, by stages, starting with one pillow, from the vicarage to an invalid he had found in comfortless surroundings somewhere in the parish. When she came upon the scene he had progressed as far as the bedstead. The mattress, however, presented difficulties for one man to carry, and so she helped him along the street with it herself. Such stories got about, and were no doubt embroidered in the telling. He was said to be a fool with his money, and therefore soon parted from it. Yet that was not quite true. If indeed he was imprudent with his own, being much addicted to impulsive giving, he was careful enough with that of other people, and very wise in the distribution of the sums which soon began to come to him, often anonymously, to be used as he would.

There was need of it. He had known the place was poor, and gone there largely for that reason. Yet, even so, the extent and bitterness of the poverty he actually encountered there moved him much, and sowed the seeds of his radical political opinions of later years. He was not alone in that; many others, whom circumstances or conscience made aware of the conditions in which a large proportion of the population were living in the early nineteen hundreds, found dangerous thoughts growing within them. Thus Seebohm Rountree: "That in this land of abounding wealth, during a time of perhaps unexampled prosperity, probably more than one fourth of the population is living in poverty is a fact which may well cause great searchings of heart . . . The suffering may be all but voiceless, and we may long remain ignorant of its extent and severity, but when once we realise it we see that social questions of profound importance await solution."[1]

It was true, and unless this search for a solution of economic and social ills, together with the grey poverty which motivated it, be always borne in mind, it is not likely that much of the flavour, at once bitter and anxious, of the whole period through which Geoffrey lived, can be recaptured. The background to it all was the coexistence of poverty and riches.

[1] Seebohm Rountree: *Poverty*. 1901.

"It seems strange today," wrote one observer of this scene many years later, "but that some children were hungry was accepted as wet weather is accepted. I can remember my mother helping to serve soup, which could be bought by the needy for a penny a jug. In most towns in the winter such soup was provided for the poor ... Neither the tradesmen who provided the materials for the soup, nor the ladies who helped to serve it, appeared to think it wrong that in a rich country families could be in such want that they would queue with jugs for a penny-worth of soup ... Poverty was something that happened, just as some people were born cripples. You helped; but you did not expect to cure them."[1]

The Socialism of the twenties, the General Strike, the dole queues, the Industrial Christian Fellowship, its crusades and its missions: William Temple and C.O.P.E.C., the whole business of the economic and political thinking of the Church with which, in the unguessed-at future Geoffrey was to be so intimately involved, is without meaning if separated from the continuous drab background against which the high drama of it all was acted out.

The need is to grasp the reality. To what desperate need, one wonders, did Geoffrey carry his bedstead down one of the streets of his Worcester parish? It could have been a case like the one quoted by Jack London, where it was revealed at an inquest on a seventy-seven year old woman, that she had occupied her one filthy room for thirty-five years, had no money, and had died of blood poisoning from bed-sores. Such may have been an extreme case; but it was easy enough to find it repeated in any town of Britain. Nor was it necessary to be aged or ill in order to be very poor. The average weekly wage of a working-man in 1913 was twenty shillings. One of the many social investigators of the time, looking into the question of how the family managed on it, concluded that the possession of four children was enough to make the task quite impossible. Given four shillings per child per week for food, there would be six for the parents and nothing

[1] Noel Streatfeild: *The Day Before Yesterday*.

at all for rent or heating or clothing or anything else.[1] Such were the depressing conclusions to which those looking into the state of the working class were faced. Yet there was nothing new about the situation: it had existed for many years, and the back streets of every town contained teeming instances of it. It was thus in the parish of St. Paul's, Worcester. When Geoffrey arrived home penniless, as he often did, to demand of his wife more money to give away, it was with many such situations of need that he was concerned.

All this made no small stir in the place. After the daily Celebration he would be out and about in the parish for the rest of the day. He preached in the streets: there were few homes where he was not a visitor. And of course there were clubs, after the fashion of the day. At Geoffrey's instigation the Church Army opened one, the Captain and his wife living in the vicarage, and evening after evening the peculiar looking vicar with the enormous eyes and noticeable ears would be in one part or another of it. The vicar was also much sought-after by children, just as he had been in Rugby. They followed him about, which can be as exhausting in fact as it is charming in theory. Even so, it was a part of his ministry which he took extremely seriously, giving anxious thought to the schools in the parish, as well as the large Sunday School. Now for obvious reasons, it cannot often happen that anyone who involves himself with the young can ever know much about the results. Yet occasionally, and usually long afterwards, a little of the truth is revealed, and it was so in the case of Geoffrey.

Thus, during the General Election Campaign of 1959 a certain Liberal Candidate in the City of Birmingham, a prosperous manufacturer, was asked by a reporter for the motivation of his political and social activities, and in particular for his championship of the elderly and the poor. He replied that it was largely an emotional matter, traceable back to his boyhood days, when he came under the influence, as a choir-boy at St. Paul's, in his native Worcester, "of that religious spell-binder, the Rev. G. A. Studdert Kennedy, known to a former generation as 'Woodbine

[1] Mrs. Bember Reeves: *Round About a Pound a Week.* 1913.

Willie'. 'When he died I resolved to dedicate myself to public service. It was not a political; but an emotional impulse.' "[1]

The interesting thing here is that the speaker, only forty-six at the time of this interview, cannot have known anything of Geoffrey until after the first war, and then but briefly and at a very early age, until Geoffrey's departure in 1921. Yet the deep impression was made, and the influence of the man was a thing of power for long afterwards.

It was at this time also that Geoffrey became known as a conductor of retreats, to use the depressing title given to a function which few can satisfactorily discharge. But with small groups of people who had gone apart for a while to think on things and to pray, Geoffrey was superb. This was the Mary side of an otherwise Martha-like personality, cumbered about to the end with too much to do. Yet somehow he always found time for this 'one thing needful': he was a spiritual interpreter of the first order, and few have more effectively put old wine into new bottles. Not many, in any event, in the years just before the first war, were interested: the idea of 'making a retreat', the religious equivalent of 'getting away from it all', had not gained the general currency it was to do in later years.

Geoffrey became in time very well known as an everyman's guide into that quiet country of the soul. Unfortunately, little of what he said on these occasions survives. Except for the book *The New Man in Christ*, edited by the Dean of Worcester after Geoffrey's death, there is little left on record of that abundance which once came from him and which so many found so memorable. This is a sorrowful loss, for he became a great teacher when, after these early Worcester days, and an age away from them in experience, he expressed in this intimate part of his ministry insights given to few. Thus there is this, from an address on prayer in *The New Man in Christ*: "When you pray like Jesus it is clear that you are not asking God to do things for you, you are asking God to give you the desire and the power to do things for him. That is a different story, isn't it? Jesus taught that there was no good thing which God does not desire to give us.

[1] *Birmingham Mail.*

The difficulty lies in preparing ourselves to receive, to appreciate, and to use rightly the gifts that he is striving to impart. The tragedy arises from the fact that God cannot give us more than we prepare ourselves to receive. There are in each and all of us unknown and immense capacities for good. We are, indeed, if we would only realise it, the sons of God. All the treasures of an infinite universe of goodness, truth and beauty are ours if we will set ourselves with single minds to seek the highest. But we must ask and keep on asking, we must seek and keep on seeking; we must knock and keep on knocking. Only to those who persevere can the glory of the Kingdom be revealed. The difficulty, according to Jesus, does not lie in persuading God to give; but in preparing ourselves to receive. The Kingdom of God; the fairer, finer, cleaner world, is ours as we ourselves develop our longing and desire for it."

There is also this, from that talk on the 23rd Psalm which, as was seen in an earlier chapter of this book, so impressed itself on the memory of one who heard it:

"A really clever man or woman finds it fatally easy not only to deceive others, but to deceive themselves, and justify conduct in themselves which is in reality utterly unjustifiable. Conscious hypocrites are rarer than people suppose, for much that the world calls hypocrisy is the honest strife of very imperfect men. But unconscious hypocrisy is much commoner than people suppose, and the very cleverest men and women are often the victims of it. Their mental powers enable them to impose their own mischievous imaginations upon more simple people and upon themselves. It is never the fool who really wrecks and ruins the family or the nation; it is the able man who has never found the true meaning of life and is still trying to build the world about himself as centre; the man whose hunger of the heart is still unsatisfied and who has not found the great love.

The heart is really the master whether you like it or not, and if the master be wrong the servants can but do his will. If the light that is within them be darkness, how great is that darkness!

The supreme question for us all is, what do you want? What do you love? And it is here that the Good Shepherd comes in to minister to our necessity—our necessity, let us repeat—comes in to give us not luxuries and extras, but comes in to give us what we must have. If we pretend that we can do without it, we do but deceive ourselves. If we do not love Beauty, Truth and Goodness as it is in Jesus Christ we will love some beauty, truth and goodness of our own, some person or reality. If we will not have Jesus for our Good then we must either find a better one, or serve a worse. If we pretend that we have not got one we are merely fooling ourselves. Atheism is not a creed, it is a nervous disease; it means life without anything to live for, and that is hell.

When a man tells me that he has no religion I simply take it that he is talking nonsense and proceed to find out what his religion is—what it is that gives life meaning to him. What one generally discovers is that the man or woman has a god, but a poor one. And because he has a poor god he is a poor person and is still in want, not knowing what he wants, but unhappy till he gets it."

But apart from these collected retreat addresses in *The New Man in Christ* only fragments remain, and even these are scattered about in unexpected places. A little book, for instance, called *When We Pray, a Method of Prayer taught by Studdert Kennedy*[1] brought out, again after Geoffrey's death, by an admirer, is clearly based on notes taken of some of his talks. Moreover, anyone who cares to compare the 'method' with which the book is concerned with much subsequent popular teaching on this theme will find in fact that there is the original and prototype of a good deal of it. The man who, in the Deanery at Worcester, or in the Chapel at Earl Beauchamp's house at Madresfield, used to conduct retreats for little groups of earnest people was, in fact, potentially a spiritual counsellor of the first order, a great deal of whose value was that he seemed to say:

> Everyman, I will go with thee and be thy guide,
> In thy most need, to go by thy side.

[1] Ronald Sinclair: *When We Pray*. Hodder & Stoughton.

But then, of course, that event occurred which came in time to render all else insignificant. The world blew up, to the profound astonishment of all concerned, who do not seem to have noticed the fuse burning and sparking in their midst for so long. Three months after Geoffrey had gone to Worcester, the first world war began. How that involved him, and how it brought him eventually, dressed up as a Chaplain, to Lady Mabel Egerton's canteen by the railway siding at Rouen, falls now to be told.

CHAPTER V

The Making of Woodbine Willie

IT was a fine summer, that one of 1914. Down among the streets of the parish of St. Paul's in the Blockhouse, Worcester, the heat drew odours from the privies out back of the row of houses facing the vicarage. That itself was a pleasant enough house. Its front door, flush to the street, gave on to a hall from which stairs led to dining-room and study. At the side, an unexpectedly large garden, brick wall enclosed, stretched down to the church. In these surroundings, for the three months remaining between his institution and the outbreak of war, the new vicar devoted himself to getting the feel of his first parish.

Meanwhile, the country at large drifted into that summer, like a man in a punt out for the day who, having had some narrow squeaks with other craft at his setting out, now sensed calmer waters before him. For one thing, industrial relations seemed to have settled down, for a while at least. Strikes and lock-outs, epidemic two years before, had tailed off. Britain prospered; some people were making a lot of money, and for those who were not, the old-age pensions and insurance schemes at long last had smoothed the sharper edges of poverty. Ireland, of course continued to give trouble. Indeed, throughout that spring by far the most alarming news had come from across the Irish Sea. Carson had raised his Ulster Volunteers, as the possibility of Home Rule drew nearer. Civil war had seemed very close. And then, to cap all, had come the mutiny at the Curragh where officers of troops concentrated for a possible move against the North, had announced that they would send in their papers rather than obey such an order. When the new Vicar of St. Paul's, Worcester, had time to read a paper in those months in his new parish, such were the events making the headlines.

Meanwhile, life went on. The British fleet paid a courtesy call on the German Naval review at Kronstadt, where the great ships of both countries lay alongside each other, bathed in the sunlight of that unusually flaming June. The occasion, overflowing with mutual goodwill, seemed a pleasant sequel to the State visit of King George V to Paris which had taken place in June.

In fact, by the end of July, things were distinctly improved compared with the situation earlier in the year.

In view of all this it was scarcely surprising that a news item which came at the end of June created at first little stir. "The Archduke Francis Ferdinand, heir to the throne of Austro-Hungary and his morganatic wife, the Duchess of Hohenburg, were assassinated yesterday in the town of Sarajevo, Capital of Bosnia." The best-documented pot-shot in the history of the world soon began to make its consequences felt. They appeared to be endless: they continued to accumulate: they touched to lives of the most obscure, including even that of the new Vicar of St. Paul's, Worcester.

But not immediately. First there had to be the period of those far-off battles among the alien corn in the golden autumn: Mons, the Marne, the Aisne: when French and German faced each other in open field, and the small British Expeditionary Force, landed in France on August 21st, learned to know the long, poplar-lined French roads. These were great, these were earth-shaking events. But because happenings of half a century old are still in that limbo which exists between the historical and the contemporary, the feel of those months, August to December 1914, is difficult to recapture. Waterloo is easier to visualise than Mons, having settled into the stylised postures of history. But the rifle fire of Mons can still faintly be heard down the corridors of living memory.

Yet it is important – at any rate to a narrative such as this – to see again that sequence of events, since only by doing so is it possible even to guess at the emotions which made people living them, including Geoffrey, act subsequently as they did. Something tremendous clearly had happened in the world to make H. G. Wells so far abandon his former attitudes as to write, in a letter to *The Daily News* towards the end of this August: "I find myself enthusiastic for this war against Prussian militarism. We are, I believe, assisting at the end of a vast, intolerable oppression upon civilisation."

Geoffrey, in his small corner, apparently shared these sentiments. His parish magazine for September contained this: "I cannot say too strongly that I believe every able-bodied man ought to volunteer for service anywhere. There ought to be no shirking of that duty. Those who cannot volunteer for military service can pray . . ."

There were many saying such things by then, who were later much mocked for doing so by those sadder and wiser after the event. Geoffrey himself became sadder and wiser after the event. It was long held, indeed, to have been especially monstrous for the Church to have urged Christian soldiers onward as to war with such crude abandon. He came to think so himself. Such sentiments were duly taken down and used in evidence at the trial of the Establishment, in the wider sense of the word, which came years later. Not that it matters now, of course. The whole scene has been long buried deep beneath other deposits of history. But he who cares to excavate down to it cannot avoid finding there, like a golden ornament among much that is worthless, traces of that astonishing wave of brave emotion which then animated so many. And unless he takes cognisance of this, recognising it as the true metal that it was, he will be unable to to make head or tail of what happened.

What happened then was that, absolutely for the first time, a genuine dragon was felt to be at large, and St. George called upon to deal with him. Out of what long camouflaged lair he had so suddenly emerged no one seemed quite to know. It was difficult at first even to credit that he had. But as Mons gave place to the Marne, as the casualty lists began to come in, as France began to bleed to death, as Paris escaped by the skin of its teeth, as Antwerp was bombarded and fell and the first Belgian refugees arrived — seventy thousand of them by October — it was seen that this dragon was real enough. He breathed fire, his proportions were enormous, his intentions wholly evil — and he was made in Germany. And then, hard upon the shock of these events came stories of atrocities, all the more horrifying because falling upon ears innocent of the sound of propaganda: tales of rape and pillage; of children skewered on bayonets by derisive Prussians, and girls set aside for the pleasure of monocled officers. Of course, most of the stories were untrue. Such was one of the many disenchanting disclosures of subsequent history. The German general staff, in fact, actually appointed a commission of neutral American observers to investigate these charges. The result was as might have been expected: occupying troops had acted with brutality: but since war was brutal anyway that was not surprising. Even so, the effect of it all in conditioning the response of many a gallant soul was considerable.

It was not difficult in those times to induce belief, however extravagant. In some cases no inducement was necessary. By the autumn of 1914 it was an article of faith that Russian troops had been seen trying to force roubles into slot machines at London termini, and several railwaymen testified to having found snow in the compartments of trains which had been used for their transportation. But there was also another cause of credulity. The war itself, especially the vastness of its scale and the suddenness of its onset, was so improbable that, to some who considered the matter, it became explicable only in cosmic terms as a fore-ordained final conflict between good and evil. In other words, God came into the picture: and if God came into the picture, so did the Church. Had there not been, for instance, as was widely believed, Angels at the Battle of Mons, interposing themselves between the advancing enemy and the thin lines of British? A certain clergyman, by name the Reverend A. A. Boddy, having investigated the matter, had no doubts, and published his conclusions in a pamphlet which had a wide sale. That is not surprising. Mr. Boddy's account of his interview with a wounded private of the Lincolnshire Regiment is interesting.

"They could now see the oncoming flood of Germans in close formation . . . There was a tremendous fire on both sides. The noise was terrific. Suddenly all guns ceased, as by magic. 'What's up?' the men cried. They looked fearlessly over the top of the barricade. This is what they saw – thirty yards away there were four or five BEINGS larger than men. They had their faces towards the oncoming Germans, and each one had its arms stretched out horizontally from its shoulders, and was slowly moving them up and down, with a sort of suggestion of 'Stop and go back. You must not come any farther'."[1]

Such testimony, and such support, were alike valuable to military authority faced with the task of raising a volunteer army. So Mr. Boddy's pamphlet appeared, "With permission of the Official Censor." What Geoffrey wrote in his parish magazine for September 1914 was being re-echoed in similar quarters all over the country. The results of such appeals, and of many other far larger ones, were impressive. The Bishop of London, Winnington Ingram, after a recruiting speech in which he described the war "as the greatest fight ever made for the Christian religion", was thanked by the War Office for adding 10,000 men to the forces of the Crown. "The acknowledgement could equally well have gone to Horatio Bottomley", a critic justly observed many years later, "and he was prosecuted for fraud".[2] By the middle of the month the daily intake of recruits was thirty thousand: and there were difficulties over billeting them. True, not everyone was for war. An intellectual minority was violently against it, and was allowed to express itself with surprising freedom. Thus A. G. Gardiner in *The Daily News* in October: "The soldier who has the luck to come out of the war alive will emerge as poor as he went in; but the shareholders of Krupps and Armstrongs will have the wealth of the Indies as their reward."

It may have been true. On the other hand, the threat behind the events, fast becoming increasingly global, which the papers daily so alarmingly reported, was a very real one. The virgins of Worcester, or of any other English city, might not in fact have been imperilled if German battalions had marched in there as they had already done into Ghent, and Rheims and Antwerp. But England would: and it was after all something to slip out from work one day to the nearest recruiting office, there to take oath before a pince-nezed officer and a big-bellied Boer War

[1] A. A. Boddy: *Real Angels of Mons.*

[2] Anthony Howard: *The Baldwin Age,* Ed. John Raymond. Eyre & Spottiswoode.

94

sergeant, to defend King and Country, in the honest belief, by no means necessarily false, that one was thereby assisting, however humbly, St. George to slay the dragon. This honest belief, this generous emotion, this absolute conviction that the contest was starkly between Right and Wrong was that alone which made the volunteer principle work in an unprecedented situation. Soon there were many blank chairs in offices, key men gone from factories, an emptiness along one side of many a matrimonial bed.

"Most of those volunteers of the prime," wrote C. E. Montague, "were men of handsome and boundless illusions. Each of them quite seriously thought of himself as a molecule in the body of a nation that was really, and not just figuratively, straining every nerve to discharge an obligation of honour."[1]

So, as the leaves fluttered down that autumn, as, on the eastern front, a hundred thousand Russian dead sank into the ooze of the Pripet Marshes after Tannenburg, as one hundred and twenty thousand German dead mingled their bones with the wreckage of the old British regular army after the first battle of Ypres, as the opposing armies dug themselves in from the Channel to the Alps, the first and the last great volunteer army ever raised in Britain began to mass. A memorable poster became ubiquitous: the face of Kitchener, staring eyes over handlebar moustache and pointing finger. Many of those who responded found themselves at first frustrated. Many were called: few seemed to be chosen, especially for commissions. If, as Geoffrey urged in his magazine, every able-bodied man ought to volunteer for service, it often proved quite difficult to get taken on, so that various voluntary organisations came into existence to expedite the process. However, by the early months of 1915 the machinery was beginning to work more smoothly: tens of thousands of men, in uniform for the first time in their lives, began military training. One of the centres chosen was Worcester.

. . . .

The Dean of Worcester, W. Moore Ede, invited Geoffrey to preach in the Cathedral to the two thousand or so men who were

[1] C. E. Montague: *Disenchantment.*

paraded there on three Sunday mornings of 1915. It was the fruitful decision of one who was already a friend and admirer. To the end of Geoffrey's life, indeed, this friendship of Moore Ede's was constant. And now both friendship and admiration were strengthened by the younger man's achievement in making, out of the highly unpromising situation of a church parade — something which was not uncommonly regarded as one of the rigours of war — an experience which many of the men remembered for as long afterwards as was granted to them.

They were not an easy audience. No congregation gathered together under duress ever is. What is more, they were men living through a rare intensity of experience. "Who," asked C. E. Montague, in a passage which enshrines forever the mood of such men in that distant time, "of all those who were in camp and still are alive, will not remember until he dies the second boyhood that he had in the late frosts and then in the spring and early summer of 1915 ? The awakening bird-notes of Reveillé at dawn, the two-mile run through auroral mists breaking over a still inviolate England ... the peace of the tranquil hours on guard at some sequestered post, alone with the sylvester moonlight ... and the jocund days of marching and digging trenches in the sun ..."[1]

Such men could be as critical as they were lively. Discipline, sometimes deeply resented, duly set them down in the Cathedral after an infinity of bawlings without, and the certainty of more to follow at the marching away. To hold such a gathering, and to hold them fast, required powers in a preacher of an unusual order. Geoffrey seemed to have them. Here was the situation he had enjoyed facing in the square at Leeds recreated in a different framework. There was not a cough, not a shuffling of feet, when he was speaking. It was all familiar, homely stuff, starting invariably from the known and going on to the unknown, so that a talk about a conversation overheard in a barber's shop on the need to treat the enemy worse than they were alleged to have treated the Belgians, passed easily and enthrallingly to the whole matter of the conquest of evil by good. It sounds banal: but

[1] *Ibid.*

96

behind it was the compelling, odd personality of the man himself. Quite soon, Geoffrey's Sunday sermon was a talking point in the camps for the following week.

Meanwhile, there was a personal problem much exercising him: the question of when and how he should get into the army himself. It was a considerable dilemma. In France the matter was settled for the priest, who was liable to be drafted with the rest, and there was a body of opinion in England which held that the same rule should apply there also. The situation was by no means clear. As a matter of fact, as Archbishop Davidson lamented in 1914, it was "chaotically unsolved", and remained so until the end. So in some clerical hearts, at any rate, there was ardent desire to serve as best they could. That meant a chaplaincy to the forces, something by no means easy to attain. For one thing, any man in charge of a parish had first himself to make provision for his duties to be carried out in his absence. For another, he had to persuade his bishop to release him. And yet again he had to commend himself to military authority in the form of the Royal Army Chaplain's Department. That meant a visit to the War Office and an interview with a remarkable character, Bishop Taylor Smith, Chaplain General. He was not regarded with unmixed approval. Already, in the closing months of 1914, his pronounced evangelical predispositions had brought down upon him the anger of the English Church Union and Lord Halifax, who considered the Chaplain General deficient in sympathy towards Anglo-Catholic applicants for chaplaincies. They even memorialised Lord Kitchener on the matter, though without decisive result. Perhaps there were other things on his mind at the time. One thing, however, which Bishop Taylor Smith did understand was death. At least he had a great interest in the subject, and his insistence upon the need, by the chaplain, for adequate preparation of the wounded for that event was long remembered. The impression was left that death would have taken place, and possibly rigor mortis set in, before the Bishop's injunctions could be carried out with the thoroughness he enjoined.

But once these various hurdles were cleared the rest of the course was often surprisingly, even alarmingly rapid. Within days a man could find himself in a position to visit a military tailor and emerge to astonish himself by his own reflection in a mirror, with only his collar and the Maltese cross of the department upon his badges to indicate the nature of his office, and his own inner resources to make of it either a mockery or a splendour.

All these things happened to Geoffrey: the initial difficulties and delays followed by the extremely rapid conclusion to the matter. On December 21st, 1915, he was appointed Temporary Chaplain to the Forces. On Christmas Day he found himself in a French village contemplating four hundred troops drawn up in sluicing rain waiting, no doubt with mixed feelings, for a service. Soon afterwards, in a letter to the people of St. Paul's, reprinted in the local paper—the first of many such—he described the scene.

"It was pouring rain, and the roads were very heavy. Everywhere along the road one met troops, mud up to their knees, dripping wet, but always with a greeting ready, or a joke. The first place we were due was a little French village which in summer and in happier times must be a beautiful place; but it was desolate that Christmas morning, the road a quagmire, cut into ruts and hollows by the heavy traffic, and the hedges covered with mud. I found about four hundred men drawn up in the rain waiting . . .

"I hurried into my robes and went to the middle of the square. There was of course no instrument, and I thanked God for a voice like a fog-horn. But once we started on 'Come all ye faithful' no instrument and no leading voice were necessary. They sang with all their might . . . Then the glorious part came—I went to a shed in the farmyard, and the communicants came to me. There were not many; but they meant it. No lights, no ritual, nothing to help but the rain and the far-off roll of guns, and Christ was born in a cattle-shed on Christmas Day."

Thus began the wartime ministry of a man destined to become, through personal qualities and the accident of circumstances, the most celebrated army padre of all time: and one who was to end hating with a rare bitterness the whole enterprise to which, at this beginning, he went with such naïvety. The same thing happened to many others; but most of them died in their anger. He survived, and told the tale.

Soon, anyway, he was to be introduced to far less idyllic scenes than Holy Communion in a cattle shed on Christmas Day. His account continues:

"On the Monday I received orders to leave for the great base of the British Army. For a while I have said good-bye to the happy part of army work, and have come to the sad part of it. I am not in a hospital; I am chaplain to the troops quartered in the town, and it is sad because here is the old enemy one fights — sin — and sin is sadder that sorrow. Had I a boy I would pray that he might never be long at a base — —"

The place was Rouen, and it was quite appalling. To recapture the reality behind the parsonic language it is necessary only to rummage among the extensive, sombre literature of that most sombre of all wars. "Passing through the town," one private soldier wrote years afterwards, "we saw stretching from the Red Lamp and down the street about three hundred men in a queue, all waiting their turns, the majority being mere lads. 'I expect they're determined to have a short time before they go West tomorrow', Duffy said."[1]

That particular brothel, as it happened, was not in Rouen; but plenty could be found there like it. As the war became static, and the bases grew until they were vast cities of men, the evil inseparable from such immense concentrations grew in proportion. They were well under way in Rouen by the time Geoffrey arrived there in the January of 1916. In that town low-lying on the banks of the Seine, the starting point for drafts going up to the unknown terrors of the line, many a newcomer, heartsick, lonely, totally unequipped for the experience, could find himself, with simple astonishment, looking in his leisure moments into the mouth of an alcoholic and bawdy hell patrolled by military police.

It is against such a background that the quality of Geoffrey's achievement during the four months he was at Rouen needs to be measured. He was as raw a newcomer as any. Fortunately,

[1] Frank Richards: *Old Soldiers Never Die.*

there was at Rouen, in the person of D. F. Carey, as assistant Chaplain General, a man of wisdom and understanding. When Geoffrey reported to him with the request to be given work in a hospital, Carey told him briefly there were no vacancies. There was, however, a canteen down by the *Rive Gauche* Siding run by Lady Mabel Egerton, where reinforcements coming from Le Havre on their way up to the line spent the last few hours before entraining. Geoffrey could go there. It seemed to Carey that was the very place for a man who, in the same interview, when asked about his background, said he had once been a revolutionary agnostic atheist, whatever that may mean, who used to stand on a tub and talk in public places in the Midlands. So to the canteen by the *Rive Gauche* Siding he went, and that is where we found him, at the beginning of this story.

.   .   .   .

To ask what exactly he was supposed to do, faced with the smoky tumult of such a place, is to pose the problem of the padre in an extreme form. It is a problem which reaches a good deal further than this particular manifestation of it. What, indeed, is the place of the parson in the scheme of things when some extraordinary circumstance pulls him out of the sometimes distressingly little world in which he lives and moves and has his being? Unlike the doctor, or any other technologist, he does not seem to have any self-evident place, a fact which can only too easily lead to the conclusion that he does not deserve one. Furthermore, if he is to become necessary, he has first to create the need. The alternative is to shelter behind such protection as rank and privilege afford, an alternative more easily acceptable in proportion as the man concerned is not of a thoughtful or a sensitive kind. It is a problem which can rarely have presented itself quite so acutely as to the army chaplains of the war to which Geoffrey went.

They were the first of their kind ever to be involved in a situation of total war, and they went untrained and unprepared from the parochial round, the common task. And though the parochial round might, in happier times, have furnished all they needed to ask, it was far otherwise when they found themselves in places like the *Rive Gauche* Siding at Rouen. Not surprisingly, some failed. The Army Chaplain of 1914–18 certainly had a bad press after the war, though any attempt to assess its accuracy must allow for the fact that in any age part of the function of the Church and its representatives is to act as whipping boys for the dissatisfied.

"If ever the conversation veered round to native troops or parsons," Private Frank Richards wrote in *Old Soldiers Never Die,* recalling post-war talks with an ex-member of his battalion, "he would launch out with a flow of language which on two occasions was very nearly the cause of us being turned out of the pubs we were in. By stop-tap he generally had thousands of native troops in one spittoon and thousands of parsons in the other." When Geoffrey came to die, hundreds of men not unlike Frank Richards and his drinking companion spoke of him with characteristic sentimentality as "our fallen comrade", and in Liverpool placed a packet of Woodbines on his coffin. But the bad press was a fact.

Chiefly, the charge preferred against the chaplain seems to have been one of inadequacy. Some of the criticisms are more touching than was perhaps intended. Siegfried Sassoon, in *Memoirs of an Infantry Officer*, in a few lines painted a picture which haunts the mind. The scene was a casualty clearing station; with many wounded, covered in the blood and filth of their condition. One person on that horrific stage who seemed to have no part to play was a chaplain, "discovering the inadequacies of the ministry of the Church of England." Was he? One wonders. Across the years, something of the plight of that unhappy man comes through the print. And with it comes also a great and looming question – the main one, then as now, the one which Geoffrey spent the rest of his days struggling with – what is the meaning of suffering? The Church of England is not alone in finding the answer to that one difficult.

But perhaps the most memorable of all the adverse criticisms which fell upon the chaplains was C. E. Montague's celebrated chapter. *The Sheep that Were Not Fed*, in *Disenchantment*. There were all sorts and conditions of men among them, he states: some good; some bad, like the chaplain "drunk at dinner in Gobert's restaurant in Amiens on the evening of one of the bloodiest days of the first battle of the Somme." But mostly the quality was indifferent. "There was the man who, urged by national comradeship, would have been a soldier but that his bishop banned it: to be an army chaplain was the next best thing. There was the man who, urged by a different instinct, felt irresistibly that at the moment the war was the central thing in the whole world and that it was unbearable not to be at the centre of things. And there was, in great force, the large, healthy, pleasant young curate . . . He abounded so much that whenever now one hears the words 'Army Chaplain' his large genial image springs up of itself in the mind."[1]

The inadequacy of such was all the more sadly evident, Montague held, in view of the rare opportunity with which they were presented. Living with death a constant probability, torn out of the complacencies of life at home, yet with long hours in trench or billet in which to think about things, some men were rendered unusually receptive to spiritual things. It is a surprising judgment. War is generally as bad for religion as for anything else. However, there was Montague's verdict: the opportunity was presented: the average chaplain was unable to grasp it. True, he was usually genial, he tended to be overpoweringly man to man; he gave away cigarettes in large quantities. But that was not enough. "When you are given an infant earth to fashion out of a whirling ball of flaming metals and gases, than good humour, some taste for adventure, a jolly way with the men . . . may not carry you far. You may come off, by no fault of your own, like the curate in Shakespeare who was put up to play Alexander the Great: 'A marvellous good neighbour, i' faith, and a very good bowler: but, for Alexander—alas, you see how 'tis—a little o'erparted.' "[2]

Yet who was adequate to the monstrous challenge of such a time? Most men, when weighed in that balance, were found

[1] C. E. Montague: *Disenchantment.*

[2] *Ibid.*

wanting. It is difficult to wander much through the vast, sad, yet endlessly fascinating museum of that old war without being impressed by the extraordinary brainlessness with which it seems to have been conducted on the higher levels. There seems often remarkably little of original thought inside the mind of a Haig or a Plumer: only a few predetermined attitudes, chiefly connected with notions of patriotism and duty, and in some a streak of personal ambition — as in the case of the disastrous French General Nivelle — all the more astonishing because cultivated at the price of massive human sacrifice. Who indeed was adequate? "It is only a very limited number of men," Archbishop Davidson sensibly observed, "of any sort of class or profession, who would be fit at such a juncture to do all that was needed." Not the generals, not the statesmen, certainly. It can scarcely be surprising if the divines were not, either. One emerges from that ghastly museum of the old war with a shudder, wondering whether we are any better off now, even after another war has been and gone or whether, even among our nuclear war-heads, the higher direction of human affairs is not still waiting for the cavalry to break through.

"Imagine the religious revival," Montague goes on to say, "if some man of apostolic genius had had the fishing of the troubled waters."[1]

It was quite untrue, of course. Religious revivals are not brought about by men, even of apostolic genius; but by the Spirit of God moving upon the face of the waters. All that such men can do — and there was one of them in early 1915 making a clown of himself for Christ's sake in the *Rive Gauche* Siding at Rouen — is to touch a few lives with a great love, to open a few eyes to a splendid vision, and often to break his own heart in the process.

There were also other elements present in the situation of a chaplain which could be disturbing. Pressure of circumstances in that war could easily transform him into a combination of entertainments manager, welfare officer, and undertaker, and often did. He could be, all too easily, made to appear and feel

[1] *Ibid.*

useless, like a man wandering round a burning ship exchanging pleasantries with the fire parties. And because of his association with formal occasions like church parade he could be associated all too easily—and indeed often justly—with the more repellent aspects of the military system. When to these considerations is added the fact that his was in some measure a privileged position, and that he could, in the first war, go home when his term of service was up, the background of his difficulties becomes even more forbidding.

Such handicaps were in some cases so triumphantly overcome by exceptional men that the first war produced padres whose names became public property, notwithstanding the severe criticism to which their kind in general was later subjected. Of these, Geoffrey's face was by far the most widespread. But there were others, like Tubby Clayton, founder of Toc H, who were able in some measure to sublimate the horrors of it all and elevate the concepts of sacrifice and service. And there were others yet again, like the saintly T. B. Hardy, v.c., m.c., d.s.o.,whom we shall meet in due course, whom no breath of criticism could reach.

Even so, there was, as indeed there must always be, one inner difficulty in the chaplain's position in time of war of which it is surprising to find so little awareness in a man as sensitive as Geoffrey—the question as to whether he had any business to be an official part of a system dedicated to the prosecution of a war which, the longer it continued, was increasingly seen as a crime against humanity. It is true that he came to see it as such himself.

> Waste of Blood, and waste of Tears
> Waste of youth's most precious years,
> Waste of ways the Saints have trod
> Waste of Glory, Waste of God—
> War!

Such emotional denunciations became, and have remained, common enough. They formed the basis of the pacifism of the twenties and thirties. But here and there it was a fact that, during the first war, the chaplain could find himself in a difficult position. Such an one was the unfortunate man in one of P. B. Clayton's *Plain Tales from Flanders, The Story of M—*, where in it is related that a devout Major of Signals became so appalled by the bloody consequences of his own handiwork that he went down to G.H.Q., entered unannounced, and informed his G.O.C. of his intention of ceasing to carry out his duties as from noon that day. The General sent for the Corps Chaplain who "tried, poor fellow, to do his best by proving once again the justice of our Cause. M— — told me, in a lucid moment later, that this was the most appalling agony of it all, and that he had the greatest difficulty in not treating him as Paul once treated the High Priest."[1]

M— — was lucky. They said he was mad, and put him in an asylum. If he had been a ranker he might have been put against a wall, in which case no doubt some other padre would have been called upon to offer the consolations of religion. Fortunately, such extreme challenges did not come the way of many. But the possibility of them was always there, and it seems strange that there is so little reflection of their inner strain upon the christian conscience in the writings of Geoffrey coming out of the war years. On the contrary, he seems at times to have allowed himself gladly to be used as a morale-booster to an extent which would certainly have been regarded as improper in a chaplain of the second war. Of the challenge to the whole christian position which the war brought with it he was, God knows, profoundly concerned. His response to the challenge forms the basis of his teaching. But he does not seem to have been aware of the challenge implicit therein to the whole position of a priest in uniform. It seems a curious blind spot; but who is to judge after all these years, or presume to say what he thinks should have been done in so fearful a situation, especially anyone who was not there on that St. Crispin's Day, or any other, for that matter? Without a doubt, the tensions of Geoffrey's work pressed terribly upon him as the years passed, and inner doubts of this sort may well have been among them. But at the beginnings there is no sign

[1] P. B. Clayton: *Plain Tales from Flanders.*

of it. The war was a just Cause. He was in that stage at Rouen in the early months of 1916. And now we can get back to him and find what happened there.

.　　　.　　　.　　　.

A yellowing cutting from a local paper, quoting a letter of Geoffrey's of that time, has at any rate his version. To those who would seek after the atmosphere of those 'old, unhappy, far-off things', it has its own fascination.

"My chief work during the day lies at the station. Men on their way to the front are often confined there from 3 a.m. to 5.30 p.m. I go down about two o'clock and go into the coffee-shop to find it filled with men. There is a piano in the corner with generally a crowd round it. I go to the piano and begin to sing, one song after another until I'm tired, then I get up and tell the men I'm there to help them in any way I can. I have found it comforts wives and mothers to hear from me that I have seen their loved soldiers and talked to them, so I always offer to send for anyone who wants it a letter I have printed saying I have seen them. Before the men come with their addresses, which they do in crowds, we have some prayers for those at home. After the service the procession begins . . . some will show me their photographs, the bright girl face in the clean white blouse . . ."

Generally, before the interviews were ended a sergeant was heard yelling out the fall-in. It was generally growing dark by then, and in the gloom a huge long train was standing.

It was then his custom to go down the train distributing cigarettes out of one haversack and New Testaments out of the other. To the end he was still giving away Woodbines.

"I begin at the top of the train; and work down it, going into each carriage. I look round into their faces. I can always tell the man who has taken that trip before. You can see it in his eyes . . . So on for an hour (it always stands an hour), with the knapsacks growing lighter and a lump in the throat that grows bigger. Often I have to cling on to finish the last carriages, creeping along the footboard. At last, I am left alone looking after the disappearing tail-lights. There is nothing glorious about this departure. It is all sordid and filthy. God only knows the hard-ships men endure on these journeys in packed and dirty carriages. No place to wash, no place to move, they sit and wait for eighteen hours or more until, I suppose, they hear far off the sound of guns and know that the end is near . . ."

He was soon himself to hear the sound of those guns and to have any suppositions removed as to what happened at the end of the line.

Meanwhile, he would wander back to the canteen when the rumble of the train had faded, to drift into that now empty place for a meal. He rarely seemed to know what he was eating. Often it was some left-overs he picked up from the plates still littering the room. And frequently, when the women running the place cooked him a meal and substituted the scraps for something better, it was observed that he did not notice the changeover.

In Rouen, in the Lent of 1916, there took place a remarkable series of meetings in the Hotel de Ville and in the camps around the town, in which Geoffrey was the chief figure. Carey had already discovered the newcomer's exceptional powers, and now had resolved to give them scope. And though it is no doubt unlikely that many of those who came to the meetings – most of them destined for the great carve-up on the Somme in a few months time – were particularly concerned with the sacred season, yet their response to the challenge Geoffrey tried to put before them was genuine enough. More than that, it was stagger-ing. The foundations of his fame were laid down at this point, thereafter to be built upon by report and rumour. Yet, examined long afterwards, what he said – published later as *Rough Talks of a Padre* – seems trite enough. Spoken against the background of the soul-rotting evils of the base, it was a challenge to self-dedication, a period piece with its characteristic first-war idealisa-tion of the soldier dead and "the cause for which they died." Something of the progress of this astonishing effort he described in a letter home.

"We started with a hall fairly full. The number grew until we were crammed, with men standing on the gangway and sitting on the edge of the platform. The whole object of the lectures was to put the challenge of Christ before the men and make them hear. It is wonderful, the change that war had already worked in the souls of many. I can see them now; crammed, packed and seething, sitting on the platform round my feet, a mass of brown, eager faces. The climax came on Good Friday when the hall was packed. When it was over, they sat still for a while, and I am sure Christ was with us, and was glad. Then they cheered, and their cheer was an answer to the call of Christ. Some may forget it; but surely not all; some will remember that Good Friday night for years."

Perhaps some did, some who survived. But that innocence of spirit which the whole incident enshrines was soon to die, with so much else. The same packet of letters and cuttings which contained this letter of Geoffrey's held also, on another yellowed piece of paper, a piece of verse, written only a year later, which evokes a very different scene:

> There's a Jerry over there, Sarge!
> Can't you see 'is big square 'ead?
> If 'e moves again I'll get 'im,
> Take these glasses 'ere and see.
> What's that? Got 'im through the 'ead, Sarge?
> Where's my blarsted cup o' tea!

Into such scenes Geoffrey passed when, in the June of 1916, in time for the Somme offensive, he was posted to that now-forgotten thing, the Front, as padre with the 157th Brigade of the 46th Division. It was the first of three periods of battle experience. The second was in the following year, with the 17th Brigade of the 24th Division, when he was in the attack on the Messines Ridge, preceded by the horrific dawn blowing of the mines which lifted the top from that geographical feature, and buried a great many Germans in an explosion heard across the Channel in Kent. In the last year of the war, with the 42nd Division, he was in the final advance. It was quite a lot. That it was not more was due, not to his own wish, but to the direction of the Deputy Chaplain General, Bishop Gwynne, sometime of the Sudan, a great man of much wisdom whose appointment as Bishop in charge of all chaplains in France had been Archbishop Davidson's quiet solution of the difficulties arising from the alleged partialities of Taylor Smith. Clearly, Gwynne recognised in Geoffrey a very rare bird, and used him accordingly. The consequence was that, between his periods in the line, he was given a series of special postings. One would seem in the retrospect to have been a task of considerable difficulty – to wander through the whole army area speaking on behalf of one of the most curious enterprises ever undertaken by a Church in the middle of a war, the National Mission of Repentance and Hope. Another was to act as chaplain, at various times, to three Army Infantry Schools. A third, the most extraordinary of all, saw him attached to a School for Physical and Bayonet Training, sometimes going on tour with a gruesome collection of morale-boosters which included a champion boxer, two wrestlers, and an N.C.O. whose title to fame was that he had killed eighteen Germans with a bayonet. One of the high spots of this performance was that Geoffrey would asthmatically box with the boxer, for the edification of troops.

What on earth does it all add up to? How could it be that, out of this mad medley of clowning and genius, of sentimentality and profound thought upon the sins and sufferings of man, out of an outward gaiety and an inwardly breaking heart, there should have emerged one of the most famous figures of that old war? Even that question would not, at this distance of time, be worth the answering were it not for another and a greater one lying behind. How did it come that this man was able to make God real to so many to whom he seemed to be dead? How was it that, over and over again, the most unlikely people came, not only to love and remember him, but through him to get a glimpse of a splendour far beyond the customary horizons of ordinary life? Somewhere in the answer lies the secret at the heart of religion; but it is a secret he took with him, and nobody seems since to have possessed it. Certainly, the common people heard him gladly. But why? As well ask, perhaps, why the common people once streamed out on to the hillsides of Galilee. The answer is but partially to be found in the written records in either case. There must have been something highly unusual, in more ways than one about the man himself. Odd stories of Geoffrey which have stuck in the memories of now ageing people testify to that.

Thus a lady, now elderly, remembers how, as a young V.A.D. nurse given to taking solitary Sunday walks in the dunes around Hardelot, south of Boulogne, she used to be puzzled by the crowds of men around a hut which lay at a distance. They filled the hut: they clustered upon the dunes. And always some would climb on to the roof and hold themselves in such a position that they could see and hear through the occasional window. The place was used for voluntary church services by men on a course at the School of so-called Physical and Bayonet Training (actually an establishment for the re-habilitation of the disaffected at a time when considerable numbers were becoming so). Who could be the padre? Investigation revealed him as the ugliest man she had ever seen, with a pair of wonderful brown eyes and the terrible cough, familiar to nurses by that time, of the gassed. That was the sound that would wake her, back in Hardelot, on some week-day mornings. She would get up, peep out of her convalescent home window down on to the grey-dawn street and the solid-tyred transport gathered there. And there he would be; looking pretty desolate, going back up the line with a returning draft. The next Sunday there would be scarcely a soul at the hut out among the dunes. Sometimes, she discovered, he only just arrived there himself. He loved riding: the Commandant of the School gave him a horse; the horse ran away with him one Sunday morning, round and round the local golf-course, cutting up the greens. He arrived breathless, gave a remarkable address, and afterwards begged no one to betray the desecration of the greens to the inquiry that would certainly follow. But what did he *say*, when he was not making a fool of himself? What did he *say* that brought men clustering around on the dunes and on to the roof? She couldn't remember: it didn't seem to matter. It was just the man himself, somehow, his odd gaieties, his touching sadnesses. After the war, in the sombre peace, when the sometime V.A.D.

married an ex-officer, they asked that Geoffrey should conduct the ceremony. "If," said the clergyman consulted, "you mean Studdert Kennedy I advise you to have someone in reserve. He will probably forget to turn up."

Without a doubt, he was fiercely disapproved of by many worthy people, so that it would be quite wrong to suppose that the personal memories of this time which have survived are all happy ones. He was widely held to be a mountebank. "Woodbine Willie: that impossible fellow! No use for him. Swears like a trooper: quite mad!" Such was a frequent opinion, as quoted by D. F. Carey. The swearing was common enough form; what made it notable in Geoffrey's case was his habit, which grew on him in these years, of doing so on platform and pulpit, as well as elsewhere. Thus it was reported how, when once two sardonic characters passed a hut labelled 'Vicarage', the one said to the other: "Bill, 'ere's the bloody Vicarage." Geoffrey immediately emerged to say: "Right! And here's the bloody Vicar!"

Perhaps it was true. The swearing in general is an accepted fact, though it has to be remembered it would probably be considered more noteworthy then than now. The habit of sitting on the ledge of a pulpit, with legs astride would, however, possibly be regarded as interesting even yet. But as to the swearing, Colonel R. B. Campbell, of the 4th Army Infantry School, remembered the effect of Geoffrey's going on to the stage, at his first arriving there, with the words: "I know what you're thinking: here comes the bloody parson." The effect was considerable; but not so considerable as the splendid words which followed, and that from a man ill and worn at the time. But such habits did not endear him to everyone.

There was an occasion when they brought him to serious trouble. It happened in the winter of 1918. The Second Army, under the command of General Plumer, was stationed in and around Cologne. Now Plumer, he whose puffed cheeks and white moustache peer out from photographs of that old-time war, was, it appears, a devout person. It was reported of him, indeed, that on the night before the blowing of the mines under the Messines Ridge, he was observed to be at prayer. As the moment approached, for which so long grim tunnellers under the ridge had prepared, as birds began twittering in the dawn while thousands of troops waited in silence, an aide, wishing to borrow some night-glasses, entered the General's bedroom. He found his chief kneeling by the bedside. But now the moment was near. Silently, the staff officer picked up the glasses, and trained them out on to the distant line. Dead on time, the mines blew, and the sound of gunfire followed the cataclysmic roar. The General continued his prayers.

Perhaps such stern and soldierly piety was not likely to be sympathetic to such wildly unconventional Christianity as Geoffrey's. However, there the General, now a victorious one, was at the great parade service in Cologne. The preacher was Geoffrey. What followed is told by one who was present:

"S.K. was grossly misunderstood. Apart from the fact that he was at that time under the impression that the soldiers understood only three universal adjectives, the pattern of his sermon was apparently the building-up of an Aunt Sally which he then proceeded to knock down. The Aunt Sally in question was the soldiers' mistaken idea of God. Unfortunately, the General did not grasp the idea, and was throughout under the impression that what S.K. was pouring out was his own conception of the Almighty. He became so shocked and incensed that he did not hear the end."[1]

Geoffrey found himself reported to the Assistant Chaplain General in Cologne. With the report went the request that the Second Army be purged forthwith of such a heretic. The order was obeyed, and the offender, at the height of his fame, sent down to the base at Havre. A more immediate consequence was an encounter with a staff officer at the station after the disaster.

"Are you the fellow who preached this morning?"

"I have that honour."

"Well, all I can say is, you ought to be cashiered or locked up in an asylum."

True, they then travelled together amicably. Many people found it difficult to be angry with Geoffrey for long. But that

[1] Private information.

detail does not affect the heart of the matter. The question remains as to why he conducted himself in this way at all. It was certainly damaging, not least in that his eccentricities tended to figure so largely in his popular reputation. Maybe the answer is to be found in another direction altogether—in the tensions which can arise in a profoundly religious man from the struggle to square what he believes of the loving kindness of God, with the squalid honours of a world said, incredibly enough, to be his.

"Now do you understand, you miserable little parson, with your petty shibboleths, this is the real thing, War!" So he imagined the shells shrieking to him as they passed overhead in the preliminary bombardment on the Somme. And when he returned with the Military Cross from the business on the ridge at Messines in 1917 and met Carey, Geoffrey said: "You know, this business has made me less cocksure of much of which I was cocksure before. On two points I am certain: Christ and his Sacrament. Apart from that I am not certain of anything."

But such tormenting uncertainties do not afflict everyone. There are always some who can find no difficulties at all in the idea of prayer before Messines or in reciting the 'Our Father' before take-off in the aircraft which carried the bomb to Hiroshima. What is more, they are often persons of much Christian devotion. There are others, again in any age, to whom the whole thing is an offence to the intelligence, just as there are some again to whom it is hypocrisy. And always, inevitably, there is the majority to whom the subject is a matter of indifference. In the centre of them all, coldly blown upon by every wind of opinion, is the man who exposes his own belief to them all and yet strives to keep it warm and living. Such an one was Geoffrey.

The war, blasting away many of his preconceptions forced upon him the task of sorting the true from the false in the resulting wreckage. What, for instance, did one make of it when one day one bent over a boy at Communion with the words " – preserve thy body and soul unto everlasting life", and the next day came upon the boy's body obscenely shattered? What was the purpose of prayer in such circumstances? What was the good of it all, in any circumstances? Who and what was this God whom custom comfortably called Almighty, and what was he playing at? How came it that some of the bravest and best had often no time for religion whatever? Above all, how did Christ fit into this picture? Did his words really hold water? And what was the inner relationship, if any, between the shattered boy and the Cross with the broken body on it?

There were various ways of dealing with such awkward questions, of course. One was to be genuinely unaware that they existed. Another was to be aware, but to rely upon the tough hide of institutional religion to turn aside such shafts. A third was to face them. Geoffrey chose the third. The result was to draw from him memorable answers, "the ruminations of an incurably religious man under battle conditions" as he once called them, to many of the questions which vexed then, and certainly vex now, a great many people of good will who look with inquiring eyes from the outside upon the Church and all its doings.

It was the consuming desire to get alongside such people, to talk their language, to think their thoughts, and yet commend his God to them which made Geoffrey act and speak so unconventionally, even shockingly. He wanted to shock, for doing so served the double purpose of capturing the attention of the indifferent and disassociating his message from the pasteboard Christ who, it seemed to him, was too often offered by his official representatives. For this his hatred was enormous. It was a falsity he was constantly attacking, as in the bitter verse he called *A Sermon*.

> My brethren, the ways of God
> No man can understand.
> We can but wait in awe and watch
> The wonders of his hand.
> O weeping mother torn with grief
> Poor stricken heart that cries,
> And rocks a cradle empty now,
> Tis by God's will he dies . . .

"When the war broke out," he wrote in *The Hardest Part*, "there was a regular run upon the bank of God, and our churches were thronged with distracted people waving cheques for protection duly endorsed 'Through Jesus Christ Our Lord.' They soon got sick of it, of course, and fell away. In a dim way they realised it was useless . . . A chaplain said to me the other day; 'Don't discourage last-resort religion: it is better than none at all.' I don't agree. It's worse than no religion. It's a base form of idolatry."

Such language did not appeal to all. But it meant a great deal to the only kind of people he really cared about, the ordinary men who, in their tens of thousands, were bearing the heat and burden of that terrible day. These were they who gave him his famous name. How it came, no one seems to know.

It emerged, and became universal. "Has Captain Kennedy gone along?" an officer looking for Geoffrey once asked of a sentry.

"No, sir."

"Have you seen the Chaplain, then?"

"No, sir."

"Have you had the padre this way?"

"No, sir."

"Look," said the officer, "have you seen Woodbine Willie lately?"

"Yes, sir: just gone by."

After the war, it was suggested to Geoffrey that he should drop the use of this curious title. He declined, being very proud of it, having once written:

> They gave me this name like their nature
> Compacted of laughter and tears,
> A sweet that was born of the bitter
> A joke that was torn from the years.

But it took some earning, and it was not to be earned only with words. Here, as always, what he was and did is inextricably bound up with what he said. What he said is important now, and always will be in a world where suffering and death lie just beneath the surface of things, however well concealed. Yet to find this message it is necessary to seek it among the circumstances that gave it birth.

An encounter which took place in a hut at the base at Étaples, between Geoffrey and another remarkable man towards the end of 1916, is as good a starting point as any.

CHAPTER VI

The Message of Woodbine Willie

THE occasion of the encounter was the arrival at the base at
Étaples of a diffident clergyman of a type familiar among the
character parts in the Anglican *dramatis personae* of any generation
—the schoolmaster-parson. This was a certain Theodore Bayley
Hardy, sometime grammar-school headmaster, at the time of his
meeting with Geoffrey, vicar of the country parish of Hutton
Roof, Kirby Lonsdale. He had wanted very much to be a
chaplain; all his quiet life he had known intuitions of some
tremendous experience awaiting him. But in 1916 he was over
fifty so that there had been difficulties. However, there he was
in Étaples at last, wondering quite what to do next. In these
circumstances he was advised to see "a certain Mr. Studdert
Kennedy, now so famous, who had by the magic of his personality
got at the heart and mind of men".[1] This, it may be noted, was
when Geoffrey had himself been in France less than a year.

The meeting which followed was a memorable one. "It was
held in an ordinary office room; but in that room was significance,
that wild thing that leaps out from unexpected places; an ordinary
hour, a period of time; but the light of the ladder pitched between
Heaven and Charing Cross shone on the faces of the two as they
talked."[2] So wrote the biographer of Hardy. The words are
mysterious; but they indicate at least something of the kind of
person Geoffrey had become by this time; a man of compelling
influence and power for the most part quite unconscious of either.
The proof lies in the kind of padre Hardy himself became. That
old war, nor its successor, never produced a greater than this gentle
priest of fantastic heroism; the oldest man, from that day to this,
ever to receive the supreme decoration. And the beginning of it

[1] M. Hardy: *Hardy, V.C.* Skeffington.

[2] *Ibid.*

was in the inspiration of this one meeting in the Assistant Chaplain General's office at Étaples.

"I remember the conversation very well," Geoffrey wrote. "He asked me to tell him the best way of working. I said: 'Live with the men; go everywhere they go. Make up your mind you will share all their risks, and more if you can do any good. The line is the key to the whole business. Work in the very front, and they will listen to you; but if you stay behind, you're wasting your time. Men will forgive you anything but lack of courage and devotion.'"

"I remember walking up and down saying this very fiercely, because I was full of it. He took it so humbly and eagerly that I was ashamed of myself, and loved him. I said the more padres died in the battle doing Christian deeds the better; most of us would be more useful dead than alive. He asked me about purely spiritual work. I said: 'There is very little; it is all muddled and mixed. Take a box of fags in your haversack and a great deal of love in your heart, and go up to them: laugh with them, joke with them. You can pray with them sometimes; but pray for them always.' I felt he would be able to do it all much better than I, because he had the power that belongs to saints, and I was such an ordinary man. I told him some yarns, and we both laughed over them. We shook hands. I have never seen him since. If I did influence him, it is just another instance of the queer instruments God can use."[1]

Hardy went out to an extraordinary career. Yet of all the critics who so fiercely assailed the Anglican Chaplains of the first war only C. E. Montague seems ever to have heard of him. "There was the hero and saint, T. B. Hardy, to whom a consuming passion of human brotherhood brought, as well as rarer things, the M.C., the D.S.O., the V.C., the unaccepted invitation of the King to come home as one of his own chaplains and live, and then the death which everyone had seen to be certain."[2] That is all, and that is a pity, for in Hardy so many of the failures of others seem somehow redeemed and forgiven. If, as some

[1] *Ibid.*

[2] C. E. Montague: *Disenchantment.*

maintain, the scenes of that ancient conflict are still visited by the ghosts of those who took part in them — and to stand by the Menin Gate on a winter evening with all those names yet crying from the walls in the fading light, or on the Vimy Ridge on a summer day, with the tourist traffic of the 1960's humming by at a distance, is to find it easy enough to believe — then Hardy's will be amongst them. Hardy inquiring, as one staff officer remembered him, when all was mud and fog and poisoned scum filling every shell-hole, "Pardon me; but could you kindly direct me to the front line?" Or Hardy staying, as once he did, for thirty-six hours by some unfortunate slowly sinking in the mud from which none could get him out. Or Hardy, lost, and wandering hazardously back in the dark from the wrong direction upon some trigger-happy outpost. The 'end which all had seen to be certain', the great experience of which, among his boys, among his Westmorland hills, he had once dreamed, came with a shot out of the dark as he was crossing a plank bridge over the River Selle in October 1918. His record ends briefly: "Died of wounds (gunshot) received in action." Three months before, he had written, in a letter to the Assistant Chaplain General, thanking him humbly for certain kind words about his V.C.; "Are you likely to meet or write to Studdert Kennedy soon? If so, will you tell him that I have often wished I could thank him properly for that hour in your office which, more than any other in my life, has helped me in this work. You can understand how I feel about these ribbons when I think of him."

Meanwhile, that queer instrument of God's purposes had himself gone out from the room in Étaples to an extraordinary career. Yet the bare records of what, outwardly, happened to Geoffrey give no indication at all of the terrific inner conflict of those years. It is necessary to search elsewhere for the voice which still speaks from out of the midst of it all. Even so, the records have their significance, if only in showing a characteristic mode of conduct much more in evidence then than now of concealing, alike from the public as from the domestic eye, what was really going on. The serving soldier of 1914-18 knew as much about the horrors of war as Goya, probably more. But at the time he does not seem to have been in the habit of talking about them. Indeed, the curtain was not really lifted until the war literature of a decade afterwards. But while it was all happening the participant in the horrors of the Somme and Passchendaele and the like preferred to keep his mouth shut before non-combatants, much as a man who has seen a ghastly accident does not, in general, go into details at home about what the victims looked like. There was, in fact, 'a conspiracy of silence' as John Oxenham put it, and one of the many criticisms levelled against some of Geoffrey's writings of this time was that he broke it by revealing something of what he had seen. Later generations, of course, have been less inhibited, though whether as a result of a broadening of mind or of a coarsening of taste it would, perhaps, be difficult to say.

If, however, Geoffrey was too frank for some in his writings, his letters home show no lifting of the curtain on reality. They are naïve and simple: while the local press, at intervals faithfully reporting the remarks of the Vicar of St. Paul's on leave in his parish, presents a similar picture of a man deliberately confining himself to the outer surface of things: a few conventional sentiments, and a joke here and there. The conventional sentiments come as a surprise until it is realised that they were common currency of the day. It is remarkable, for instance, to find Geoffrey, in a letter home which he clearly thought might be his last, advising his wife as to the upbringing of their son in terms which spring almost ready-made from the world of Ernest Raymond's *Tell England*. "Make him a sportsman, encourage him to play games and play the game. Teach him to despise cowardice . . . Teach him that a gentleman should choose one of the poorly paid but honourable professions . . . Teach him to love and reverence women . . ."

It is puzzling that such an original thinker as Geoffrey, who spent so much of his time blasting out of their complacency people who lived by such fatuous concepts in the religious as in the social field, should himself have appeared to subscribe to them. It is also interesting, as indicative of the values of a culture not even yet, after all this time, quite dead. Perhaps it never dies;

but only fades away, like the old soldier. Certainly, no true picture of Geoffrey, nor any appreciation of the distance he had to travel in drawing away from these ideas is possible, unless it is understood how once he accepted them.

Only when some of his letters of this time, some yellowing newspaper cuttings, some hints from his official record are put together and fitted into the enormous tapestry, full of violent death, and battle scenes, of the historical background, does some little of the truth of what really happened to him begin to emerge.

For instance, in 1916; to his wife:

"My own darling Em,

I have had rather a sharp attack of asthma which is now over. How I wish I could see the last of it. I have succeeded in throwing this off more quickly and I must be glad of that. But it takes me more suddenly now and hurts more than it did. I don't know quite what to make of it — —"

He never did discover what to make of it, except to say that it made him feel 'like a rat pulled by its tail through a hedge on a wet morning'. The affliction plagued him constantly until the end, and is mentioned often enough in his medical records as to make plain that for much of his time in France, which was not the best place for a delicate man, he was ailing. 'Debility' and 'Trench Fever' also occur. And the source of the memorable lung-tearing cough which so many heard in aftertimes is probably indicated in the entry 'gas-poisoning'.

Perhaps that happened on some fearful occasion just hinted at in another letter:

"I have been up the line again. We got deluged with gas shells and had a very terrible time. I got a bit of gas, which makes me feel very miserable: sore throat, running nose, aching eyes. Tomorrow there is a fight, I believe. By the time you get this it will all be over and done with. I am writing this on the eve of it, wondering whether I shall be safe when I write again. One can't help wondering, though I am not anxious—."

He may not have been anxious; but he was often enough terrified, distraught and miserable, no doubt with many others. But little enough of the reality of what he was saying and feeling comes through reports he gave, sometimes in written messages which were read from the pulpit in St. Paul's, sometimes in person when on leave. There was this, for instance, after the Somme:

"The Vicar first explained why his despatches, which he sent from time to time, have ceased. His experiences were so awful that, if he had written home about them, he would have frightened everyone to death. It was difficult to describe life there without giving the impression that it could scarcely be possible for anyone to come back alive ... The officers seemed bored at first at the idea of having a clergyman with them. They seemed to assume he would stay behind, keep out of danger, and bury the dead. He had to make them feel differently. But the men gave him a good reception. Burying the dead was very unpleasant sometimes. In some cases he had to bury them where they lay, lying on his stomach in the dark to say the service ... The work he was doing was being done by all the padres ..."

Or this grim picture, later that same year;

"We always have a service before a trench raid, the fellows in tin hats, hands and faces blackened. I always go up with the men to a raid, and this has tightened the bond between them and me enormously. If you get men into such a state that they will ask for a service, you have hold of them—"

Or again, this; after that fighting at Messines, before which General Plumer had said his prayers;

"He told them how a large shell dropped just behind him, when he had his arms full of wooden stakes. When he heard the noise he cried 'Lord, help us', dropped the stakes, and fell flat on his face. His companion turned round and said, 'You've got the wind up!' Then there came heavy fighting in which he was engaged in tending the wounded. In one engagement the supply of morphia at a dressing station had given out, and he volunteered to fetch some. 'After that,' he added, 'I was rung up on the telephone and told I had ten days' leave and the M.C.'"

The *London Gazette* for August 16th, 1917, put it differently:

"For conspicuous gallantry and devotion to duty. He showed the greatest courage and disregard of his own safety in attending wounded under heavy fire. He searched shell-holes for our own and enemy wounded, assisting them to the dressing station, and his cheerfulness and endurance had a splendid effect upon all ranks, whom he constantly visited."

Perhaps there was little at all exceptional in any of it. And more expert hands painted in after-times infinitely more graphic pictures of what the squalid and murderous war was for the combatant, living and dying in those fantastic slits in the ground which stretched for years from Ostend to Switzerland. Answering the question, "What was it like?" Robert Graves, forty years later, called the trenches "our homes, our privies, our graveyards; like air-raid shelters hastily dug in a muddy field, fenced by a tangle of rusty wire, surrounded by enormous craters, subjected not only to an incessant air-raid of varying intensity, but to constant surprise attacks by professional killers, and without any protection against flooding in times of rain."

And the smells: of corpses, latrine-buckets, rotting sandbags, human sweat, chloride of lime, frying bacon. And the sounds; clatter of working-parties, rattle of dixie-lids, squeak of rats; laughter, curses and, at sunrise and sunset the cry of 'stand-to'.[1]

Geoffrey's picture of the muttered service for luckless ones setting off on that singularly appalling enterprise, the trench raid, takes on a more sombre colouring in Sassoon's account of just such an event: "It was now midnight. The fire parties had vanished into the darkness on all fours. It was raining quietly and persistently. An occasional flare revealed the streaming rain, blanched the tangles of wire that wound away into the gloom and came to nothing, bringing down the night." Later, when the survivors returned, "Among them was a grey-haired lance corporal, who had one of his feet almost blown off . . . He said; 'Thank God Almighty for this; I've been waiting eighteen months for it, and now I can go home'."[2]

Such reportage was far beyond Geoffrey's powers. It recreates something of the feel of the darkened world in which he, with

---

[1] *Sunday Times*. November 9th, 1958.

[2] Siegfried Sassoon: *Memoirs of an Infantry Officer*. Faber & Faber.

so many others, was living. But what remains to be accounted for is the extraordinary fame which, even by the time of his meeting with Hardy, had begun to gather about him.

The beginning of that starts in a small way with a press-cutting of 1916. Once again he is reporting back to the people at St. Paul's.

"When I left you at the end of last October I got a notice saying I was being withdrawn from my battalion in order to preach the National Mission. I was very much cut up at going away to a soft job. I reported to the headquarters of the Chaplains' department and saw Bishop Gwynne and poured out all my dissatisfaction. He heard me out, and then said; 'It doesn't matter what you want. As you have been given by the Lord Almighty the gift of the gab you have to do as you are told.' He said I was not much good except for talking. So for ten days I preached three times a day to an audience varying from 500 to 1,500 but before the proceedings ended I had an attack of the 'go wrong with my wind-box" (Laughter.) My temperature rose to 103, and between the wheezes I preached."

What actually happened followed the pattern which became familiar to those who helplessly watched him killing himself in the decade after the war. He would become possessed, after the uncomfortable, disturbing way of the prophets of old, whom some thought mad. It was a process Geoffrey himself hated and feared; but while he was thus the words poured from him with incredible force, every sentence loaded; the style novel, the manner unforgettable. And then at the end of it he would be left shaken and exhausted. All those words, all that matchless eloquence has long vanished into the indifferent air. It is possible to grasp something of its power only by observing its effect on him and its impact on others.

Its effect on him was to put him in hospital, gasping for breath. He was there several weeks. When he emerged he was sent to paradise in the South of France. And then, at the beginning of the great frost of the winter of 1916, he can be found moving north again to the bleak land of the armies where in that season corpses left in the open were before long iron hard and where not a few men died in some freezing listening-post, by night, in the phenomenal cold. Fourteen hours to cover forty-two miles, in twenty-two degrees of frost, in a train without a door was Geoffrey's minor share in these discomforts. He was on his way back to his own battalion, still under orders, ostensibly to preach the glad tidings of this National Mission, actually to deliver himself yet further of the message which was shaking him. Thence he was sent back to the Channel coast where, among their mountains of stores, the dockers and the transport people lived. And after that he passed through all the great bases behind the lines, wandering on like some novel kind of prophet who, unlike any of his predecessors, considered it as important to make his hearers laugh as well as listen. "He didn't know," according to the faithful local paper, "whether he touched their souls. But he touched their sense of humour. They split their sides laughing at him."

That was among troops and dockers. The next stage was a grand tour among military high society; from brigadiers to brass-hats of the heaviest calibre whose very word, even when it was not a very intelligent word, determined the destinies of armies. Sassoon has an interesting picture of one such in *The General*.

> 'He's a cheery old card,' grunted Harry to Jack
> As they slogged up to Arras with rifle and pack.
> But he did for them both with his plan of attack.[1]

It would be interesting indeed to know what these potentates with their attendant retinues made of the Irish padre sent amongst them to talk about a National Mission of Repentance and Hope. The mind quails before the difficulties inherent in the enterprise. However, they treated him with much distinction, which he found very frightening. They also, as he told the people at St. Paul's, gave him a splendid horse, which threw him the second time he got into the saddle. Yet apparently something of what he said got through, since it was not long afterwards, at one of the infantry schools to which he was posted, that the Commander of one of the Armies sent for him. They were

[1] Siegfried Sassoon: *Collected Poems 1908–1956*. Faber & Faber.

together two hours, while the rest of the establishment marvelled, like the people of Israel during the absence of Moses on Sinai, at this extreme sign of divine favour.

On the whole, however, he was more than glad to claim from the Assistant Chaplain General the reward he had been promised for taking part in these efforts – permission to return whence he had come. By the autumn of 1917, therefore, he was back in the line.

. . . .

But meanwhile he had begun to write, and this, as far as his wider fame was concerned, was the beginning of things. It happened quite haphazardly. The National Mission of Repentance and Hope, which must now be identified, represented one of those periodic outbursts of anxious energy to which the Church of England is peculiarly subject. The parallel between this enterprise and the events which culminated, in the second world war, with the publication of the report *Towards the Conversion of England* at the end of it, is so uncannily close as to move the historian to the conclusion that in times of crisis it is almost an Anglican reflex to create a committee which will in due course, when the crisis is over, issue a report, with recommendations and findings. In the case of the National Mission of 1916 the issue involved was the religious condition of England. For in 1914, as in 1940, or indeed in any time of great collective anxiety, there had been signs which the sanguine could construe, if they wistfully wished, as those of a religious revival. People resorted to the churches in unusual numbers, though as time wore on, and the first excitements faded into the light of common day, the numbers lessened. Whether the original fervour had sprung from true piety or had been a result of what Geoffrey himself called 'a run upon the bank of God' was a matter requiring judgement. Archbishop Randall Davidson, moved to the conclusion by the representations of numerous earnest persons, at any rate considered the phenomenon of sufficient importance as to appoint the inevitable committee to consider what ought to be done about it. Its conclusions, in spite of a few weighty minority opinions to the contrary, were that the spiritual tide was at the flood and, if taken, would lead on to fortune. The result was the National Mission of Repentance and Hope: repentance for the collective sins which had thrown up the kind of society which had made war possible; hope in the mercies of God and the fact of his forgiveness. Not surprisingly, such concepts, though of impeccable theological derivation, were frequently misunderstood. The demagogic Horatio Bottomley fulminated in *John Bull* against the Church for calling men to repentance—at any rate men in the army—since in fact they were saints. This gave Geoffrey a splendid opportunity. "I see *John Bull* says you're all saints," he said at one mass meeting in connection with the mission; "well, all I can say is, 'eyes right', and look at your neighbour.'"

But whatever the public misunderstandings may have been, the response of the Church was as fervent in spirit as it was familiar in form to any who have, in later times, been involved in similar movements. It therefore began with a year devoted to the spiritual preparation of the clergy, so that a lifting of history's dusty curtain at this point reveals, as in a tableau, the Archbishop in his cathedral at Canterbury, as other bishops elsewhere, gravely addressing a congregation of clergymen, among the pillars and arches of that noble place as all hell continued to break loose, by day and by night, sixty miles away across the Channel. Just so, in 1944, in a room in the Old Palace nearby, Archbishop Temple was speaking to a group of clergy upon the challenge of the future as overhead, in a steady roar, the gliders were towed towards Arnhem.

After the preparation of the clergy the message of the mission was to be taken out to the people in the parishes and to the nation at large. By that time it had naturally been translated out of the language of theology into more everyday terms. Thus the propositions which Geoffrey found himself pledged to support, in common with others involved in carrying the message to the armies, (who, surprisingly enough, listened to it) were chiefly these: that there was a war which would never end until Christ was King, enthroned in the hearts of all men; that God was love and all mankind his family, that the family would continue to destroy itself until the fact was recognised, and that for Christ's sake, as for that of the many dead, Britain would need to be rebuilt, like Jerusalem, as a fairer and a juster place – after the war. Thus do people sustain themselves with a vision in a time of great darkness. And that the vision seems so often to fade when the lights go on again means neither that it was a mirage nor that those who pointed to it were deluded. True, the dole-queues followed the first war, just as other phenomena equally far removed from the New Jerusalem followed the second. But in each case a vision was seen. The Anglican expression of the vision of the first was the National Mission.

It was not a success; perhaps people were too weary by that time to respond. But it was a notable effort which stirred many to earnest prayer and self-examination. Unfortunately, as so often happens, the self-examination turned into self-criticism, and then into the washing of a good deal of dirty linen in public, which, though better than keeping dirty linen unwashed in private, is not very good for morale. The call for corporate action emphasised disunities which were the result of years of party warfare. Everybody saw the vision; too many differed as to the ways of attaining it. What is more, the National Mission, in addition to having to navigate among all these dangers, was loaded to the waterline with organisation. So after a while it ran aground in the shallows and was cast away, with so many other generous ventures. Eventually brought ashore from the wreck was an enormous report, presented to the Archbishop in 1918, divided into five sections. One of the conclusions arrived at therein was that it was the primary duty of the Church to evangel-ise England. "We desire to see ... nothing less than the evangelisation of England and the English people." In 1945, at the close of another war, the first recommendation of the *Conversion of England* report said that "the state of the Christian religion in this country urgently calls for definite action – no less than the conversion of England to the Christian faith". *Plus ça change, plus c'est la même chose.* The temptation is strong to conclude that nothing ever comes of these periodic outbursts, and that as things have been, they remain. But such a conclusion is belied by the facts. The Life and Liberty movement of the twenties, with which Geoffrey was also to be involved, owed at least something to the self-critical ferment of the National Mission. And though England yet remains to be converted, and no doubt always will, the need for it has at least been more clearly recognised than for many a long time past.

.　　　.　　　.　　　.

The main effect upon Geoffrey's fortunes which came from his part in the National Mission was that it drew from him his first sustained attempts at verse. It began by chance, in a manner described by a fellow padre, Frederick Macnutt, later Canon of Canterbury, who also was involved in the Mission. In the February of 1917 this man was at Boulogne where he met "An Irishman charming, amusing and eloquent. He was known in the line as Woodbine Willie. I never knew anyone with such power ... We met every morning and talked over our message. One day I quoted some poetry to him, and he told me 'he did a lot of the poetry stunt'. I suggested he should write a poem for the men on the National Mission. The next day he brought me the result ..."

This was *A Sermon in a Billet,* the beginning of Geoffrey's dialect poems.

> Our Padre says I'm a sinner, and John Bull say I'm a saint,
> And both of 'em's sure to be liars, for I'm neither of 'em, I ain't;
> I'm a man, an' a man's a mixture, right from 'is very birth,
> For part of 'im comes from 'eaven, and part of 'im comes from earth.
> There's nothing in man that's perfect, and nothing that's all complete,
> He's nobbut a big beginning, from 'is 'ead to the soles of 'is feet.

No one would be likely to claim, and Geoffrey himself never

did, any literary or artistic merit whatever for this kind of thing. But there is at least one reason why his verse in general, and these early dialect poems in particular, is not lightly to be dismissed. It represents a break-through in the age-long problem of com-munication—a problem of quite critical importance which needs to be solved in every generation by any who have, or believe themselves to have, a body of truth to communicate. For those concerned with religion the issue is obviously crucial. But they are not the only ones; the matter concerns the scientist also. If he is to have the respect of the great mass among whom, and presumably for whom, his work is ultimately done, then he too must find a language in which he can make plain at least the outlines of his various mysteries. Lacking that link, with no lines of communication between his laboratory and the street outside, he is likely to sink in popular estimation from that of a saviour of mankind, as the Victorians tended to see him, to that of a faceless egg-head in some danger of destroying the world, which is what in fact has happened to the public image of the scientist in proportion as his activities have become increasingly complex.

It is possible, of course, that this does not matter, although it is noticeable how earnestly those scientists who take a high view of their calling seem to desire, even to need, the understanding of their fellows. But to the divine it matters tremendously. His business is essentially with the souls of all men—not of a small proportion which happens to be sufficiently literate as to under-stand what he is talking about. No Church can afford to go on indefinitely talking to itself once it has become concerned with meaning and no longer largely dependent upon mystery. The mediaeval worshipper did not have to understand the Latin mutter of the Mass. The mutter itself was enough. But once the Scriptures and the language of worship has been translated into the vernacular the question of meaning arises.

Obviously, the language in which the broad truths of religion can be communicated to the mass of the people varies from age to age. Nobody appears in the present, for instance, to have found the secret as regards the millions of secondary-modern educated citizenry with its television background. And certainly

Geoffrey's dialect verses would scarcely have meant much to the more sophisticated soldiery of the second war. But the men he had in mind and heart were of a very different sort, for the most part the simple working-men of pre-1914 Britain, the kind of people he had known so well and loved so much in the back streets of Leeds and Rugby and Worcester. That they were men in uniform did not alter their essential nature. The dialect he used was truly their speech. The sentimentality was truly of their very being. Not surprisingly, the *Rough Rhymes* as he called them, swept through the armies in France and the people at home like a fire; burning some; warming many. His favourite, ever recurring theme of the involvement of God in the sufferings of mankind—that very matter he had debated with Mozley so long ago—comes out in one of the earliest of these verses, *The Sorrows of God.*

> I wonder if that's what it really means,
> That figure what 'angs on the Cross.
> I remember I seed one the other day
> As I stood with the Captain's 'oss . . .
> Well, what if 'e came to the earth today,
> Came walking about this trench,
> 'Ow 'is 'eart would bleed for the sights 'e seed
> I' the mud and the blood and the stench.
> And I guess it would finish 'im up for good
> When 'e came to this old sap end,
> And 'e seed that bundle o' nothen there,
> For 'e wept at the grave uv 'is friend.

It was a long time indeed since spiritual insight had come in this workaday form; and longer still since any cleric had so abandoned the customary reticences as to mention matters on the whole much more firmly left unsaid then than now:

> I met 'er one night down in Leicester Square,
> With paint on 'er lips and dye on 'er 'air.
> With 'er fixed glad eye and 'er brazen stare—
>   She were a gal on the streets.

So the leave-expired man in that old wartime London goes with her to the usual sleazy room. There, he chances to mention the name of a comrade who had also, apparently, in his time been to that same place. He adds that he is dead.

> She stood there and swayed like a drunken man
> And 'er face went green where 'er paint began
> Then she muttered, 'My Gawd, I can't' and ran —
> She were a gal on the streets.

"Verily I say unto you," quotes the text italicised at the head of these lines, "the harlots go into the Kingdom of Heaven before you."

It was all most uncomfortable, most startling. And yet it was incredibly satisfying to the many who had longed to be able to see where, if at all, Christ was to be found in the horrors which had come upon the world. The answer appeared to be that he was to be found in the most unexpected places:

> Easy does it — bit o' trench 'ere,
> Mind that blinkin' bit o' wire,
> There's a shell 'ole on your left there,
> Lift 'im up a little 'igher . . .
> 'Ere we are now, stretcher-case, boys,
> Bring 'im aht a cup o' tea!
> *Inasmuch as ye have done it*
> *Ye have done it unto me.*

And counterbalancing this was the deep sense of guilt, inexpungable as the blood on Lady Macbeth's hands, which lay on many a simple soul by reason of the dark deeds war and his betters had forced upon him. So the casualty awaiting the doctor ruminates:

> Well, I've done my bit o' scrappin'
> And I've done it quite a lot;
> Nicked 'em neatly wiv my bayonet
> So I needn't waste a shot.

> 'Twas my duty, and I done it,
> But I 'opes the doctor's quick,
> For I wish I 'adn't done it:
> Gawd! it turns me shamed and sick.

This sort of thing was listened to because it was real. And it was real because the writer could get inside the carefully guarded door behind which the inarticulate kept their deepest feelings. Nobody else was writing for the inarticulate; nobody else ever did. Nobody since his time has done, which is a sobering thought. And what was he trying to say? The outlines of a message later far more carefully worked-out and written for a different audience altogether are nonetheless to be found in some of these early dialect pieces. The purpose is always the same — to try to make sense to the ordinary man of some of the incomprehensible things religious people, especially parsons, when encountered in the form of the occasional army chaplain, were in the habit of saying to him. The contradictions, in Geoffrey's passionately held opinion, between the harsh facts of life and the current presentation of religion, bothered the average man far more than was generally realised. That which appeared to be plainly untrue was naturally written off as nonsense. A first need, therefore, was to make that which was true appear true. Thus several of these longer pieces begin with a statement of bewilderment and go on to try and replace it by meaning.

The question of Judgment: for instance.

> Our Padre were a solemn bloke
> We called 'im dismal Jim.
> It fairly gave ye bloomin' creeps
> To sit and 'ark at 'im,
> When 'e were on wi' Judgment Day
> Abaht that great white throne,
> And 'ow each chap would 'ave to stand
> And answer on 'is own.
> And if 'e tried to chance 'is arm,
> And 'ide a single sin,

> There'd be the angel Gabriel,
> Wi' books to do 'im in —

Did in fact any parson ever say any such thing? Possibly not. What mattered was that he was thought to do so. And that matters still, half a century later, when by very many he is still thought to be uttering the same enormities.

However, it is of little use to remove a misconception without replacing it with something better. And so Geoffrey in these verses — quoted time and oft by a post-war generation until the memory gradually faded — goes on to create a picture of a personal, Everyman's judgment at once understandable and haunting. The speaker, here as elsewhere imagined as some homespun philosopher yarning to his pals, tells how he dreamed a dream of himself, dead, and standing by some solemn sea.

> Its waves they got in my inside
> And touched my memory,
> And day by day and year by year
> My life came back to me
> I seed just what I were, and what
> I'd 'ad the chance to be . . .

So he stands there until, after an age, a figure comes to look down at him. This figure has a most remarkable face.

> It never changed yet always changed
> Like the sea beneath the sun.
> 'Twere all men's face yet no man's face
> And a face no man can see —
> All eyes were in his eyes — all eyes,
> My wife's, and a million more
> And once I thought as those two eyes
> Were the eyes of the London whore . . .

There is no court of judgment, no white throne. Only this figure beside that queer, moaning sea. And when at last the figure speaks it is to utter only one word; "Well — ?" Yet somehow the word is so loaded with sorrowful accusation that there seems nothing left to do but to ask immediately for the punishments of hell itself. But the request is not granted:

> . . . that 'Ell is for the blind
> And not for those that see.
> You know that you have earned it lad,
> So you must follow me.
> Follow me on the paths of pain
> Seeking what you have seen,
> Until at last you can build the 'Is'
> With the bricks of 'Might 'ave been'.

Of course, it is confused. Anyone could pick holes in it; anyone could ask what exactly 'seeking what you have seen' is supposed to mean, or what is the nature of the 'Is' which is to be built out of the ruins of a man's past. But equally critical — and equally useless — questions could be asked about much of the language of eschatology. The Four Last Things: Death, Heaven, Hell and the Judgment do not lend themselves to precise statement, being concepts to be grasped as much by the emotions as by the intellect. And here, in these verses, was a novel breakthrough on the level of emotional understanding. Geoffrey's dialect poems, thus written to meet the need of getting across something of the message of the National Mission, were an immense success, not only in that context, but far beyond it.

Their derivation is obvious. Anyone who cares to compare Geoffrey's —

> Yes, I'm fighting for old England
> And for eighteenpence a day,
> And I'm fighting like an 'ero
> So the daily papers say . . .
> *with*
> My name is O'Kelly, I've heard the Revelly
> From Birr to Bareilly, from Leeds to Lahore

— will catch the similarities, of vocabulary and style with Kipling's *Barrack Room Ballads*. There was the great original which Geoffrey took as his model. What is more, the man he was speaking for was the direct descendant of Kipling's Tommy Atkins. Not so many years separated the old British Regular Army with its horse-lines, its leathery N.C.O.s, its vocabulary spattered with Hindustani words like *blighty* and *cushy*, from the vast citizen army which fought the first war in France and Flanders. Indeed, they often intermingled; the old army taught the new before it eventually perished at the early battles of Ypres. Many a recruit to Kitchener's Armies encountered in the course of his training men who were the spitting images of those whose hoarse voices mutter from the pages of *Barrack Room Ballads*. The worldly-wise sergeant mentioned by Montague in *Disenchantment* whose idea of a route-march was to conduct his charges to the nearest pub, there himself to sit enthroned while they bought his drinks, might be the very man celebrated in Kipling's *The Sergeant's Wedding*. Consider also Kipling's ranker-philosopher who, as on some calm evening his troopship crosses the Indian Ocean, meditates on life:

> For to admire and for to see
> For to be'old this world so wide —
> It never done no good to me
> But I can't drop it if I tried.

This very man seems to speak again in Geoffrey's;

> I've tramped the whole world over
> Through 'Frisco back to Dover
> And I knows my 'uman nature through and through.

The difference is that in this latter case the subject of the meditation, strangely enough, is the Cross, and how much courage — here saluted by a connoisseur of a wandering life's many and varied brutalities — must have been required of Christ not only to endure that exquisite torture; but to forgive its inflictors.

Similarly, it is not immediately apparent that the thoughts troubling the man surprised by gas while sitting quietly in his trench in *Thy Will Be Done* are to be concerned with prayer and the answer:

> I were sittin' me down on my 'unkers
> And 'avin a pull at my pipe,
> And larfin like fun at a blind old 'un,
> What were 'avin a try to snipe.

Suddenly, into this placid scene there breaks the ghastly sound, a true period piece, of the 'Strombo', a gas-alarm operated by beating with a bar upon an empty shell-case. And when the philosopher springs to his feet he sees the yellow cloud drifting across towards his parapet. Like Shakespeare's Mariner on his sinking ship in the opening scene of *The Tempest* he turns in his extremity to prayer, that the wind may be changed. After all, he had been told often enough that prayer was a certain winner, if backed by something called faith. So he prays. But the wind does not shift; the gas cloud comes inexorably on, and the poem finds him meditating in verse and in hospital on yet another mystery of religion. He finds the answer in a 'story' he has been reading, presumably in one of the soldiers' New Testaments handed out in quantities in those times by the well-meaning. The story turns out to be Gethsemane:

> 'E prayed to the Lord, and 'e sweated blood,
> And yet 'e were crucified —

But at least the Christ of the Garden was given the power to see through to the bitter end that which he had felt called to do. So it is always with prayer which is truly christian. Unfortunately, it so rarely is in practice, a fact which Geoffrey, in these times and afterwards, never tired of stating. Thus, in *The Hardest Part*:

"Too often we model our prayers upon the false interpretation of Gethsemane. Our prayers are too often either a wail of agony or a kind of indent upon God for supplies to meet our needs, with 'Thy Will be done' put in at the end in case God cannot take away the pain or grant us the supplies, 'Thy Will be done' ceases to be the great prayer, and becomes the necessary apology for praying. It becomes an act of passive submission instead of an act of positive and powerful aspiration ... We have taught people to use prayer too much as a means of comfort ... the comfort of the cushion, not the comfort of the Cross. Because we have failed in prayer to bear the Cross, we have also failed to win the crown."

And that, of course, is as true now as ever. The trouble is that it is so tough a truth that not many will ever want to have much to do with it. Geoffrey, in saying these things, often resented, was certainly being true to his prophet's vocation. For that, after all, is not to popularise religion; but to make plain the truth about religion. And that usually involves saying things which comes strangely upon ears unaccustomed to such starkness. So the quivering intensity of his final definition of prayer, surely one of the most splendid ever written, makes a nonsense of much which commonly goes under that name: "Prayer is the means of communication by which the suffering and triumphant God meets his band of volunteers and pours his spirit into them, and sends them out to fight, to suffer, and to conquer in the end."

The Rough Rhymes made a big impact. A letter of Geoffrey's to his wife, in the February of 1918 from the Fourth Army Infantry School at Flixecourt, might be taken as his final word on them. "I got my presentation copies of the *Rough Rhymes* this morning and sold them all in about ten minutes for about twice their proper price. So much more for the fund— —"

The 'fund' was St. Dunstan's. Geoffrey's handing over the whole of the proceeds from his enormously successful book to that admirable organisation for the blind was merely a continuation of the kind of impulsive generosity which at Rugby had led him to give away his overcoat and at Worcester one of the family beds. But it was hard on the family, and continued for a while, understandably, to be a sore point domestically. It is doubtful whether he ever had much understanding of the earning power of his pen. He was a child in such matters, though fortunately a child with kindly guardians. Moore Ede, Dean of Worcester, drew the attention of Hodder & Stoughton to his work — sent to the Dean, apparently, from time to time in the humble hope he might be interested. The early contracts between Geoffrey and his publishers were all made out 'Care of the Deanery'. And thereafter his interests were looked after by Sir Ernest Hodder Williams.

This same letter in which he refers to the *Rough Rhymes* also indicates that he was at work on other verses. "I am enclosing two poems so I hope you won't be disappointed that all the fatness of the envelope isn't letter. I have now five poems for the new book, so I'm getting on." The 'new book' refers to a further and later collection of his verse. The habit once begun of 'having a go at the poetry stunt' as he put it to Macnutt in Boulogne, remained with him, and continued to the end. The dialect verses, largely written to meet the needs of the National Mission, form only a small part of that which he eventually produced in the war years, and which reached edition after edition, "saying for the soldiers the things they wanted to say for themselves", as his publishers put it, and bringing home the truth to those at home. And to the verse of the war years was added later that of the decade afterwards. Geoffrey's verse therefore falls into the two parts of *War Rhymes* and *Peace Rhymes*, and in fact originally appeared under those titles. The final collection, containing all the poems which he himself wished to live, was *The Unutterable Beauty,* now in its fourteenth edition.

But somehow that damaging word 'rhymes' used by him with characteristic modesty, has stuck. It is true that the dialect verse might fairly be thus labelled, and seen as perhaps little more than a novel, and in their day brilliantly successful, form of Christian apologetic. But these, in the final collection in *The Unutterable Beauty,* amount to only twenty in a total of a hundred and four poems. Yet their effect in forming the public image of Geoffrey as a man who wrote ephemeral verses was as unfortunate as the nickname Woodbine Willie to any assessment of him as a serious thinker. The fact is that he was far more; very, very much far more than a rhymster. He was a poet: the seeds of it were in him from the beginning; they were peeping out when people used to be startled in his curate days at Rugby, as Bishop Herbert recalled, by the arresting beauty of the language in some of his sermons. The agonies of the war brought them painfully to bloom, poppies on the rim of a crater. And in what years afterwards remained they continued to flower from time to time in other places. How the gift developed in him during the war years can best be seen by comparing the power of his bitter lines on the Treaty of Versailles in *Dead and Buried* with the naïvety of some of the dialect verse.

Yet that word could not be fairly used of his other *War Rhymes*. Some of his best work is here; some of his longest remembered; some of his least perishable. To turn the pages of it now is to experience at least two emotions — a feeling that one is here drawing nearer than at any other point to Geoffrey as he really was; and an excitement at the power and originality of the work. Yet the general effect is curiously sombre, as though here were the poetic testament of a soul continually racked by some inner, personal pain, presided over, as it were, by the ever-present image of a crucified Christ, his dolorous body a constant reminder of the involvement of God in the world's sorrows.

> If he could speak, that Victim torn and bleeding,
> Caught in his pain and nailed upon the Cross,
> Has he to give the comfort souls are needing?
> Could he destroy the bitterness of loss?

It is in this poem *The Suffering God,* that there is to be found Geoffrey's major poetic statement of the basic doctrine of his faith — the one concept which for him made sense of the problem of suffering. And here are to be found the famous lines, the key to the whole philosophy of his life:

> Peace does not mean the end of all our striving
> Joy does not mean the drying of our tears;
> Peace is the power that comes to souls arriving
> Up to the light where God Himself appears.

And the same theme occurs yet again in *The Comrade God*. The war made it necessary for him to fight very hard for the faith he had, and this inner conflict is reflected in his verse *Faith*.

> How do I know that God is good? I don't.
> I gamble like a man. I bet my life
> Upon one side in life's great war—

Similarly, in *If Jesus Never Lived*, he faces the possibility that Christ could have been a product of wistful human imagining, and meditates upon what the world would be without him. And sometimes faith went altogether, to be recaptured unexpectedly in a moment of joy.

> I lost my Lord and sought him long
> I journeyed far, and cried
> His name to every wandering wind
> But still my Lord did hide . . .
> I sought him where the hermit kneels
> And tells his beads of pain.
> I found him with some children here
> In this green Devon lane.

Even the very titles of the poems indicate this continuing element of inner struggle; such as *The Soul of Doubt*, with its strange beginning:

> That's it. Doubt's very soul of doubt
> Lies here. Is God just faith in God,
> Or can God work his will without
> Our human faith?

And *Truth's Betrayal*, and *Tragedy* have echoes of the same struggle. Yet all the time, cheerfulness keeps breaking in. Comedy and tragedy co-exist in the spiritual life as in the physical, and it was Geoffrey's acute awareness of this which made him one of God's clowns, in whom laughter and tears were always getting mixed up.

> I scorn the sun
> I con the books of years in bitter rage.
> I swear that faith in God is dead and done:
> But then I turn a page,
> And shake my sides in laughter at his fun.

So inward doubts, outward sorrows, the piercingly felt brutalities and horrors of the world pressed upon him hard, and from the pressure emerged his poetry. The horrors especially affected him deeply, and no aspect of the manifold beastlinesses of a war which abounded in such moved him more than the sexual licence to which it gave rise. The venereal disease casualties of that old war were phenomenal, and as a man who lived among men he knew it and saw it. In *Idols* he spoke about this memorably, and his words are as applicable, perhaps, to our own pornographic society as to his. The ancient Gods, he says, still have their power:

> Still Venus stands with swelling breasts
> And sidelong glancing eyes
> And lures lust-driven devotees
> To trust her when she lies . . .

And here again the ever-recurrent image of a beaten and mocked-at Christ appears, dragged in the train of a triumphant Venus for her especial pleasure.

Yet his picture of the world, as it emerges in the poems, is not all ugly. Beauty, as well as cheerfulness, keeps breaking in; and the loveliness of the natural world stirs him to thanksgiving as often as its man-made squalor moves him to tears. Those — and they are many — who found matter for displeasure in his so often dwelling upon the Christ of the *via dolorosa,* stumbling and derided on his way to the Cross seem, oddly enough, to have missed the point that the dying Christ was the necessary precursor to the risen and triumphant Christ. But Geoffrey knew it: and realised also that he had to go that way himself:

> Blessed are the eyes that see
> The agony of God,

Blessed are the feet that tread
The paths his feet have trod.
Blessed are the souls that solve
The paradox of pain,
And find the path that, piercing it,
Leads through to Peace again.

.   .   .   .

A letter home, again from the Fourth Army Infantry School, this time in the October of 1917, makes mention of another book he was busy with.

My own darling,

Here I am settled for three weeks at least. I had rather a ghastly journey down in a cattle truck, but now that I have got here it is a splendid place . . . I think they will let me have one evening a week for lectures so that I will have some decent work to do. I will also be able to get on with my book, and get it finished . . . Here one is far away from the fighting, and cannot even hear the guns . . . "

Where and what was this 'splendid place'? Since he was at Infantry Schools for four separate and lengthy periods, each far longer than the three weeks the letter mentions, it is worth looking at the kind of scene where he spent so much of his time; his mind seething with impressions, questions, memories, agonies, from his latest tour in the line. At the Infantry Schools he had the comparative leisure and quiet sufficient to get some of them, at least, down on to paper. So the places were important to him, though he nowhere attempts any description of one. Fortunately, however, Siegfried Sassoon does, so that anyone who cares to accompany Lieutenant Sherston, that former fox-hunting man, through the opening chapter of *Memoirs of an Infantry Officer* will arrive very soon at the place from which Geoffrey dated so many of his letters home—The Fourth Army Infantry School, Flixecourt.

It lay between Amiens and Abbeville, a clean little town thirty miles behind the line, so it is not surprising that Geoffrey says he could not there hear the guns. Parades and lectures filled the day, the latter not always on matters closely relevant to the realities of the muds and guts fighting thirty miles away. Thus a big-game hunter would lecture on the use of the telescopic sight, and the instructors rhapsodise on the virtues of open warfare. The motto of the Commandant was "always do your utmost", and in the mornings there was bird-song, and the bell tolling in a church-tower. Did Geoffrey ever meditate, one wonders, as Sassoon did, upon the multiplicity of regimental badges in the audiences at lectures; the lion, the lamb, the harp, the phoenix and crown? Sassoon was there before the Somme; Geoffrey afterwards. But the place was the same. And the 'Sandy-haired Highland Major' who lectured on 'The Spirit of the Bayonet', and the sinewy sergeant who gave horrific demonstrations of the use of that weapon bear a remarkable resemblance to the kind of group, called by Geoffrey 'The travelling circus' with which he used later to go on morale-building missions.

It is difficult, at this distance of time, to understand what exactly his function would be at these Infantry Schools. It was at Fourth Army Infantry School that he met Colonel R. B. Campbell, with whom he formed a close friendship. Colonel Campbell wrote: "I was much impressed with his personality and fire, and induced him to come and speak at our service the following Sunday. He came to St. Pol, but owing to an attack of asthma could not take the service; but he spoke at a smoking concert given that evening to all manner of people who were living at St. Pol; civilians as well as soldiers. He asked me if he could speak for ten minutes, got up on the stage smoking a cigarette and commenced with the remark; 'I know what you're thinking: here comes a bloody parson'. But as he spoke he seemed to get hold of his audience more and more.[1]

It was in consequence of this meeting that Geoffrey joined Campbell's unit at Hardelot, already mentioned, and began his travels with the 'circus', of which the boxer Jimmy Driscoll, was a member. Geoffrey would spar with the champion before intrigued audiences of troops, and later himself demonstrate unarmed combat. It appears fantastic, and no doubt was. Possibly

[1] G. A. Studdert Kennedy: By His Friends.

it was intended to be, for here again was Geoffrey as the clown, totally disguising the breaking heart, which the poems reveal as he tumbled in the ring. He could be genuinely ridiculous, sometimes unconsciously. Campbell, it appears, was a keen egg-collector, and instructed his padre in the technique. He observed, however, one day when lecturing in the open, that the attention of his audience was markedly distracted by strange movements in the surrounding grass. It was Geoffrey, looking for nests.

But, as always, there was another side to the coin. On taking Geoffrey as chaplain to Hardelot Campbell had made the condition that there were to be no parade services, and that if he could not attract men voluntarily to his services, he would be got rid of promptly. The result was those odd scenes around the church hut, which the V.A.D. nurse witnessed from a distance, the dunes around dotted with men who had failed to get in, and others on the roof trying to hear, through open windows, what Geoffrey was saying. "Never once," Campbell said, "did he fail to hold their attention, and inspire them with the big things of life. He was a man with a wonderful insight into character, and I never met one who was more fearless. He would box anybody, he would ride any horse, and he would face any General who attempted to criticise him and his methods." It was not only Generals who did so. There was a certain kind of officer, Campbell remember, who were much offended, as Plumer was, by his unconventional manner. But others were not, and perhaps the extreme limit of his powers of attraction was reached when he succeeded in getting Australians, those formidable and unforgiving characters of the Western front, to listen to him.

The book which Geoffrey said his being at the Fourth Army Infantry School would enable him to get on with was *The Hardest Part*. Moore Ede went so far as to say it represented the attempt of 'an earnest man to do for the British soldier what the writer of the book of Job and the prophet Isaiah endeavoured to do for the men of their times'. The praise seems at the same time too lavish and too limiting: the book is Geoffrey thinking aloud. And while its thoughts arise from conditions in which the soldier was the chief figure, it is difficult to think that the book was intended for him. Some of the verse was, true enough; but *The Hardest Part* is in fact a theological book of a novel kind: and while it came out of the war, it outlasted the war. It was being reprinted seven years afterwards, and is quoted to this day.

Naturally, since the book represents Geoffrey's thinking, it has central to it the theme of God as one who suffers with mankind, rather than looks down 'a staring splendour, like the sun' in remote omnipotence. The very title comes from one of Geoffrey's dialect poems, *The Sorrows of God*.

> The sorrows of God must be 'ard to bear
> If 'e really 'as love in 'is 'eart.
> And the 'ardest part i' the world to play
> Must surely be God's part.

In his very early days as a padre, Geoffrey writes in his introduction, he went to see an officer in a base hospital. This would be at Rouen, about the time when he was frequenting the *Rive Gauche* canteen. The sick man, voicing thoughts which may well have been with him in long hours of lying in bed, asked his visitor what God was like. There was a crucifix over the bed. Geoffrey pointed to it. The result was not what he had expected. The young man found the sacred emblem puzzling and repulsive: puzzling because the victim figure seemed quite irreconcilable, when one really gave the matter a moment's thought, with the idea of God Almighty; repulsive because it was apparently held by Christians in some extraordinary way to represent a perfectly futile plan for saving the world from sin. And he went on to say that the plan, if such it could be called, appeared to be a thoroughly bad one because it hadn't worked. Anyone who supposed the world was in any sense free from sin had better take a trip to the front, not so far away, and see for himself. "I asked you," the young man concluded, "not what Jesus *was* like; but what God *is* like. To me he is still the unknown God."

It was a challenging beginning. Geoffrey went through at least two battle periods with the question burning in his mind, and the stark experiences which came his way made it burn all the more intensely. One thing was clear; the traditional presentation of Christianity had been weighed in the balance and found wanting when it came to reconciling what was taught about God, about prayer, about the sacraments, with the harsh facts of life as war revealed them. If God was omnipotent, why did he allow such horrors to exist. If prayer was the power it was said to be, how came it that it appeared to be so ineffective? What was the real meaning behind such phrases as 'the resurrection of the body' and 'eternal life'? Above all, what was the answer to the question posed from that Rouen hospital bed; what was God like as seen in the Bible, in history, in prayer, sacrament and the Church? Such questions were given urgency amid circumstances where prayer could be mistaken for cowardice, where death frequent and bloody, came suddenly upon the just and the unjust, and where the whole world seemed to be mad and bad. Geoffrey's purpose in *The Hardest Part* was, in Moore Ede's words to 'bring religion into relation to the stern realities of life, and free it from the deadening conventionalities of thought and practice'.

It was a bold undertaking, and the method was striking, even shocking at that time. "During active operations," Geoffrey wrote, "I was very busy and intensely preoccupied, unconscious of any connected thinking. Yet when a lull came I found in my memory whole trains of thought that had been working themselves out all the time. Each I have tried to write down as memory gave it to me."

Thus each of his trains of thought starts from the memory of a particular event and thereafter wanders wide. A sector of trench is caught in a heavy bombardment. It lasts two hours, during which it is possible only to cower down and keep still. In occasional pauses between the immense crashings and howlings a sergeant can be heard cursing vividly, and a man next to him praying aloud, despairing and shivering, for safety. The realisation comes to Geoffrey with some force that it is the praying which is by far the more disgusting, and the thought was made more disturbing by the realisation that a great deal of the prayer, in peace as in war, was in fact of that order, if not of that urgency.

What, then, was prayer which was not contemptible, or selfish, or useless? His answer has long survived the passing of the conditions which posed the questions. True prayer, when it is of that kind which asks, is for courage to endure, never for permission to survive. It is not a protection against any calamity in any day or age. It will not preserve in that sense any more than it saved the Christ of Gethsemane from the imminent cross. But it will ensure that, whatever particular cup of bitterness has to be drunk, neither fear nor the consequences of it will destroy the essential self. Such a condensation does violence to the quality of Geoffrey's answer to the question posed for him by the two voices heard in the lulls between heavy shelling; the one cursing; the other praying to be spared. (Incidentally, the man of prayer was duly blown up.) The question abides, and always will, while human suffering endures.

And then again there was the corporal who, with others, attended Communion before one of the summer battles on the Somme in '16. Geoffrey noticed the splendour of his physique as he bent over him with the words: "Preserve thy body and soul unto everlasting life." Three days later, in one of his customary post-battle wanderings about, he found the same body, terribly mutilated, in a shell-hole. The incident is the starting point for a thinking aloud upon what the sacrament really means, as distinct from what it is often said to mean. Why did this boy make his Communion before the fight? Did he take 'preserve thy body' literally? Or was it thoughts of home? Or was it a kind of self-dedication, something it was felt 'ought to be done' before an important occasion? If it was any of these reasons which brought the boy to his last Communion, then the fault lay at the door of all the faulty teaching which has abounded for so long upon this vital matter. He proceeds, in a brilliant chapter, to outline some of the consequences of thinking of the great sacrament as something remote from life, reserved for the zealous few: 'Many old and middle-aged women, some young girls, and a few very respectable men.' And why was this so, why was it that the norm in so many churches was a tiny nucleus of such 'regular communicants' as they were called, surrounded by a much larger circle of the irregular, which was in its turn encompassed by a still wider circle of those not interested at all?

His answer is worth quoting: "I wonder if we have not made the Sacrament an end in itself rather than a means to an end, the great end of Christ-like life. It has seemed to the man in the street that we were trying to persuade him that regular and frequent attendance at this service would of itself avail to save his soul, and secure him entry into heaven hereafter. We have failed to connect the Sacrament with life ... Of course, in theory we are just as much opposed to magic and mechanical religion as he is; but in practice we sail close to it ... The Churches tend to become ends in themselves ... We have been calling men to services when what they wanted was the call to service." And when to all this, he goes on, is added the complexity with which the doctrine of the Eucharist has been surrounded, and to that the bitter, age-long controversies which have divided Christians at this very point, can it be wondered at, he asks, that so many in the outer circles stay away altogether?

So much is destructive only, a manifestation of the critical spirit which the war had aroused in many of the best chaplains regarding what all had come to see as the inadequacies of the Church as they had known it. There were others, besides Geoffrey, feeling keenly that — "We have our small band of devotees; but the great tide of restless, vigorous life sweeps by our doors and finds outlet in a thousand other ways."

This critical spirit is reflected in the book *The Church in the Furnace*, a collection of essays by seventeen Anglican Chaplains serving in France and Flanders at that time. Four future bishops were among the contributors; Barry, Woodward, Kirk and Woods: so was a future Dean of York, Milner-White, and the novelist George A. Birmingham, alias Canon Hannay. Geoffrey is among them, and took vast trouble over his essay, on *The Religious Difficulties of the Private Soldier*. They were all very angry, full of the things which would have to be done in the promised time when war should be no more. Some of them have been done, too, so that Geoffrey's picture in the chapter on God and the Sacrament in *The Hardest Part*, of a pietistic inner core as the chief frequenters of the altar is no longer true. The growth of the Parish Communion has altered that to some considerable extent. Nor are the divisions between what he calls 'Church and Chapel' anything like as deep and bitter as in his day.

Many things, indeed, have altered — and for the better. The Church has been through another furnace since then, and is possibly, with many other institutions, now in sight of a third, this time having nuclear temperatures in which objects do not so much melt, to resume other shapes later, but vanish altogether. Meanwhile, however, one challenging truth remains still as regards the Church in this modern world: that past its doors "the great tide of restless, vigorous life sweeps by, and finds outlet in a thousand other ways".

But there was a constructive side to what Geoffrey here has to say in this book about the Sacrament which was so absolutely central to his own life. And this abides, speaking still, the very words throbbing with some of the passion which could make his voice so memorable: "The Sacrament . . . is the heart, the blood-centre, of the great army of people who, having seen and loved God in Christ, are resolved to fight for and suffer with him unto death and beyond it. It is the appointed means and method of meeting God. That bread is the ration of a fighting army. That wine is the stirrup-cup of a band of knights who ride out to an endless war—"

It is a personal testimony, a noble vision of what he felt ought to be, rather than an accurate picture of what is. Yet it is part of the function of a prophet to see visions and to dream dreams, and here he was doing both. And still his cry goes up; "God, turn the Church from an ambulance into an army, and make it really militant upon earth. Do we love God? Do we love the suffering God, and do we want to suffer with him? Do we find him in the Sacrament? Ritual does not matter; the manner of the Presence does not matter. They are not essentials. Nothing really matters but the love of God in Christ."

Such matters may seem to range far from the starting-point of the body of the corporal in the shell-hole. But the impression is a false one. That pathetic image looms behind the argument of the whole remarkable essay, like some blown-up photograph filling the back of the set in a television discussion. It is the same throughout the book; only the picture changes with the topic, and each picture is a period-piece. So the chapter on God in History begins with a 'still' of a captured German strong-point lit by a candle which keeps going out in the draught of concussions outside. The floor is covered with wounded. And the chapter on God and the Life Eternal has a horrid picture of Geoffrey's friend and batman, nineteen-years-old Roy Fergusson, leaning against a pile of sandbags, his head buried in his hands, a great hole in his back. And when the theme moves to God and the Church, behold, the picture changes yet again, this time to a big man, heavy jawed, deep lines round eyes and mouth, kneeling on the lip of a shell-hole, somewhere in the Ypres Salient in '17, still gripping his rifle. He had been shot neatly through the forehead. From his pay-book Geoffrey discovered his name—Peter. And immediately his thoughts go to another Peter, the big fisherman of Galilee, and how he was an 'average man', too. The difference between them was that the first Peter had had all the latent strength and goodness in him aroused. But no one, and certainly not the Church, seemed able to do much in that line for his modern namesake. Here in this chapter can be discovered the beginnings of that emotional self-identification with the 'ordinary man' which was the key to Geoffrey's thought and action in the post-war years.

.   .   .   .

And now those years were fast approaching. For Geoffrey, in spite of the fame which by then had gathered about him—war's end came, not with a bang, but a whimper. The man who disembarked at Folkestone on March 21st, 1919, was a very different person from the eager, ingenuous priest who had gone out at the Christmas of '15. Like the wedding-guest after his encounter with the Ancient Mariner, he was a sadder and a wiser man. Both words fit him exactly; the sadness which had always underlain his surface exuberance became henceforth more marked; and a deeper wisdom, that of a man who had learned much in a very dark valley of the shadow, added weight to the rest of the message which he had still to give.

Like so many of his generation, he returned to civilian life embittered, above all conscious of the many, the very many, who did not come back at all. Among these, a little group, were some of his own sort. Tubby Clayton of Toc H, mentioned some of these chaplains in aftertimes:

"Rupert Inglis, serving with my own Brigade, went out upon the Somme to bring men in, and brought some; then went out again and disappeared. Hardy, orphan son of a struggling commercial traveller, the greatest of them all. Dick Dugdale, transferred to win a hostile Colonel. He won him in a month; they died together." And then he added words which may serve as an epitaph, when all the critics have had their say, upon these padres of that old war. "They were true priests, true men. The Church scarce knew she held them. Their names are now forgotten; but many men's hands welcomed them into Paradise."[1]

Perhaps it might have been a happier end for Geoffrey if he had been among them. But there was work yet for him to do. Meanwhile, it fell to him to express, in tremendous and bitter lines, what so many came to feel about the monumental, historic anti-climax to the years of tragedy which came with the Treaty of Versailles. He called this cruel poem *Dead and Buried* —

> I was crucified in Cambrai
> And again outside Bapaume;
> I was scourged for miles along the Albert Road,
> I was driven, pierced and bleeding,
> With a million maggots feeding
> On the body that I carried as my load.
>
> Yet my heart was still unbroken,
> And my hope was still unquenched,
> Till I bore my cross to Paris through the crowd.
> Soldiers pierced me on the Aisne

[1] P. B. Clayton: *Fishers of Men.*

But 'twas by the river Seine
That the statesmen brake my legs and made my shroud.

There they wrapped my mangled body
In fine linen of fair words,
With the perfume of a sweetly scented lie,
And they laid it in the tomb
Of the golden-mirrored room,
'Mid the many-fountained garden of Versailles.

Some little while after the March of 1919 'an ugly little man, with wonderful eyes, wearing an immense collar', presented himself in the study of the vicarage of St. Martin in the Fields. The vicar looked at him with curiosity. It was the famous Woodbine Willie.

CHAPTER VII

The Development of Woodbine Willie

WHAT first brought Geoffrey to St. Martin's H. R. L. Sheppard could not afterwards remember. What did stay in his mind was the impression his visitor made, and that in spite of a good deal of unfavourable report about Geoffrey which had already reached him. It had reached many people, and the shadow of disapproval never left Geoffrey to the end of his days. It might at this very time have engulfed him altogether but for the understanding of the King in making him a royal chaplain. Sheppard knew of these things. He had suffered himself, and was to suffer more, from adverse criticism.

He found at that first meeting those mannerisms of which ill-report had spoken – language strange and strong, an apparent determination to make an impression at any price. But he found also something else, a sincerity so absolute as to redeem all.

As usual, Geoffrey began by speaking off the top of his head, continuing verbally the topic he happened to be thinking of. On this occasion it chanced to be the subject of Christ, so that Sheppard found himself listening with some astonishment to a monologue on the theme. There began then a friendship between these two which lasted until each in his turn passed from the scene, and which survived the irritation which from time to time the one caused in the other. Each meant much to his day and generation. F. R. Barry, Vicar of St. Mary's, Oxford, and later Bishop of Southwell, held that Studdert Kennedy, with Tubby Clayton (founder of Toc H) and Dick Sheppard were probably the only parsons of whom that celebrated character, the man in the street, in the twenties ever heard, or in whose opinions he showed the smallest interest.

It may well have been so. The early twenties were strange times; embittered, disillusioned, poisoned by a sense of anti-climax so absolute that the only possible answer, among thinking people, at any rate, seemed to be one of an all-pervading cynicism. "The extraordinary fact remains," wrote C. F. Masterman in 1922, "that in both the two great interpreting branches of literature, fiction and poetry, not only has the war given no real inspiration but, among the young, bitterness and contempt of the foolishness of men is far more noticeable than any new inspiration." The picture presented, he goes on to say, was usually of a contrast between a materialist pre-war society having given place, for a brief while, to the self-sacrificial temper of the war itself, only to be succeeded by a return to the former ills distinguished by an even more determined resolve, on the part of many, to grab the pleasures of the hour. This third stage was "one of complete disillusion and disgust: of hatred of the old men who have sent the young to die . . ."[1]

The Church came in for its full share of the blame which was held, however unjustly, to lie at the door of any established institution which had seemed to acquiesce in the death of a generation. It was a difficult time for religion. Two incidents which befell Geoffrey himself in the immediate post-war years had a dark significance in this context. The first was recalled long afterwards by Sheppard. Geoffrey was to preach in St. Martin's at a service for men and women in uniform. "It was a time," Sheppard recalled, "when the whole world seemed to be tottering, when anything might have happened, for many of those in uniform were tired of discipline, and angry—" And then this dangerous congregation saw in the pulpit "a strange little man, wearing a Military Cross on his surplice". He held them spellbound as he acknowledged in burning words the justice of their resentments and then passed on to show the futility of a barren rage. Many, Sheppard said, "had come to the Church almost insane; they left it perfectly cured . . . yet the lesson was taught with infinite sympathy, and with an obvious and passionate love for those who were passing through a difficult time."[2]

But then, Geoffrey was himself doing the same thing. There

[1] C. F. G. Masterman: *England After War*. 1922.

[2] *G. A. Studdert Kennedy: By His Friends.*

were those who met him in these years who judged him to be definitely off-balance, as were so many who came back from the war to find what was left almost intolerable. If others were bitter, so was he: if others had been sorely tried, so had he. And the pain was made all the more acute by the uncomfortable capacity, common to those of deep sensitivity, to identify himself with the sufferings of others. True, the agony did not now come from encounter with the physical brutalities of war so much as from the spiritual mass-casualties who staggered back into civilian life, as often as not to find themselves unwanted. "That chap *must* have been on the dole," one such unfortunate once said of Geoffrey, after hearing him speak, "or he could never talk like that." So similarly, in these immediate post-war years, there were many who felt likewise when they heard him speak. He *must* have been through it all himself. And that, of course, was true.

The second incident befell in, of all places, the London School of Economics, and came to light in a curious way. A woman who for forty years had sent, without explanation, an annual subscription to the offices of the Industrial Christian Fellowship with which Geoffrey came to be associated, was asked eventually why she did so. She replied that it was in token of long-remembered admiration for his courage and patience when, during her student days, he visited the School. She wrote:

"He received a hostile reception. The message of a Christian padre was not a welcome one, and I expect the occasion was thought of as a chance to show Woodbine Willie a thing or two. The students were noisy from the start; stamping, throwing bread rolls, tomatoes, rolled-up newspapers. S.K., after trying to make himself heard, stood in silence, not moving. He was a small man, not of commanding presence. In the end he was heard. Afterwards, he seemed very exhausted.

"How did he impress one? He made an impact that could not be avoided. He seemed to know — really to know — that he had found what men sought, and must tell them of it. But he knew also that they would not listen and I think, like our Lord, wept over Jerusalem. Perhaps he knew his time was short. As he stood on that platform I felt, though I was not then a Christian, that we saw another Stephen, of the twentieth century. I never saw him again. But I never forgot him. I could still take you to the exact bus-stop in Regent's Park where I opened an *Evening Standard* and read of his death, which came as a personal shock."[1]

Both these events took place in what was for Geoffrey essentially a time of transition. At the end of the war he returned, as so many others returned, to the place he had left, at the close of 1915. In the March of 1919, three and a half years later in time, but an age away in experience, he was still Vicar of St. Paul's, Worcester. His work was there; his family was there, a family to be increased, in January 1921, by the birth of a second son, Christopher. Yet—also like many others—he was to find it difficult, indeed impossible, to resume a life that in truth, had changed radically. Or perhaps it would be more accurate to say that he had himself changed, or been changed, so fundamentally, that the framework of life which had once fitted him well, was no longer large enough to contain him.

There were, in Geoffrey's case, at least three other reasons why any resumption of the old life was not really a tenable proposition. In the first place, he had become a national figure— his fame followed him around, and with it came the inevitable demands on him to speak here, there, everywhere. The press-cuttings of the period show him turning up in an odd variety of places: from St. Martin's to Buckingham Palace to preach before George V (who took care to hear him at least once a year henceforth). And of course all the time there were the invitations to be the *pièce de résistance* at provincial occasions. *Famous Army Chaplain's Visit to Wellingborough,* is the headline on one cutting representative of many. "The Vicar of St. Paul's, Worcester, known under the pseudonym of 'Woodbine Willie', visited the town on Sunday and spent a very busy day."

He did indeed. Geoffrey preached in the morning, inspected a parade in the Market Square afterwards; preached at a service for men in the afternoon; preached at evensong, upon which

[1] Private information.

occasion "the church was crowded and the choir sang un-accompanied their prize selection; 'He that shall endure to the end'."

It was an appropriate choice. How long any man, especially one who lived on his nerves to the degree Geoffrey did, can endure that kind of thing, is an unsolved problem which remains still of great importance. It killed Geoffrey within ten years. It removed from a world which bitterly needed him one of the greatest of all Archbishops, William Temple, likewise at a sadly early age. The loss in both cases was tragic—and unnecessary. The words which F. A. Iremonger, Temple's biographer, used of his subject after the second world war could with equal truth have been said of Geoffrey after the first: "As I looked across the hearthrug at that spent man with the tired eyes and ill-regulated engagement-book whom Christians of every name were trusting for leadership and inspiration in the post-war years I could only ask, with shame and amazement; 'Is the Church so rich in prophets that it can afford to squander the gifts of God?' "[1]

Of course, it is often the prophet's own fault. Prophets are not good at saying 'no'. But it is a pity when no one at least tries to do it for them.

Geoffrey's need at this time—though he may well have been reluctant to acknowledge it—was for a platform, a secure base from which he could have gone out to carry his message and to which he could have returned to refresh himself as occasion offered. Some saw the need; representations were made at this time with regard to a possible canonry of Worcester. But it was not to be. And so yet another great man was allowed, no one hindering him, to start upon that fatal path of sick hurry and divided aims, somewhere along which there lurks in ambush the inevitable coronary or failing heart. No one wants a prophet to be comfortable, least of all the prophet himself. But nobody is any the more edified when he has to write his books in the train, flog himself to speak when the tired brain rebels, or listen to a thousand choirs giving their prize selections.

However, for Geoffrey the full impact of this kind of life had

[1] F. A. Iremonger: *William Temple*. O.U.P.

not yet arrived. He was still Vicar of St. Paul's, Worcester. Meanwhile, if his fame pressed upon him many extra burdens, so also did the ferment within himself. This was the second element which made any return to a pre-war pattern of life so difficult. If he had become a national figure, he had also become a different man. The Chaplain of the *Rive Gauche* Canteen was dead. In place of that ingenuous participant in a just war there stood now an infinitely more mature person equally convinced that no war could be just.

This is not the place to examine Geoffrey's pacifism which, never being of the same emotional simplicity as Dick Sheppard's, did not have the same popular appeal. He had not as yet, in these years immediately following the war, sorted out his own mind on this, as on many other matters. But he was in process of doing so, and that is the significance of this period in Geoffrey's life. He was thinking his way through the huge barbed-wire entanglement of problems in which the war had left him. What is more, he did a good deal of his thinking aloud, and it was very brilliant and very helpful to many who in those times found themselves enmeshed in a similar situation. If, for instance, the whole of Western civilisation had been unable to prevent itself drifting into that vast corporate sin which the war had been, was it not necessary to probe deep into the causes, and to find what was wrong with a society in which such things could be?

Yet war was but one symptom of a general malaise of which poverty was another. The threadbare society which he had encountered in Leeds and Rugby and Worcester—indeed all his life with its background of slum parishes—now came up in his mind for much closer examination. Why was it necessary: what was the remedy? Was Socialism the answer? Was Marx the answer? Did there in fact gleam beyond the darkness which had come upon Russia in 1917 the possibility of a juster world order? Such questions, forty years on, may well look antique, like a car with bulb horn and gears outside. But they were pressing enough then, and were the origin of much of the Christian thinking on social and economic matters which characterised Geoffrey's message in the next decade. And since

159

his was a profoundly Christian mind at work on them, the message itself does not date as do the events which drew it forth. And it may here and at once be said that it was seminal to a degree which has scarcely been recognised. Many, including William Temple himself, owed much to the passionately hard thinking which Geoffrey was doing in these years.

Naturally, when he thought aloud on such matters, he chose his audience. Certainly, to such gatherings like the one at Wellingborough he gave of his best, because he loved them so dearly. As was once said of him—"he and a crowd were made for each other". "He has a rich Irish brogue," noted one reporter, "and everyone much enjoyed the breezy utterances that fell from his lips." But it can scarcely have been breezy utterances which led to the inscription on a cigarette box still to be found in his widow's Worcester house: *To The Rev. G. A. Studdert Kennedy, M.C., In grateful remembrance of visits to the British Embassy Church, Paris, 1919.*

He could be so many things, to so many men. Perhaps that is partly why he has been so forgotten, since his effort was spread over so wide an area of understanding. How then shall we see him as he was in the early twenties? As good a picture as any, and as sound a judgment, came from James Adderley, in a press-cutting of the time, who encountered him in these years and indeed succeeded him as Rector of St. Edmund's, Lombard Street: "I have seen and heard most of the great preachers of the last thirty years. I have never seen anyone who created such enthusiasm, unless it was Father Ignatius. I have sat under Father Maturin, Stanton and Dean Hole. I was an intimate friend of Dolling and Knox Little. None of them approached Kennedy. Continually one is hearing of fresh fields in which he is making a name. Very few parsons can take a retreat, thump a tub in the park, advise business and working men, write readable theology and passionate poetry, and be acceptable at Court, all at the same time. The only fear," he added prophetically, "is that he should do too much."

A third element which made resumption of pre-war life so difficult was that there was very little pre-war life to resume.

Everything was different: even though outwardly things might appear the same. True enough, St. Paul's, Worcester, was still there, and the people went about the streets, and the Cathedral clock chimed the hours by the Severn which still flowed unalterably by the county cricket ground. But in fact it was a time of the breaking of nations; a time of discord, a time of the bursting forth, like prickly buds on a bare tree, of many discontents. "Those who tried to put the clock back found merely that it no longer told the time. The Edwardian epoch, which continued in essentials until the first world war, was found, when hostilities had ceased, to have receded into the background of history. It was as remote as the *ancien régime* after the Napoleonic wars."[1]

So some fame, and profound changes in himself, and equally, radical and bewildering ones in the whole pattern of contemporary life, made these years of return, 1919 to 1922, difficult for Geoffrey. All the time he was writing. Two books which came from him at this time, even by their titles alone, reflect the prevailing mood: *Lies* was one: *Food for the Fed Up* the other. A reporter on a Worcester paper, who met him in connection with the first of these books, twenty years later from memory drew an admirable picture of Geoffrey as he must then have been.

"It was in his role as a writer that I first made contact with Studdert Kennedy. Overwhelmed with applications for articles and books, as well as travelling all over the country preaching and lecturing, he came to a friend who was editor of an evening newspaper in Worcester, asking him to recommend a stenographer. So he was sent into the reporters' room, where he sat himself on the back of a chair and told his errand. I was fascinated with the man and arranged to see him later.

"There followed many pleasurable evenings together – most of my duty-free time being spent at St. Paul's Vicarage. Studdert Kennedy was doing the series of articles which he subsequently published as *Lies*. He would dictate at tremendous speed, smoke and choke; then, if he had not made his meaning thoroughly clear, he would scrap it all and start again.

[1] James Laver: *Edwardian Promenade*. Hulton. 1958.

"In a very real sense it may be said that Studdert Kennedy helped to make Jesus Christ real to the ordinary man. At Worcester I often met him and his curate in the immediate post-war days at a midday meal in the Communal Kitchen. In the Christian Social Union in the city he was a leader, and he was sure to draw a big crowd as a speaker at the Worcester Brotherhood. This meeting was held on a Sunday afternoon in the Congregational Church. He loved the rostrum. There was room for him to walk up and down. He began by quite unconcernedly throwing his leg over the side and asking, 'You remember that bloke that came to Jesus by night?'"

It was another journalist—a kind of man for whom Geoffrey seemed to have particular attraction—who, tracking him down when Geoffrey was on holiday at Eastbourne in 1920, also left an interesting picture of him. "He is one of the most inspired talkers that you could meet. He has all the real conversational *flair*: the vivid phrase, the heaven-sent adjective, the fire of the controversialist: and then, suddenly, the rapt air of the mystic, of the communer with old forgotten, far-off things, and, swift as the turn of a kaleidoscope, the balanced pronouncements of someone who has really studied a subject and gone down to its roots."[1]

.   .   .   .

But it would be false to suggest there was any vestige of a success story about Geoffrey's life at this time. There never was at any time: his true life flowed too deeply for such surface phenomena to be of importance, and often the stream of it was dark and sombre. That suffering Christ of the broken body whose image had so haunted him in France was equally an ever-present reality in these times of peace. Suffering, ugliness, poverty and injustice he saw everywhere. Some maintained that he was unbalanced in this, also, as in other attitudes to life. So, in spite of the surface outward ebullience, he remained what he had always been, a sad man; full of doubts and difficulties, kept going only by the steady gleam of faith, like a light seen across darkness amid the benighted wilderness of life.

[1] *Eastbourne Gazette.* August 25th, 1920.

For wilderness it was — indeed, as it still is. Yet there would seem to have been an especially bitter quality, a kind of sourness in the air of those early twenties not known before. The impression received by the wanderer through the silent corridors of those times is a very strange one, as of an enormous, circumambient grief. A man of some psychic sensitivity, known to the writer of these words, even in the later thirties visiting at evening a military cemetery near Passchendaele, found himself so affected by the atmosphere of the place that he had hurriedly to leave it. The cult of the war-dead which was such a feature of the twenties had no parallel after the second war, even though its outward forms may have been to some degree maintained in the form of custom. Too many men had died too recently to allow life to be comfortable for the living in the twenties. Too many memories fluttered like moths in the windows of too many private lives. Bereavement was everywhere. Tens of thousands of women in the prime of life who should have been bearing their children found themselves condemned to the secret, never to be discussed tortures of the unsatisfied, until the fires of desire burned out with time, and all that was left of a husband, maybe, was a photograph, a telegram and perhaps a pipe, still faintly redolent of masculinity, and bitten at the stem. And too many parents were left like the shy father, described in a terrible passage in A. L. Rowse's *A Cornish Childhood* who, having attended the unveiling of a memorial window in the local Grammar School, stopped an uncomprehending prefect to explain that his son's name had been wrongly spelt.

Such were some of the realities behind the cult of 'Lest we Forget'. The trouble was that the sorrow was so large-scale, and darkly suspected of having been unnecessarily incurred. As Geoffrey himself reflected in the verses *Dead and Buried* the prevailing bitterness, so also is the grief caught in:

> Let me forget — let me forget,
> I am weary of remembrance
> And my brow is ever wet,
> With tears of my remembrance,

> With the tears and bloody sweat—
> Let me forget.

But that was not so easy. The circumstances of the living also often gave little enough cause for cheer. Too many had too obviously done well out of the war, and were looked upon with sullen anger by those who, it seemed, had lost their places in the rat-run of a competitive society by gallantly absenting themselves a while. So the unemployed old soldier, and the ex-officer with frayed cuffs, formed a sombre background to times out of joint. And always there were the disabled whose tragedy was lived out behind the closed doors of many a home to which a shattered man had been returned. Typically, in one of the dialect poems, *The Pensioner,* Geoffrey chose to show what this could mean in a humble household. The speaker is a working-class woman of the little streets landed, until death chose to part them, with a human wreck:

> I should be most 'umbly grateful
> And just do as best I can.
> But my pension won't buy kisses,
> An' 'e'll never kiss again.
> 'E ain't got no kissin' in 'im,
> Ain't got nothing now—but pain—

The blow dealt by all this grief and disillusionment to the basic concept of a beneficent God was, naturally enough, staggering. Geoffrey summed up the prevailing mood in his introduction to *Lies.* "This post-war world is black with lies—biting and buzzing round everything. There's a bad smell about; like the smell of the dead. It is the smell of dead souls—"

And at the same time, as regards the life of the Church, other factors were at work equally inimical. "Many of the social habits whose continuance was calculated to sustain religious conventions, even where personal fidelity was weak, were quite suddenly destroyed by the war. There was the sudden fluidity of the nation, invading every home, as men left for army life. Great

164

numbers of women entered industry on a scale without precedent. The habitual became humdrum, and there were all the new pressures on leisure time and the traditionally quiet Sunday."[1]

But above all it was the prevailing atmosphere of indifference which was so spiritually deadly, and this was the atmosphere in which Geoffrey was to live and labour for the brief remainder of his life. "History already sees those inter-war years as the unnecessary and wasted years throughout all of which the open cracks in society and the writing on the wall were visible . . . The pre-war social trends continued unabated, and after a few years of unsettled industrial activity, the deterioration, leading to the Great Depression, set in."[2]

.   .   .   .

Food for the Fed-up, the best of Geoffrey's books of this period, was a tremendous piece of sustained apologetic. The 'fed-up' he saw as those many who had continued into civilian life those soul-rotting attitudes towards all that they had once believed which the brutal futility of war had implanted in them. And his method is, as though a sullen audience of such were before him, to go through the Creed clause by clause, re-stating its ancient truths in modern terms, straining every nerve to show its relevance and its necessity, and clothing all in memorable language. More here than in his later books, Geoffrey wrote as he spoke, the headlong prose disguising the careful thought that had gone to the making of it. Thus, on whether any credal statement is merely a formal dogma: "The Creeds are no more complete statements of truth than a soldier's love letter was a complete statement of his love." His wife "slept on it, lived with it, found it life and love and laughter; sun, moon and stars. That is what creeds are — ridiculous as expressions, but wonderful as symbols . . . Poetry does not say what it means: it hints at it. So do creeds—"

And so on. It is difficult to believe that he ever sat down and wrote this kind of thing. It is spoken word. One can almost see,

[1] E. R. Wickham: *Church and People in an Industrial City*. Lutterworth Press. 1957.

[2] *Ibid.*

165

as probably the Worcester journalist who acted as amanuensis did see, the excited gestures which went with it as Geoffrey paced the study, late at night in St. Paul's Vicarage, chain-smoking the while. "If our Creed is only a form, that may be our fault. You can bet on this—you don't really believe your Creed until you want to say it standing at spiritual attention with the roll of drums in your ears, the light of love dazzling your eyes, and all the music of a splendid world crashing out a prelude to its truth."

Such dramatisation may well have seemed unbalanced, had it not been accompanied by a ballasting weight of thought. But it was. *Food for the Fed-up*, in spite of its cheap-jack title, was and is, a closely argued case for the validity of Christian truth, written, not for the already convinced, not for the theologian, but for the man with no time for either.

Nor was that all. The book is notable for its encounters with most of those arch-enemies of faith—materialism, determinism, pessimism, cynicism—with which he was to be in frequent conflict, in print as on platform and street corner, for the rest of his life. In particular it is noticeable how his old adversary of pre-war days—the doctrine of sexual freedom as popularly held to be manifested in Freudian psychology, exercises him here.

"There is the solution," he says, echoing first the arguments of the opposite side—a habit which even the gentle Sheppard found particularly annoying—"if you could somehow choke the priest with his pale-faced Christ, in which he does not believe himself, you would be free to live according to the true creed, which is that man is an animal. Get rid of the King and his enchantments, and be content to abide without, among the cattle of the field."

Perhaps because he felt personally involved, or maybe because he was particularly well informed, he attacked this enemy with singular intensity.

"It is a ghastly thing for one who has studied and come to understand the powers of suggestion to contemplate the un- natural alliance which has been formed between the specialist in his study and the fool in every street to debauch the minds of the people with a flood of new sex teaching."

There is an echo of the poem in his collected verse, *The Psychologist*.

> He takes the saints to pieces
> And labels all their parts,
> He tabulates the secrets
> Of loyal loving hearts.
> His reasoning is perfect
> His proofs as plain as paint.
> He has but one small weakness,
> He cannot make a saint.

But the real value of *Food for the Fed-up*, like the true worth of the writer of it, lay at a deeper level, and the many to whom the book came as an invigorating tonic in a spiritually debilitated age received it well. It was Christian apologetic of a new kind, in its combination of raciness with wisdom and understanding. Not surprisingly, it was, and indeed continues to be, imitated; though rarely with success. As Sheppard said, imitations of Studdert Kennedy were usually disastrous. For as the man was unique, so was his style.

Nor did he always succeed himself. *Lies*, which came out a year or so before *Food for the Fed-up*, lacks its cogency, smacks more of the street corner stand, and therefore has less in it of abiding value. Significantly, the anthology of Geoffrey's writings, *The Best of Studdert Kennedy*, published in 1947, quoted extensively from *Food for the Fed-up* and not at all from *Lies*. The latter as a book has died; the other lives still, a testimony to the truth of the statement made by his publishers at the appearance of the Anthology: "This generation needs Studdert Kennedy. His is the teaching for the kind of world we live in, and for the kind of people we are."

    .   .   .   .

Meanwhile, as was inevitable, Geoffrey found himself increasingly drawn into the larger life of the Church of his day; so that to retrace his paths therein is to come upon many signs of the men and movements which, at the time, appeared to loom large within it.

Thus *The St. Martin's Review*, for the June of 1923, printed the following notice: "The Sixth Anniversary of the Life and Liberty Movement will be held on Monday evening in the Queen's Hall, Langham Place. Among the speakers are the Bishop of St. Alban's, the Dean of Manchester, and the Rev. G. A. Studdert Kennedy."

What was this movement, the anniversary of which it was thus thought proper to mark? Six years from 1923 gives 1917. One day early in that year, two notable men with whom Geoffrey was to be much associated, Sheppard and William Temple, were talking in the study of St. James's, Piccadilly, the latter being at that time Rector. "Sheppard said with explosive suddenness, 'Don't you think, William dear, that there ought to be a ginger group in the Church?' So began a movement that played a prominent part in English Church history during the next few years . . ."[1]

A 'ginger group'? The phrase is a curious one in association with a movement which turned out to be an attempt to bring in a revolution by democratic process in the life of the Church. Its origin lay partly in that National Mission of Repentance and Hope which had occupied Geoffrey during part of his time in France, partly in the serious situation with which the Church found itself faced when the war was over. Both contingencies revealed the same fact – that before the Church could act dynamically and corporately essential reforms in its own organisation were necessary. The matter was stated with his usual succinctness by Temple in a letter to *The Times* on June 20th, 1917, not long after the conversation with Sheppard.

"Amid the ruins of the old world, the new world is already being born. In the ideas of reconstruction now being formed there is hope of a new and better era. The Church has felt, and to some extent imparted, the new impulse in the National Mission . . . But as soon as we consider the changes that are needed to make the Church a living force in the nation, we find ourselves

[1]F. A. Iremonger: *William Temple*. O.U.P.

hampered at every turn by an antiquated machinery which we are powerless to change except by a series of Acts of Parliament . . . If the Church is to have new life, even if to maintain the life that it has, it must have liberty . . ."

Liberty in the sense of power to order its own internal affairs the Church most certainly did not possess. The fact that it had required nine sessions of Parliament to settle the salary of the Archdeacon of Cornwall was some indication of the difficulties likely to attend even more important matters. Moreover, it was clearly improper that a body such as the House of Commons, which may or may not include a Christian majority, should have ultimate powers over the Church itself. Here the wide gulf of disestablishment suddenly yawned before the startled gaze of some within the movement who had been unconsciously advancing towards it. True, some still cried forward; but equally others, including Temple and Sheppard, cried back. And back it was, so that the Church has not yet leaped into the gulf and performed that act of self-immolation which would, in the opinion of some, at any rate, in the days of Life and Liberty, have mysteriously aroused many of the indifferent to a new loyalty.

But disestablishment or no, there were plenty of other reforms crying aloud to be brought about. Nearly a century before, in 1820, a curious publication, *The Black Book, or Corruption Unmasked*, had set forth some of the more spectacular financial aberrations of the Church, as that there could be four thousand clergymen receiving salaries of less than £180 a year out of a total ecclesiastical income of £900,000, while the average episcopal salary was in the neighbourhood of £10,000. Of course, such things had long vanished away, by 1917. But had they, entirely? The Church Reform League, for one, was quite sure they had not, and had striven for years, not very successfully, to rouse interest in the matter. Clerical poverty was as much a part of the English scene as fog. It came and went in patches, so that one parson could in Geoffrey's time receive, for reasons as baffling, as obscure, and as legally respectable as anything that went on in the Court of Chancery in *Bleak House*, £2,000 a year in a country parish of 800 or so people, and £400 – which in fact was Geoffrey's salary at St. Paul's — in a congested slum. It was still possible to sell the right of presentation to a living, exactly as it had been in the days before the Reform Bill.

And now suddenly, in this new age which had come with the end of the war, all these things — not exactly perhaps fatal in themselves; but annoying, inefficient and discreditable — seemed ridiculous anachronisms, to be swept away. So the Life and Liberty Movement came into being to do that, among other things, engendering both enthusiasm and criticism. Both could be embarrassing. When such a man as B. H. Streeter maintained that emphasis on organisational reform argued a care rather for the body than the soul; or when the formidable Dean of Durham, Hensley Henson, maintained that the whole thing was precipitate, there were always some to take note. There were also those only too ready to smile, and maybe to imagine something curiously typical, in the spectacle of the old lady, a staunch supporter, who every morning, "was wheeled up and down the sea-front at Eastbourne in a bath-chair, tinkling her way with a bicycle-bell attached to the steering handle, displaying a poster inscribed 'Life and Liberty for the Church of England' ".[1]

Even so, Life and Liberty was a cause which lit a warming fire of purpose in many minds. What is more, many of those in the forefront of the crusade — for as such it was seen — were persons of weight in public life. Temple himself gave up St. James's, Piccadilly, to devote himself to the movement. There were meetings up and down the land, of which a mammoth inaugural one in the Queen's Hall in the July of 1917 was the prototype in the degree of enthusiasm engendered. And thereafter names of note in their day slip in and out of the story — Gore, Selborne, Lord Hugh Cecil, Maud Royden, Sheppard, Iremonger. Passions were aroused, anxieties expressed, not least, in the early stages, by the ever-cautious Randall Davidson. And then, quite suddenly, and far sooner than had been thought possible, it was all over. Frances Temple recalled long afterwards how a church-warden of their acquaintance, a staid and respectable citizen, came breathless, as one who brought the good news from Ghent to Aix, to

[1] *Ibid.*

the London house in which she and her husband were then living, on the day when the Enabling Act passed the Commons. "It's passed—it's passed!" he gasped, for he had been running.[1]

And the result? The result, among other things, was the Church Assembly, and it was not long before impatient parsons like Sheppard were complaining that it was packed with the respectable and engaged upon trivia. The result also was a vast machinery, offering opportunity for an important degree of self-government, of which the quintessential local manifestation came to be the parochial church council. Not only, therefore, amid the debates of Church Assembly, but especially wherever and whenever the 'P.C.C.' of some church meets, maybe in country village schoolroom after dark with wild flowers in jam-jars round the walls, or in some urban parish room, the excitements of Life and Liberty stand behind it. And perhaps, while the secretary reads the minutes, and an incumbent looks anxiously from the agenda to the mixed bag of humanity before him, it is possible to feel a sharp sense of anti-climax. The priest of vast experience who once said that, were he ever to get to Paradise, the first thing he would do would be to seek out Temple and ask him if, looking down from the ramparts of Heaven, he were satisfied with the way Life and Liberty had turned out, was expressing a feeling at least understandable.

Yet such a judgment misses at least three important considerations. The first, that the legislative revolution with which Life and Liberty was concerned was an overdue necessity, alike for the Church's honour as for its effectiveness. The second, that it was at least seen as the preliminary to a spiritual advance rather than as an end in itself, though whether that advance has been made is another and a deeper matter. And thirdly, here as so often with English things, a movement which started with a brightness, like a summer day in these latitudes, giving place by noon to rain, itself tended to become prosaic as time passed. However, the deed was done; Life and Liberty carried its primary objectives. And this was the movement which, together with

[1] Private information.

171

other shared concerns, brought Geoffrey into contact and indeed into friendship with two great though diverse personalities of his time, William Temple and Dick Sheppard. Both, in their reactions to him, reveal something of Geoffrey himself.

.   .   .   .

The story of 'Dick' has been told well and often. How this intensely lovable man, eventually ordained in a steam of emotion after many private hesitations, in twelve years throughout the war and into the mid-twenties at St. Martin in the Fields exercised an amazing ministry, is a narrative which belongs to the history of his day. Sheppard, in the naïvety and gallantry of his idealism, typified one kind of reaction to the stresses of his time. Supremely a man of sensibility, truly a lover of his fellows, he was born to be loved, to be hurt, to have his heart broken in the course of his sentimental journey through life. True, there were other chapters in that life besides St. Martin's: before it Oxford House, Bethnal Green; and Grosvenor Chapel: after it the arid splendours of St. Paul's and Canterbury. But St. Martin's was the core of it, and St. Martin's was where Geoffrey, for some six months after the war attached to Sheppard's staff, met him in his prime.

"He made the Church the most widely known in London; himself the best-known and most loved parson in England: hundreds and thousands of men, for whom religion had meant routine, boredom, mumbo-jumbo, found it was exciting, moving, helpful, alive . . .[1]

The words are so similar to those used so often of Geoffrey that it is almost possible to think they refer to the same man. And when the story of Dick at St. Martin's goes on to reveal the passionate love for the destitute, the lonely, the troubled; the brilliant unconventionalities, the startling enterprise, and the laughter which was always getting mixed up with the tears, the similarities between the two grow more startling still. And beyond and beneath the surface similarities there is always the fact, curious and strange, that each eventually had to drink a cup of suffering to the dregs.

[1] R. Ellis Roberts: *H. R. L. Sheppard.*

In their own day they were often compared. Thus the *New Statesman*, in a mid-twenties review, quoting a then recent book on contemporary preachers:

"The boyish wistfulness of Dick Sheppard is always winsome; but his prescription of a sympathetic good nature for the ills of tortured humanity is hardly convincing. Mr. Studdert Kennedy definitely says as much; he evidently thinks that an unarmed man might as well offer a biscuit to a hungry lion in its native jungle. Mr. Kennedy is a passionate and indeed almost savage critic of society and current politics. He has a knack of versifying, and a gift of coining phrases which bite and sting and reveal.

"His God is rather formidable and ruthless . . . 'all down the ages He has stung, whipped, called, wooed, driven, sometimes it would almost seem, tortured men into life; for the last enemy which shall be destroyed is sloth'."

Therein lay the essential difference between them. Sheppard was nearly all heart: Geoffrey, contrary to popular opinion, was, if not all head, at any rate a man in whom head usually had the last word. Of the two, his was by far the greater intellect—an intellect which Sheppard at times found disturbing.

"He is a Saint—a real Saint," he once wrote of Geoffrey; "I've never met a great orator before who wasn't pleased with himself, only sometimes I wish he hadn't got quite so big a brain that causes him to worry over problems until they become positively insoluble . . . The result of Studdert on me is to send me away thanking God for him; but trying to think as he thought and tending towards despair at the immensibility of all that he has put before me."

And again, when Geoffrey's novel *I Pronounce Them* appeared; "Please tell me what you think of Studdert Kennedy's novel. I just can't read another word of him. I don't know why, and it's not jealousy."

Indeed it was not. No one wrote more movingly of Geoffrey at his death than Dick. Yet the mind dwells with curiosity upon this antipathy which at times momentarily overshadowed the loving relationship of two great Christian men. The world of Dick Sheppard, of the Peace Pledge Union, of good intentions overthrown by the hard-faced without too much difficulty, has vanished away long ago. The dictators went through its emotional idealisms like tanks through a hoarding bearing the legend, once the slogan of Sheppard and his many supporters, "War—We Say No." As Nurse Cavell discovered that patriotism was not enough, so perhaps it may be said of them that theirs was the sad discovery that emotion was not enough, either.

"Year by year," Sheppard wrote, "I grew to know Studdert better and to love him more deeply, for we often met and had hours of talk. We did not always agree; but we knew each other's ways."

And, from that knowledge of Geoffrey, Sheppard drew a sketch of him which lives still: "As a companion Studdert was a sheer delight. His laughter was a thing of joy, and his smile had a never-to-be-forgotten radiance. He would sit in an armchair, smoking endless cigarettes and drinking countless cups of tea, while he thrilled us with his wisdom and humour. To go to a theatre with him was to have your attention removed from the stage to the companion by your side, who was laughing with enjoyment. Then suddenly, at a touch of pathos in the play, those wonderful eyes would grow large and sad, and he was not ashamed of letting tears fall down his cheeks—"[1]

The association between Geoffrey and William Temple was of another order, being necessarily that of the lesser with the greater. Few, if any men of his day, and certainly not Geoffrey, can survive comparison with that tremendous figure without being revealed as of smaller stature altogether. Acclaimed by some as the greatest Archbishop since Augustine, Temple stood, and indeed stands yet, alone. Those who watched his bulky coffin being borne down the nave of Canterbury Cathedral on a November day of 1944, when even the heavens seemed to weep, were surely right in feeling that there was passing from their midst a man of a calibre not likely to be seen again for many a long day. To have enjoyed the love, respect and admiration of such an one is a testimony in itself to notable qualities, and Geoffrey from Temple had all three.

The two first met in unpromising circumstances. Temple, as

[1] *G. A. Studdert Kennedy: By His Friends.*

Sheppard had been, found himself prejudiced against Geoffrey before personally encountering him, expecting to find one who affected extravagance of language as a deliberate means of calling attention to himself. But at the first meeting, in the house of the Headmaster of the King's School in Worcester, he received a different impression. Instead of the expected poseur he found a man so un-selfconscious as to be able to speak and act without any consideration of his own appearance, one way or the other. Geoffrey on that evening of the early twenties arrived late, talked for twenty minutes at high speed, then fell silent and remained so. The Temples observed him with curiosity and surprise. But it was not long before both, to use Temple's own words, "were under his spell".

Thereafter, for almost a decade, they were in frequent association. Any friend of a great, many-sided man has to accept the limitation of knowing him only on one or two of the many sides, and that would certainly have seemed to be so in the case of Geoffrey with Temple. Chiefly he met him in the area of concerns where the Christian as such looked at contemporary society, acknowledged his responsibility for it, and considered how best he may help to redeem it.

From the first, then, Temple recognised Geoffrey's quality. "Soon after the end of the war," he wrote, "men knew that there was among us a prophet of social righteousness in the true succession of Henry Scott Holland."[1] Such a testimony from such a man was remarkable enough in itself. And it is clear also that Temple was deeply struck on the one hand by Geoffrey's intellectual capacity, and on the other by the wholly unusual degree to which this was balanced by a profound sense of the divine compassion. Sympathy for individuals, Temple saw, was at the centre of Geoffrey's life, even though social and economic problems of man in the mass exercised his mind. Thus the numbers of people in all varieties of need — material and spiritual — the hard-up as well as the lonely or the lost, continued to seek him out.

There are some odd stories from these years. There was for

[1] *Ibid.*

instance, the woman who came to the Headquarters of the Industrial Christian Fellowship, and who, being asked to leave her name, said she was Queen of the Tarts. There was the representative of the Rationalist Society who, at an I.C.F. debate arranged to bring opposites into confrontation, rather clearly had the best of Geoffrey. A little later, seen at one of Geoffrey's meetings, and asked why, he said, "I'd go anywhere to hear him." And then again there was the woman, embittered to the point of violence by the loss of a husband, who was changed totally after an hour of talk with Geoffrey.

Temple judged him to be, in this capacity to carry others on the heart, as he put it, the finest priest he had ever seen. Even so, it was a testing combination, this one of demagogery with a genius for personal counsel. At times, to some, it could be off-putting. A woman who came later to serve him with devotion in the I.C.F., at first encountering him at a Life and Liberty meeting, found him in every way excessive. It was difficult to believe, she found, that the retreat conductor she heard a day or so later reading from his Greek Testament, and then expounding so helpfully, so quietly, could really be the same man. "Don't forget," Geoffrey himself used to say, "the gift of eloquence is the most dangerous a man can be given." Certainly, he knew he possessed it; but the effects of the power he had continued to puzzle him to the end. As the years went by, and he became increasingly able to draw crowds he would say to himself often, as he entered a pulpit or mounted a rostrum to see an ocean of faces beneath "Lord, I can't understand it."[1]

Thus, then, in the early twenties, was the man who so profoundly affected Temple. How far his outlook affected the future Archbishop's is a question which becomes all the more interesting when certain passages in Temple's writings are compared with Geoffrey's. Thus Temple on Humility in *Christ in His Church*: "Humility means that you think of yourself, as a distinct person, out of count, and give your whole mind and thought to the object to which they are directed, to God Himself . . ." Geoffrey, on the same subject, in a broadcast address from St. Martin's, has

[1] Private information.

this; "Humility means, not thinking little of yourself, but ceasing to think of yourself at all, becoming swallowed up in the great job and the great work which God has set you to do . . ."[1] The resemblance is striking, and similar instances, as in the case of Geoffrey's teaching on the Eucharist in the pamphlet 'Bread' with Temple's own doctrine on the same matter, can be found elsewhere. Between Temple and Geoffrey there does seem to have been, in fact, a cross-fertilisation of ideas in which, for once, the former was not altogether predominant. Temple's name will be remembered long among those of the illustrious; honoured as that of one who, amid many other concerns, gave leadership to that cause of social justice which looked back to Christian Socialism for its beginnings. It may likewise, perhaps, be included among the honours of the quaint Irishman who was his friend for a while, and whose name is not among those of the illustrious, that now and then, at least, he stimulated the mind and warmed the heart of so great a man.

. . . .

Geoffrey resigned the living of St. Paul's, Worcester, in 1922. It was high-time. He had by then for more than a year been living the kind of public life, already deeply involved with the work of the Industrial Christian Fellowship, which made it impossible to continue in such a position. The press-cuttings of the time show him all over the place: now preaching in York Minster in the February of 1921, "the finest exposition of economics to which we had ever listened" in the opinion of one reporter: now involved in a public dispute of some moment with, rather surprisingly, Ernest Bevin.

These two events are connected, and the connection is important to the story of Geoffrey's final years. In York Minster, on February 21st, he had said; "The service of humanity, the dignity and priesthood of work, are the ideals which alone can heal the interminable wranglings of Capital and Labour." A few days later, in the Queen's Hall, London, he turned suddenly on 'the docker's Q.C.' formidably sharing the platform with Lang,

[1] Quoted in *St. Martin's Review*, January 1925.

Archbishop of York, Temple, Bishop of Manchester, and other notables of the day. Bevin had been urging, with the emotion which it is always safe to impart into a statement which commits one to nothing, 'that the Church should join hands with Labour, and together march against the curse of war'. This was too much for Geoffrey. He accused Mr. Bevin of attempting to reduce a complex question to a simple issue in order that they may fight on it, going on roundly to declare that the Labour Party was shirking thinking. They were bold words, at the time for anyone with any interest in mass acclaim. Even so, he was to suffer much, from those, more numerous then than now, to whom left-wing associations smacked of anti-Christ. Geoffrey was dead nine years after this collision with Bevin. The day following his death, his old chief, P. T. R. Kirk of the Industrial Christian Fellowship, went to the Dean of Westminster with the proposal that Geoffrey should be buried in the Abbey. "What!" was the reply, "Studdert Kennedy? He was a Socialist!" And since equally there were those who held that not to be left-wing smacked of anti-Christ, it may fairly be held that Geoffrey, together with Temple, for that matter, fell neatly between the two.

Somewhere among the press-cuttings of the early thirties is an account of a sad little ceremony at St. Paul's, Worcester, at which Geoffrey shed some of his tears, received a presentation, sang *The Mountains of Mourne*, while his wife played the piano, and made a speech. It was his farewell to Worcester. Two events had made this possible; his appointment to the living of St. Edmund's, Lombard Street, and his acceptance of the post of chief missioner for the Industrial Christian Fellowship. He was about to begin the last lap of his journey, and enter upon a new scene.

CHAPTER VIII

The Man in the Train

WHAT that scene was in its wider implications may be illustrated by certain events which took place towards the close of the gloomy year of 1926. The General Strike was months over. The much more prolonged Coal Strike had miserably faded away. At this juncture there appeared a press article by the Dean of St. Paul's, under the heading 'Interfering Parsons'. There was nothing surprising, of course, in yet another piece of journalism from Inge, that pillar of the Church who, as someone unkindly remarked, had become two columns in the *Evening Standard*. The Joad of his day, 'in divine and secular wisdom alike one of the principal public oracles for the last twenty years or more', according to *The Times* on his retirement, was usually writing about something. It might have been 'Sex Ignorance among the Clergy' or 'The Revised Prayer Book'. Most things were grist to Inge's peculiar and highly profitable mill. In this instance, however, his target was those clergymen—and they had been numerous and distinguished—who had intervened to try to effect a settlement of a dispute which had been as ruinous to the country as poisonous in its social consequences.

The sombre facts were these: trouble in the coal industry had been accumulating ever since 1918. A national strike in the following year was postponed by the appointment of a Royal Commission, whose recommendations were on the whole ignored. Two years later, de-control of the industry shattered its wage-structure. Upon the coalfields, in fact, had fallen already the economic blizzard which was to moan so dismally about the industrial scene for years to come, building up great drifts of bitterness and disillusion. There was plenty of both now, among the still pit-heads from Rhondda to the Tees. Meanwhile, yet another Commission was appointed. This, in the *Samuel Report*, published its findings early in 1926. Almost coincidentally with its rejection by the miners, the Government decided to discontinue its subsidy to the industry. And at that stark point, the Trades Unions, led by J. H. Thomas, decided to add their weight to the miners in their struggle. The General Strike, the most formidable industrial dispute Britain has known, opened at midnight of May 3rd, 1926. How and why it collapsed nine tense days later, on May 12th, belongs to the history of the twenties. Here it may be noted only that henceforth the miners were left to fight on alone – a fight which ended with virtual capitulation on November 20th of the same year. The Dean's strictures of 'interfering parsons' appeared shortly afterwards.

He was correct in his main contention, that there had been parsons, and that they had been intervening, if not interfering on this economic 'darkling plain'. The debatable point arose from his second contention, that they would have been better employed minding their own business. And since that question lay at the heart of the work which engaged Geoffrey for the rest of his life, it is relevant to look into the matter in some detail.

There had been clerical interventions on two occasions in the prolonged struggles arising from the coal strike. The first had begun with the initiative of a man by that time Geoffrey's chief, P. T. R. Kirk, General Director of the Industrial Christian Fellowship. He it was who had been active in forming a group pledged to endeavour to bring together the contending parties. Davidson of Canterbury gave active support, and the General Strike itself gave urgency to the matter. Thirty-nine Bishops and all the Free Church leaders were signatories of a call to prayer broadcast from Savoy Hill when the country was already, to its profound astonishment, preparing for siege conditions. By May 7th, this group of Churchmen had been in contact with the Prime Minister and Ramsay Macdonald, both of whom had welcomed a further appeal for the withdrawal of the strike which the Archbishop was to broadcast on the night of May 7th. This time permission was refused.

Even so, the appeal was printed in an attenuated *Times*. It created much excitement, not only on account of its contents,

An Industrious Christian Fellow

Reproduced from *St. Martin's Review*, June 1923

with their three-point basis for a settlement; not only because it had been suppressed—Churchill had refused it also for the official *British Gazette*—but especially by virtue of its origin. Here was the Church interfering in a noticeable manner; here was the Christian voice being heard in economic and political affairs on a scale not equalled since the personal efforts of Westcott of Durham had made possible settlement of the coal strike of 1892. What is more, the intervention was apparently welcomed in those frightening May days. At any rate the T.U.C. sent a delegation to Lambeth to thank the Archbishop, and the Prime Minister expressed gratitude shortly afterwards. Later on, however, he did inquire in the House "how the Bishops would like it if he referred to the Iron and Steel Federation the revision of the Athanasian Creed".[1]

But it had been a notable effort. The second, on the part of the same group, brought together Owners and Miners in a series of meetings, mostly at the headquarters of the Industrial Christian Fellowship, appropriately enough, in those warring times, located in the Sanctuary, Westminster. It would be too much to say that they were successful. Seebohm Rowntree, indeed, the critical Quaker of York, who was also involved in efforts at reconciliation, claimed that the Church's intervention delayed settlement for many months. But the Church as such had been in the battle. That was the great thing. Some approved. Temple's biographer summed up one reaction thus:

"One result at least had been achieved by the Churches' group. Coming immediately as it did after the Archbishop's action in the General Strike, its intervention changed completely the miners' attitude to the Churches. By organised labour organised religion had hitherto been held to embody the reactionary spirit of a privileged caste."[2]

But some reactions were very different. Inge's, in his article, was very different. The 'interfering parsons', Inge maintained, were "obvious time-servers—a new type of parson, sprung from the ranks and soured by poverty and thwarted ambition who,

---

[1] William Temple: *Christianity and the Social Order*.
[2] F. A. Iremonger: *William Temple*.

finding their people bored with religion, and perhaps not having much to say on that subject themselves, gladly escape to politics, in which they see so much more excitement and actuality." Above all, if illogically for the purposes of his argument, they were "incorrigible sentimentalists who refused to look economic facts in the face".

Here was the heart of the matter. The main implication was that if they did look economic facts in the face they would be confounded by them. And behind that lies another, echoed in much correspondence of the time, that they had no business to do so in any event. How true was either? As to the first, the supposedly inexorable nature of economic law was a doctrine which, in a multitude of applications had made possible, as the whole process of industrialisation intensified, some of the horrors which were the price of it. Such degradations as Engels noted years later in Manchester and as Hook found in his parish in Leeds, were consequences of it. The saddest consequence was that the shape of society which emerged from the process seemed to many fundamentally unchristian. But how could it be otherwise if, as was so generally assumed, the economy was subject to iron laws of supply and demand which could no more be deflected from their operation than the stroke of a piston could be made to go any other way from that for which it was built? And if people at times got caught in the machinery, that was unfortunate: but to blame the machinery was unrealistic. In fact it was more: it was subversive if done in the name of any political theory; it was at best sentimentality if done in the name of Christ.

Such views, sincerely held by generations even of the devout, made possible simultaneously two things: the acceptance of poverty in some parts of the economy as inevitable, like rain: and the deep suspicion by those most usually subject to it, of any religion which could acquiesce in such a view. The desperate man who, in a moment of bitterness, tore up Bible and Prayer Book in a slum of Hook's Leeds as the bells were ringing to church, was the forerunner of many who, like the miners before the Coal Strike of 1926, regarded organised religion as embodying the reactionary spirit of a privileged class. So the first implication in Inge's article – that it was vain to argue with economic laws, whatever their consequences to human nature – had a long history.

So had the second, that the economic and political field of human affairs was no place for specifically Christian intervention. "Seek ye first the Kingdom of God and His righteousness, and all these things will be added unto you" Inge had quoted, to which the *New Statesman* had rather well replied that it would be equally irrelevant to offer such counsel to a hungry child as to the industrially dispossessed. It was simply not true, as a writer in the *Methodist Recorder* about this time, in the course of this same controversy, pointed out, that the Church could admit any field of human interest and activity as beyond the frontier. It took cognisance of art and science; why not then also of economics and of working conditions? The same point had been made more succinctly by Henry Scott Holland years before: "The more you are interested in the Incarnation, the more you must be concerned about drains," or again by Bishop Weston of Zanzibar in 1923 at the Anglo-Catholic Congress: "It is folly, it is madness to suppose that you can worship Jesus in the Sacrament when you are sweating him in the bodies and souls of his children."

But such voices were by no means the first to be raised on this issue. Nor is Inge's petulant outburst to be seen as more than a very minor footnote to the massive and complex theme of the re-discovery by the Church of its social responsibilities. Even so, it represents an attitude of mind by no means yet defunct. A cartoon of Low, published in the *Evening Standard* as late as 1943, and reproduced in Iremonger's *Life of Temple* shows the Archbishop being rebuked for concern in such matters. "Be warned sinner, turn to higher things," is the caption under one, showing Temple venturing to tamper with a golden calf labelled 'Sacred Tradition of Economics'.

It was Geoffrey's destiny to spend the last decade of his life among similar concerns. And to see what he was doing there, it is necessary also to find out who they were who had been there before him. A way into all these questions is to be found through some understanding of the origins and objects of that body which henceforth claimed him—the Industrial Christian Fellowship.

.   .   .   .

The origins of I.C.F. were varied. It was a body which, if called upon to look to the pit whence it was digged, would have to lay claim to several fairly small excavations, like little lead mines on a moor, which had been made in the nineteenth century here and there on the industrial wastelands. The purpose of these workings had varied; some had sought an ultimate Christian law or sanction by which society ought, ideally, to be powered. Others had sought for ways of bringing practical Christian concern to the task of binding up some of the many sores of industrialism.

So here and there in those dark and smoky years of early Victorian England were some, at any rate, who felt the weight of Christian responsibility for the ills of society. That, on the whole, such persons figure comparatively modestly in the story of their times is indicative of the unglamorous nature of their concern, of its lack of precise definition as to aim and of the suspicion with which the whole enterprise was generally regarded. Exactly the same three difficulties attended the work of the I.C.F. in Geoffrey's day. The emergence of Christian Socialism, which had, as its chief adversary, indifference merging often into hostility, alike from the official Church as from the very working classes whose cause it sought to champion, exhibits all these characteristics which again can be found reflected in the I.C.F. story seventy years later.

Christian Socialism emerged after the failure of the Chartist Movement in 1848. Its founder, John Malcolm Fowler Ludlow, a member of the bar at Lincoln's Inn had in Paris witnessed the revolution of that year. Out of that experience was born in him the conviction that Socialism, as a new political portent, needed to be Christianised, needed a spiritual and moral basis. The sharing of this conviction with another remarkable man, F. D. Maurice, who had been equally stirred by the events of the year of revolutions, led, in association with Kingsley, to the birth

185

of the movement. Intellectually, Maurice was the dominant figure. Kingsley for a time, under the pseudonym 'Parson Lot', was the movement's propagandist. A man of immense learning, the son of a Unitarian minister, ordained after many a doubt, Maurice was chaplain of Lincoln's Inn when, on an evening of 1846, the barrister Ludlow called upon him. The immediate purpose of the call was to ask the Chaplain's advice upon a project for "bringing to bear the leisure and good feeling of the Inns of Court upon the destitution and vice of the neighbour-hood".[1] Little came of this initial approach: the barrister found the chaplain, a shy theologian, much withdrawn into his own affairs. Even so, a beginning had been made. And though the subsequent development of Christian Socialism as a movement was not propitious, its long term effects were considerable. The paper of the movement, *Politics for the People,* suffered the double indignity of arousing opposition and failing through lack of support. The evening classes which developed into the Working Men's College established in Great Ormond Street in 1854, had to struggle hard. The 'Society of Promoters', with its co-operative workshops, did not flourish. It was all, in any event, a very small enterprise, a modest little mine in the industrial wasteland in which Victorian England laboured feverishly to grow richer. It was the thinking behind the movement rather than its attempts at practical expression of its ideas, which was to prove seminal as time went by.

Such then, was one of the pits from which the Industrial Christian Fellowship of Geoffrey's day, as of the present, had part of its origin. Its actual birth just after the first world war, when Geoffrey had returned to Worcester, arose from the fusion of two of the many societies which the emergence of a Christian social conscience in the nineteenth century had encouraged; the Christian Social Union and the Navvy's Mission. The Christian Social Union, founded by Henry Scott Holland and Charles Gore in 1889 had as its forerunner a body started in 1877 amid the slums of Bethnal Green by the Rector of St. Matthew's, Stewart Headlam, the supposed original of the Reverend James

[1] M. B. Reckitt· *Maurice to Temple.*

Mavor Morell in Shaw's *Candida*, "a Christian Socialist Clergyman of the Church of England, and an active member of the Guild of St. Matthew". There in the play he may still be met, accurately observed, vigorous and enthusiastic, with Maurice's *Theological Essays* on his bookshelves, a complete set of Browning, and Marx's *Capital*. The Guild had as its special object "to get rid, by every possible means, of the existing prejudices, especially on the part of Secularists, against the Church, her sacraments and doctrines, and to endeavour 'to justify God to the people' ". The last phrase, a quotation from Kingsley, indicated the ancestry of the union. The endeavour, expressed often in protests at social injustice, could at times take dramatic form, as when Headlam led the funeral procession of a workman, ridden down by a police horse during a Socialist demonstration, from Bow Street to Whitechapel Cemetery via the Strand. But the Guild was a small, esoteric affair, never very influential. Its importance, as was so often the case with these pioneer efforts, lay in subsequent developments to which in some measure it gave rise.

The Christian Social Union, a body of a different order and dimension, included among its founders some of the contributors to *Lux Mundi*. Its nature may be seen in its three objectives; to claim for the Christian Law the ultimate authority to rule social practice, to study how to apply the moral truths and principles of Christianity to social and economic problems, and to present Christ in practical life as living Master and King. The objectives thus laid upon its members the twin obligations of study and action.

So research amid such apparently unrewarding fields as *Charitable Agencies and Industrial Relief*, and *Housing and Town Planning*—two among the many subjects selected for study by the Christian Social Union in its Edwardian heyday—were in fact of the essence of the matter. Even so, emotion does sometimes break through—

> Judge eternal, throned in splendour,
> Lord of lords, and King of Kings,
> With thy living fire of judgment
> Purge this realm of bitter things—

The writer was that Henry Scott Holland, sometime Regius Professor of Divinity at Oxford, co-founder with Gore of the Christian Social Union.

Here, then, was one of the bodies from which the Industrial Christian Fellowship derived. The other, the Navvy Mission Society, was again of an entirely different nature.

Here was the social conscience expressed principally in action, but within a specialised area of concern. Navvys, 'navigation men' were the pick and shovel diggers of early nineteenth century canals. The name stuck to any engaged in a labouring capacity upon public works. The years saw armies of them come and go. They built docks and reservoirs; the railway age brought them out in force. And to meditate before some such work today, and to note the magnitude of the labour this curve of embankment, that cutting, must have involved long before the days of earth-moving machinery, is to be moved to spare at least a passing thought as to who they were who sweated there. Where did they live? Who cared for their families?

The Navvy Mission, begun in 1877 by Mrs. Charles Garnett, was very interested in these questions; to which the answers were usually hard ones. Navvys were casual labourers; they lived where they could, and what happened when they or their families fell ill was nobody's business. They were outcasts. "Living in their own temporary villages, separated from the ordinary influences of a town or rural population," the first annual report of the society stated, "they consider themselves to be in a sort of Edomite relation to all around them, their hand against every man, and every man's hand against them."

The Mission moved in on this situation with four objectives. The first, expressed in the customary phrase of the time, was to promote the spiritual welfare of the navvys, which being translated, usually meant simply showing them that someone cared. The other three: to gather information as to the real living and working conditions, to make known to the hitherto uncaring Christian the true facts, and to promote practical help, together represented those elements of research and action characteristic of this kind of endeavour.

The Navvy Mission became a sizeable affair in its day. In view of the importance of the lay-missioner, the resident man on the spot, to the Industrial Christian Fellowship of Geoffrey's time, it is interesting to find this early enterprise working in the same way. There were thirty-nine of them by 1890, in mission rooms built on most big public-works sites.

Some crossed the seas. In Canada, as members of the Church Camp Mission, they followed the building of the Pacific Railway, in Australia of the Trans-Continental. In the first world war the Mission had a concern with the labour-battalions in France. It has quite a story, for the most part unknown. It vanished as the navvy vanished, with the passing of time. The embankment, the tunnel, the reservoir, the dock and the canal, are the navvy's memorial — and the Mission's. In 1919 it was incorporated into the Industrial Christian Fellowship. The Christian Social Union followed in 1920, and this story moves nearer to the point at which Geoffrey became chief missioner of the new society.

.   .   .   .

Its architect was, like Geoffrey himself, an Irishman, P. T. R Kirk. Before the war, vicar of a large London parish, during it a chaplain, Kirk returned from it, as did many others of his generation, deeply concerned at the degree to which the Church was out of touch with a large part of contemporary society. Especially was it failing to get across, to any significant degree, to the great working masses who, the war having brought them together and revealed their hearts and minds, were plainly to be seen as separated by enormous gulfs of misunderstanding from anything the Church had to say. Such a concern was not peculiar to Kirk: it exercised many. The symposium *The Church in the Furnace*, published by a number of Army Chaplains during the war — Geoffrey was working on his own contribution to it while at Flixecourt in 1917 — had been full of it. But Kirk's particular concern was the failure of the Church to bear witness to the lordship of Christ — the phrase echoes the language of the Christian Social Union — in industry, in the daily working life of men and women. And since the parochial organisation of the

Church was unsuited to this task the Fellowship was formed, as a body of men and women sharing the same sense of need, to break through with the Gospel into the industrial hinterland. It stood for Christ as the living Lord and Saviour in every department of human life: it proclaimed the Gospel of redemption and renewal both for the individual and for society: it held this world, in spite of impressive evidences to the contrary, to be God's, and human sin to be the continuing causes of the separation of that world from the divine order.

The organisation brought into being to give effect to these aims was extensive, working outwards through Council and Executive Committee. It had a headquarters staff – people destined to acquire unforgettable memories of Geoffrey as time went by. It had Clerical Area Directors, charged with the task of organising the work of the Fellowship, especially of bringing home to church people their obligations as Christians, for the social order in which they lived – rarely an easy task, nor always successfully accomplished. And, basic to the whole enterprise, it had its lay-missioners, drawn from the ranks of industry, specially trained and then sent to bear their witness for Christ in factory, on street corner, and wherever they could find those to listen to them. This was hard and unglamorous work, to which some gave the best years of their lives. "In 1921 I was a miner," one of them recalled years afterwards, "1926 came along. By this time I was a trade union official. However, for some years I had been a lay-reader. I believed in social security, but I was also convinced we must have a new world order. If we were going to solve the problem of industry, we wanted something more. We wanted social righteousness. I became an I.C.F. Missioner . . . The work is hard; the life strenuous. We are missioners without glamour."

That was always true. Perhaps it was always true of the whole movement. One searches in vain for an end-product, some clearly definable objective, by the attainment of which, or by the failure to attain it, the success or otherwise of the whole enterprise can be measured. And here one comes upon a haunting similarity with Geoffrey's own life, to which the customary criteria of success cannot be applied. It was a self-giving, a proclamation of great truths, a stirring of many hearts, and an opening at least of some eyes, with no earthly reward and little honour at the end of it. So the work of the Fellowship might perhaps be said to have been the creation of an atmosphere of Christian concern, involving the education, on the one hand of the Church, and on the other of the outsider, of their joint responsibilities. None of it makes sense unless the continuing background of it all is borne in mind; the indifference of the many, both Christian and non-Christian, the manifest evils of the social system, and the constant effort to proclaim, amid all this, Christ as the Lord of all Life.

To do that is never easy. But it was quite exceptionally difficult in the decade after the 1914–18 war, for these very reasons. Those who complain of the amount of stony ground upon which, in these later times, the word of God is likely to fall, might usefully reflect that there was a good deal more of it, and that it was considerably stonier, forty years ago. This was the situation which the Industrial Christian Fellowship had to face from the beginning. Its business was specifically with that stony ground, and therefore it was perhaps scarcely to be expected that any immediately spectacular fruit should grow there from its efforts. But this is the story of a man, not of a movement, and now is the time to see where Geoffrey fitted into the whole picture.

.　　　.　　　.　　　.

Few less propitious nor more challenging times for the creation of such a body as the Industrial Christian Fellowship could have been chosen than the early twenties. A long winter of industrial discontent was about to begin. The bad years, the wasted years, lay ahead, the age of the gathering storm internationally, and the queues ever lengthening at the ironically named Labour Exchanges, of folly and sourness and defeat when so much went wrong, and so little went right. Above all else, at such a time, the movement needed a prophet. Kirk found him in Geoffrey. How he found him he has himself revealed.

"It was my privilege, under the hand of God, to offer him the work which occupied the last years of his life. The Industrial

Christian Fellowship ... was preparing for a wider embassy of goodwill among the trades and industries of our land. We were in need of a Messenger. After hearing Geoffrey speak I had no doubt that his was the voice, and his the message, for which we were waiting. A long conversation, some correspondence, and he had accepted the call."[1]

Another major change in his life at this time made it possible for Geoffrey to give his whole energies to that work—the appointment to the living of St. Edmund's, Lombard Street. Henceforth, since his family remained in Worcester—a family increased in the March of 1926 by the birth of a third son, Michael —he was to have in effect three homes: Worcester sometimes, St. Edmund's at week-ends, and the train often, the train taking a usually tired, frequently exhausted man to yet another challenge to all that he had to give. We must try to see him in all three if we are to see a little of him as he was.

Once, at the conclusion of a particularly exhausting campaign in the North, Geoffrey was found to be preparing for a night journey to London in order to catch a train there which would land him in Worcester at dawn. Because he was so clearly in no fit state for such an undertaking there were remonstrances, and he was asked why he did it. The reason, he said, was that the birthday of his eldest son fell on the morrow, and he felt he had to be there to see him wake up. The incident is symbolic of the anxious, divided life, torn between love and duty, difficult for all concerned, which was to be his and his family's until the end. Yet his home at Worcester, the house in which he settled his family after resigning St. Paul's, drew him always, and in the three sons of his marriage—Patrick, Christopher and Michael—he had deep joy. So the first of his three abiding places in these final years— Worcester, was where his heart was even though his body was condemned to the weary pilgrimage through the world which is so often the portion of the prophet.

The second, the Church of St. Edmund, King and Martyr, Lombard Street, bears to this day traces of him—a portrait in the vestry, a memorial in a side chapel, and the memory of a

[1] *G. A. Studdert Kennedy: By His Friends.*

remarkable incumbency. The church is dark and quiet, the famous old street in which it stands surrounded by banks.

He was given the living in order that he should have time to devote himself to other things, such being the tradition of the parish, and others like it, where caretakers tended to be the only week-enders in the silent city. The pastoral demands were not heavy. Previous incumbents had been for the most part scholars and students. The fact gives a measure of what the place could be for the man holding the living: it could be what he made it. Geoffrey made it the opportunity for ceaseless, almost superhuman service. All sorts and conditions of men used to make their way to St. Edmund's when he was known to be there. That was not always: but his engagements were generally planned for him—he was hopeless at doing so himself—so that he could be at St. Edmund's usually for two Sundays in each month. And then, just as in those far away, pre-war days at St. Paul's in Worcester, people would come to him. Always a high proportion of them— and this was a very marked feature of his whole ministry—were people of no specific religious affiliation at all, but rather the doubtful, the seekers, of whom in any age there are more than meet the eye. They are not of the indifferent majority, equally, they are not of the 'faithful' who form the hard core of any Church's existence and for whom so depressingly many churches seem exclusively to exist. Rather are they the 'floating voters' of religion who, if faced with a voting card for or against belief in God would tend to place their cross in the affirmative square and then wonder wistfully if it were true. In any age there are people who will flock to that particular shepherd whose voice they seem to know, calling to them in their own half-sad, half-humorous accents. Geoffrey's was that sort of voice.

Thus it came to be remarked upon how after a while at St. Edmund's these occasional visitors, for the most part quite unknown to the Church, came to make their Communion on the Sundays when Geoffrey was there. Their number grew until they were somewhat of an embarrassment, especially as the church was not large and had no side aisles, so that those passing to and from the altar had to do so along a centre already congested with chairs. So one of the 'faithful' was deputed to tell him about it. His reply was short: "Who am I to prevent them? How can I tell what one such contact may not mean in their lives?" Who indeed can tell? It is of the essence of such a highly personalised ministry that its effects are hidden, and vanish with the passing generations. Here some heart suddenly moved; there some eyes opened to things unseen before; a life maybe given direction. Such perhaps makes the sum of it all. But it is a considerable sum, for all that.

One feature of his services at St. Edmund's which many came to find altogether memorable were his dramatic, intense, yet exceedingly carefully prepared intercessions. "He would bring before us," wrote a woman remembering it forty years after-wards, "some one case of distress of mind or body known to him, or some national or world calamity. Then he would lead us to see such things as incidents in a battle between good and evil that was always going on. When he did this it was strange how one forgot one's self concerns altogether. And after that, in a complete quiet, he would ask us to remain absolutely still and allow ourselves to become the channels by which God might work his will through to that particular situation." There were many elsewhere, who met him during retreats and missions, who remembered this oddly intense intercession more clearly than anything else. It was an experience, though at times it could be startling, as when, during the General Strike, politicians and trades union leaders were presented severally by name, with considerable biographical detail, to the prayers of the con-gregation.

Such methods require very special powers in the executor if they are not to topple over into absurdity. It is true that there were always some who thought that Geoffrey was unduly histrionic. But at least that was natural: he was a histrionic person, a fact very evident in his preaching, although there it was a small element in a far greater whole. The fact is that in these years of campaigning for the I.C.F., constantly exercising his art, those rare gifts came to full fruition which Boyd Carpenter had noticed in the library at Ripon so long ago as the young men from the Clergy College came nervously to preach before him.

What, then, were the elements which made up Geoffrey's preaching? Here is a matter worth looking at in a day when the very art itself seems to be dwindling away. That shrewd journalist, Sidney Dark, who in his day strayed so surprisingly from Fleet Street to the *Church Times,* went so far as to say: "I imagine that no religious leader since General Booth has had so great a popular appeal. I heard S. K. once in the Dome at Brighton. The great hall was crammed to the back of the gallery. The preliminary speakers were heard with a certain impatience, and there was a curious rustle of expectation when the little dark man in his cassock stepped to the table. For a minute or so he knelt in quiet prayer, and then he began to talk, and he talked in what were actually burning sentences. He was indeed an orator of genius. He went easily from grave to gay; he played on his audience as an organist plays on an organ. He was an inspired demagogue in the best sense of that term."[1]

But the effect, he adds, was due to the quivering sincerity of the man even more than to any conscious art. Such was the impression given; such no doubt was the impression Geoffrey sought to give. But in fact there was a great deal of conscious art about Geoffrey's preaching. It was indeed no more artless than the performance of a great pianist. "He lived in a state of fierce indignation against the cruelties and injustices of modern life, and this came through," Dark added, and that, of course, was true enough. So a sense of purpose, a conviction of an adversary to be fought, was certainly a prime element in Geoffrey's preaching. A further one was an extraordinarily vivid feeling for Christ as a person, terribly closely involved in the whole drama of human life, just as Geoffrey had found him to be so on the battle-fields. And the strength of this feeling within himself enabled him at times to evoke it in others to an astonishing degree.

On Good Fridays in Dick Sheppard's time, Mr. Arthur Bourchier would put the Strand Theatre at the disposal of the

[1] *Church Times.* March 20th, 1929.

Vicar of St. Martin's. A grey ticket of admission to the Three Hours' Service on one such Good Friday of the early twenties announces Geoffrey as the speaker. What happened is told by a cutting from the *Morning Post* of the following day. "On the stage, throughout the whole of the time, stood the priest, burning with nervous zeal. Men—there were hundreds of them—and women sat as if hypnotised, moved often to tears, held prisoner by the eloquence of a man whose soul was on fire. The stage was at length, towards the end, invaded."

This in a London theatre in the middle of the day in an age scarcely notable for fervour of any sort. It makes a strange picture. One wonders if it could ever be repeated. But it was equalled often and often in these closing years of Geoffrey's life. American tours he made under the auspices of the Berkeley Divinity School in the mid-twenties led to similar scenes. "I heard him first at the Indianapolis Convention of the Student Volunteers in 1923. He electrified that vast audience," wrote one who was there. And again; "He came to the seminary at Alexandria, Virginia, where I was a student. I can see him now standing in the chapel wearing one of the professor's gowns which was way too long for him, and picking up the skirt and wrapping it round his arms as he spoke—wrapping and unwrapping this black gown with red facings. He gave a talk which I can remember still, and his voice saying; 'One of my earliest recollections is of my mother reading to me in a soft Irish brogue the opening words of *Pilgrim's Progress*.' He quoted it, and I remember still his pronunciation of the word 'lamentable'. 'He broke into a *lar*mentable cry.' "[1]

To most who heard him his speaking appeared to be brilliantly extempore. In fact, it was nothing of the sort. Meticulous preparation backed by a powerful memory was of the essence of it. He once said he 'dared leave nothing to chance'. Most of his set-piece orations were committed entirely to memory so thoroughly that he could, and frequently did, transpose whole sections verbatim. The same American who heard him often soon discovered this: "I became aware that he combined elements from

[1] Private Information.

many sermons in different ways according to circumstances; but the passages, though variously arranged, were always the same in content. This taught me much about his preaching method."

Geoffrey's memory, so vague in other ways, was certainly phenomenal in this respect. His secretary noted how, once he had dictated a speech to her, he had only to read through the typescript once to become word-perfect. He would go to the meeting without notes. But she, following him from the script, marked how his words followed the text line by line. Everything was there, even the apparently casual interjections. This was his art; he excelled in it. But the price paid in labour was enormous, and it was scarcely surprising that those — and they were numerous — who tried to emulate his style so often failed not only because they lacked his unique fire, but also because they fell short of the rigorous preparation which was the price of its effectiveness.

Kirk of I.C.F. also noted something of this care in preparation. Geoffrey's method, as he observed it, was to write his addresses on a pad which he carried with him and would work upon as occasion offered. If he made one correction on a sheet, he rewrote it all immediately. Ultimately, he had the whole off by heart. Every phrase, which in the hearing seemed so spontaneous, had a fixed, predetermined place, and the whole was delivered with enormous energy, humour, and raciness which some found distasteful, exactly as some had found it so during the war years. He spoke usually for at least an hour — on one occasion for two, quite carried away, and disturbed afterwards to find he had been so long. But his audience had been held.

In these years, his resting-place — often his only one — was the train, and he was not always left undisturbed there. One of the headquarters staff of I.C.F. remembered travelling with him to a crusade on a train which happened also to be returning from a race-meeting. The two of them had to squeeze into a compartment where a card game was in progress. Gradually silence fell as Geoffrey, quite unconscious of his surroundings, continued the discussion — one of the endless arguments he loved — which he and his companion had been having on the platform. Then one of the card-players, who had heard that voice before, not so many years back, muttered to his neighbour, "Woodbine—" The name was enough. By the end of the journey they were all arguing together.

But the flavour of these years was for the most part a bitter one. At the end of Geoffrey's day, men from the Rhondda were singing *Jesu Lover of my soul* in the London gutters while the red buses blew exhaust at them. That was only one aspect of the disjointedness of the times. God knows, there were plenty of others. But it was the one which affected Geoffrey the most deeply, and with which his work for the I.C.F. brought him into closest touch. "His passionate concern for the down-and-outs has probably done more to arouse public conscience than all the endless discussions in Parliament," P. T. R. Kirk considered, "for he taught by example as well as by precept. He had the human touch, if ever a man had it; and bore in his body the marks of the Lord Jesus. There was a world of sorrow in his deep eyes."

But if all this was bitter-flavoured, he could yet find sweetness in the personal contacts which his work involved. The head-quarters staff of I.C.F. he loved dearly. The General Director, Kirk, accepted the living of Christ Church, Westminster, in 1922, and it was in the vicarage there throughout these years that a room was always kept for Geoffrey and companionship and guidance offered when, as was often, he needed both. The guidance was something he had always needed. Now, without Kirk, he might well have become an unguided missile of evangelism, just as Kirk without him might have been a man with a message lacking the means of projecting it upon the world. As it was, the two complemented each other. And if Geoffrey was able to do more than any other man of his generation to commend the Gospel in the Market Place and the factories of his day and age, and if I.C.F. was a power for good, it was due in no small measure to the fact that these two were close friends, brothers in the work. That did not prevent Geoffrey from being worked remorselessly hard; but the cause was a great one, and in any event he was a man born to burn rather than rust out. There was also Miss E. C. Knight-Bruce, Geoffrey's opposite number as a woman messenger for the Fellowship, whose hand-some features look out from I.C.F. group photographs of the period. She had, it was said, in addition to presence and formid-able intelligence, a lovely voice, and would sing Geoffrey's sentimental verses, put to music by the organist of St. Edmund's, Lombard Street—"When through the whirl of wheels and engines humming—"

This is the verse which speaks of the miner, far below ground 'wielding his pick more splendid than the sword', and of the second coming of the Lord:

> God in a workman's jacket as before,
> Living again the eternal Gospel story,
> Sweeping the shavings from his workship floor.

The sentimentality, the idealisation of labour, all bring back Geoffrey and his day. However, it was easier then to see Christ in the worker, when that worker was so obviously, it seemed, being once again the victim of economic theory.

And then again there was Alice Charles, for twenty years Director of Studies. She it was who wrote of Geoffrey:

"To me, as a teacher, what I admired most was the wonderful gift he had of expressing the most profound dogmatic truths in language that could be understood and appreciated by simple and unlearned people. This is obvious in his writings, but when the stuff in his books was delivered by him in his addresses—as it generally was—backed by his powerful personality and his intense desire to bring men to Christ, and his complete self-dedication, it availed greatly. In the mass meetings and open-airs which he addressed, there were many who took their first steps towards the Christian faith through him.

"No one who worked with him in the Crusades will ever forget the urgency of the crowds by which he was surrounded in the cities and squares, nor the vast length and eagerness of the queues that waited to get into his mass meetings. The Holy Ghost was truly there to 'inspire and lighten with celestial fire'."[1]

[1] Private information.

Such people were a few among many; but they did happen to be among those who were able to observe Geoffrey at close quarters. It is clear that the staff adored him, to whom his general helplessness in the practical affairs of life could make a powerful appeal. It was a long-remembered excitement to have to help him out when he turned up penniless, or to see him coming in with a huge toy in his arms for one of his children, or to encounter some of the incredible people who came looking for him in Westminster; that Queen of the Tarts already mentioned, or some of the ex-prisoners from Wandsworth who came after he had visited the prison and offered help to anyone who, on release, felt in need of it, or to listen to him in theological argument with Miss Knight-Bruce during some long journey. Now the tale of that particular day is finished. But among such memories of small things which are still to be detected around the scene, like some previous occupant's scent in the wardrobe of an hotel bedroom, is still to be found something of that extraordinary warming of the heart which Geoffrey was able to inspire. As with those who knew him long ago in Leeds and Rugby and Worcester, and France, so now it was with these who encountered him in his last years, that they felt something very remarkable, something very moving, had been glimpsed passing upon the usually grey highway of life. And when he was able, as he often was, to lift up their hearts in his retreat addresses, the impression was deepened. Thus Kirk, of just such an occasion in 1923:

"The talks given to a little company at a retreat at High Leigh were unforgettable. One who was there writes of the setting of glorious spring weather — sunshine and a blaze of flowers. His message seemed to be a part of their setting. He sat in the big chair of the chapel, looking past his hearers to the glory of the garden."

What was he saying? This is one of the far too rare occasions when we can know, because his notes have survived. He would be looking out on the flowers Kirk speaks of when he said: 'He maketh me lie down in green pastures: He leadeth me beside still waters.' This is a picture of beauty: the shepherd wandering with his sheep to the quiet pool through the green and gold of nature—the pool exceedingly still, with shadows in its heart. But the sheep follow the shepherd, not because of the beauty; but because they are hungry. So if we crave beauty, it must be not as a luxury but as a necessity: if we follow the shepherd it must be from necessity. God is never real until he is just that."

He certainly craved beauty himself. Among Kirk's memories is one of Geoffrey, on the first visit to the Alps, having to be sought until at last found, quite overcome by the tremendous spectacle of those 'snowy summits old in story'. Many have felt the same, of course; the only exceptional feature of this sort of reaction was its intensity. But the importance of the matter to Geoffrey's thinking lay in the fact that he so emphatically identified God with such outward phenomena, thus laying himself open to the charge of pantheism often brought against him. A man who could say, as he did, that there was the Kingdom and the Power and the Glory in the towers of York and Bach's *Mass in B. Minor* was obviously rendering himself vulnerable.

But to get back to the train—Geoffrey's movements had to be carefully planned not only because he was liable to forget date, destination and purpose of journeys; but also because there were so many of them. So generally he would be issued with a list stretching far into the future—during one Crusade there was a man charged with the sole duty of getting him to the right place at the right time. One such list, still extant, presents a picture of him being shunted ceaselessly from one end of the country to another, from the Rotarians of Warrington, to a mission at Barry, to a mass meeting in Carlisle, to Leicester Cathedral, to Liverpool Cathedral, to St. Mary's, Oxford, to the Town Hall, Wallasey, the Brighton Corn Exchange, to uncounted churches, a miner's demonstration in Durham, and to some long-forgotten, unspecified, curiosity-arousing meeting with persons unknown in the middle of the afternoon in a theatre in Swanage. Such became the common form of his life. But the great occasions, those which showed both him and the work to which he had devoted himself at fullest stretch, came when a train delivered him at the station of some town for the beginning of that characteristic activity of the I.C.F. of the time—the Crusade.

It is certainly true that such things have been common in all ages to the history of religion. It may well be equally true that their ashes can rarely be stirred with profit. A mission, a campaign, is held; many words are spoken, a varying degree of warmth is engendered. Then it is over, the fire dies down, and the winds of everyday appear to blow as coolly as ever over an unchanged scene. But sometimes—not often, perhaps, but sometimes—it is different; the fire does not die wholly away, but can be found years afterwards still glowing comfortingly in a few private lives. And that at least can be claimed for some of these I.C.F. crusades.

The time was apt for the invigorating exposition of the Christian faith in relation to social, economic and political life. There was need to get out into the streets and talk about Christ the Lord of All Life when he seemed so singularly absent from the discouraging scene. What is more, it was still possible in that time, before radio and television had altered social habits in these respects to gather people together in large masses. Above all, these Crusades of the twenties, though they represented, and were made possible by, the labours of many, had in Geoffrey a central figure of genius, while the economic tragedy of the times gave them vivid relevance. These factors together made possible results, in terms of fervour and enduring inspiration, which even at this distance of time are surprising.

Geoffrey was involved in many such Crusades. They were always carefully prepared, the process beginning perhaps a year before-hand with local committees of clergy and business men co-operating with the I.C.F. priest director and headquarters staff in arranging the programme. By the time the Crusaders themselves arrived the ground would have been thoroughly made ready for the 'ploughing-up' which was intended. The Crusaders themselves invariably included I.C.F. missioners who had been working-men themselves. Those to be glimpsed, in the first chapter of this book, struggling bravely to hold a packed street corner meeting until Geoffrey arrived, were of that valiant band.) In addition there would be four or five clergy accustomed to the rigours of open-air speaking, a number of women and the Crusade leader, often a bishop, sometimes, in his day, Geoffrey himself. And also special speakers would be brought in—George Lansbury was one, Sir William Cash another, and Christian economists, employers, trade union leaders. The whole effort would last a week or two, gradually building up to the climax of mass-meetings towards the end. Meanwhile there would have been daily factory and canteen gatherings in the lunch-hour, and at night—most challenging of all—open-air pitches for the proclamation of the Crusade message and for the uninhibited and at times bitter debate of bitter times.

The message of a crusade was based on the syllabus drawn up in the early years of I.C.E., *Christ the Lord of All Life*. Geoffrey had a hand in this clear exposition of Christian fundamentals. To read it is to realise at once how far removed these Crusades were from the kind of mission, often focused upon the personality of one man, which in recent times appears to have taken up the torch of emotional evangelism.

Here is something quite different. Even the purpose of the Crusades differed utterly from the "decision for Christ" objective of a later day. "It is an endeavour," the book stated, "to present the Christian religion to the people of a town or district as the solution of the problem of modern social life as they see and experience it . . . The appeal to the individual is made to him as a member of society. A Crusade endeavours to give this message to those whom the Church does not otherwise reach . . . It does not aim directly at getting people into the Church, though that has sometimes happened to a considerable extent; but it offers a magnificent opportunity for the removal of deep-seated misconceptions, and for putting truer ways of thinking before people who have hitherto left organised religion altogether out of account."

Emphasis was laid also upon the importance of meeting people upon their own ground, of starting from the known and going on to the unknown. Above all, speakers were urged to have constantly in mind that principle at the heart of all successful communication—a principle so often forgotten or ignored—of speaking in a language that could be understood. Conventional religious phrases were to be avoided at all costs. "We have to aim at presenting the truth in all its depth and power, but in quite a different sort of language." It was a task exactly suited to Geoffrey's genius. Many shared it with him; but these many were the first to recognise how overwhelmingly much whatever success the enterprise had, owed to him.

These dry bones came together into life, each day having its theme, and each theme having its place in the message as a whole, so that from a beginning at the contemporary order of society, its origins, its evils and its challenges, the argument passed on by stages to the relevance of Christ and his Church and to the common life which had to be lived therein. Above all, personal contacts were made often during the course of a Crusade, some of which can be found having their effect to this day.

In the middle twenties a train deposited Geoffrey at the city of Stoke in the Potteries. This was the scene of a notable Crusade, perhaps the greatest of his time. Indeed, for many years afterwards an annual service used to be held in those unlovely places, Tunstall, Hanley and Longton, commemorating the effort, as though it had been a battle. There, in the six towns with their potbanks, the iron and steel works at Shelton Bar, and the collieries around, was a fit setting for an effort symbolised in the poster which had been visible around the area for some time past. It showed the tower of Hanley Parish Church shrouded in the smoke of potbanks curling up to the legend "Is it nothing to you, all ye that pass by?" In the event, it turned out to be much. The interest, even the passion aroused, was enormous. One who was there, as curate of Stoke in those days, remembered how:

"Each day the missioners, about eighty of them, met in Hanley Old Church. Bishop Kempthorne of Lichfield, was leader, but it was S.K. who gave the message for the day. In this he excelled. Many people crowded into this meeting just to hear him ... Every evening, in one of the Town Halls, there was a mass meeting, often representing some industrial interest. S.K. was a necessity here. There was a dinner-hour meeting every day in Stoke Parish Church, which held two thousand. It was packed daily—for S.K. My last and most distinct memory of him was on the last Sunday, in Hanley, after the evening services. The Victoria Hall had been set aside, and the largest Methodist Church had been added. Both were packed. I sat on the floor in the Victoria Hall at the edge of the platform. It was like that."[1]

Geoffrey, it seemed, spoke first at the Methodist Church, an all-out effort. He then had to face the crowd waiting in the Victoria Hall and repeat the whole thing. He was exhausted by the ten previous days. By the time he reached this final meeting he was; "visibly reeling with fatigue. How he kept on his feet I don't know, but he kept on till he had done his work. I cannot describe the impression he made in that Crusade, except to say that he was the best-known man in the place, and continued to be a name for many years after."

As always where Geoffrey was involved the memories surviving are a mixture of the absurd and the touching. So one will recall touring the 'pitches' with him and seeing, as it grew dark, the light of a street-lamp on his face while questions came out of the shadows. "He always answered on the level of the questioner, but going deeper as he went on, until there was silence all around." Or again a man coming shyly up to him in a similar dusk scene, some private words passing between them, and Geoffrey afterwards saying to the helper doing the rounds of the 'pitches' with him, "He was at Messines." Or again Geoffrey startling a gathering of Potteries business-men in boiled shirts by opening an after-dinner speech, after a long look round the tables, with the words; "My God, but it's funny, the kind of people he allows to have money!" Or again, but this time in a pulpit, in the brogue he put on with such ease: "David in his haste said all men were liars. If he'd taken his time he'd have said it just the same." This, of course, was the kind of thing which had so annoyed General Plumer and others, years before. It continued to annoy. Clergy especially started with a prejudice against him. But, as Bishop Kempthorne recorded of this Stoke crusade, they were soon won over by his obvious humility and the reality of his spiritual power. And then, as always, there was a great number of individuals

[1] Private information.

who came to him for personal counsel. "I remember one time," is another memory, "that he had so many to see him after a meeting that when he came in he was so exhausted he literally could not speak —"

And the results? Who can say? Who can now presume even to try to measure so insubstantial, so gossamer-like a quality? The thing is secret, and perhaps should be, unless the whole business is to sink to the level of that kind of evangelism which counts the number of the alleged converted as a brave once reckoned his scalps. There was nothing of that, either in atmosphere or intention, about these I.C.F. Crusades of the twenties. In any case, the only results of any value, in this as in any other kind of high endeavour, are those which last. Whether, when the excitement had died down, and the missioners had departed, any abiding impression had been made, may well be difficult to decide. Even so, it is something to discover for how many years the effect endured of the Stoke Crusade, to take that one instance alone. Thus there was the manufacturer to whose heart, in some way or another the whole thing, and Geoffrey especially, spoke direct, and who as a consequence tried down all the years since to run his great concern on Christian principles. And then again there was the stout-hearted man who was appointed full-time missioner to carry on the work, and did so, for many years, until other times and other manners rendered it all less meaningful. 'Is it nothing to you, all ye that pass by?' the poster advertising the Stoke Crusade had asked. Perhaps it was enough that there were some at least who found, as a result of it all, and of the many efforts like it, that a little light was cast thereby upon the business of living.

It was during this Stoke Crusade that the same man who watched Geoffrey's supreme effort during the packed final meeting noticed how each morning, while the day's business was being arranged, he was to be seen in a corner, abstracted amid the surrounding noise, quietly writing. The book was *The Wicket Gate*. With the other product of these I.C.F. years, *The Word and the Work* it represents, apart from his verse, the most important writing he managed to distil from the pressures of an absurdly overcrowded life. It is a brilliant demonstration of the art of communication of basic truths in the language of the kind of person for whom it was intended—that 'plain man' with his inarticulate longings and unanswered questions who, as Geoffrey passionately felt, usually found precious little of satisfaction to his soul in organised religion as he commonly encountered it. Yet his needs were great for 'the plain bread of religion which a man must have in order to live'. It is a bad time for the man in the street. He is aware he dwells in the City of Destruction ... In the unutterable depths of his inarticulate soul there is trouble, and he breaks out with a lamentable cry saying, '*What shall I do?*' ... We cannot see the wicket-gate, or walk in the narrow way of our forefathers: and to the ancient Evangelist who kindly points it out, we can only answer 'No!' But when he further says, 'Do you see yonder shining light?' there are thousands who would reply doubtfully, hesitatingly, and yet with a thrill of hope, 'I think I do'." So Geoffrey wrote in his introduction.

Such thousands are still around, of course. And they are certainly more conscious, and with reason, of being in the City of Destruction. And here, at this very point, is the importance of Geoffrey for today. To read these two books of his now is often to be astonished at their topicality. Thus, in *The Word and the Work*:

"European man, whom the Dean of St. Paul's describes as 'the fiercest of the beasts of prey, who is not likely to abandon the weapons which have made him the lord and bully of the planet, is threatened with extinction unless he becomes either a more tyrannous lord, using without restraint or remorse the powers of destruction that have been put into his hands, or dies with Christ, and finds a more excellent way."

That 'more excellent way', in *The Wicket Gate* on the basis of the Lord's Prayer, in *The Word and the Work* on the Logos passage of St. John, is tellingly set forth, pleaded for, given contemporary significance. Both books arose directly out of Geoffrey's constant confrontation with the spiritual problems of people outside the enclosing walls of churches. As a consequence, both books seem quite exceptionally real, in the sense of lighting up questions which belong to the very stuff of existence. Both cry aloud for quotation; both are rich in aphorism, which together suggest formidable qualities. Thus, in *The Word and the Work*:

"The world and the life of men have meaning and purpose. At its heart the world is not mad; but sane. That is the bare minimum of faith for man. If that goes, everything goes, and we can neither live nor think about life; but only take a long time to die."

Or again; "Nobody worries about Christ as long as he can be kept shut up in churches. He is quite safe there. But there is always trouble if you try to let him out."

Or once again, from *The Wicket Gate*:

"However difficult it may be — and it is difficult — to see and to realise the unity of the secular and the sacred, it remains true that to see it and to realise it is the essence of religion."

"This book will make people *think*," the Bishop of London said of *The Word and the Work*. It was a true judgment, still valid. The pity is that there were not more books of Geoffreys. For the need is still great in every generation for the very special kind of approach which they represent, at once exciting and illuminating, to the vast army of those who are yet prepared to see 'yonder shining light' if only there is someone to point it out to them across the wide field of human experience.

The other two books Geoffrey managed, somehow, to produce are of lesser calibre altogether. He was right in saying, as he did in the introduction to it, that *The Warrior, the Woman and the Christ* bit off more than it could chew. The result is confused. He was attempting to think aloud over the fact that "the traditions, the habits, the conventions which surround the relation of the sexes are all breaking up, and we have nothing to put in their place". The impression is of someone attempting to cover so wide a ground of speculation that sight is lost of the original point of departure. Thus a book which begins at the fact of sex — a fact with which he admits to have been himself preoccupied for years — and of which many had spoken to him 'not a few in tears' in the course of his pastoral ministry, is soon talking about the 'Creative Conflict'. It does not quite come off, even though the justification of this discursiveness is significant. No thinking about sex, he maintains, can be straight thinking if the subject is considered in isolation from the rest of experience. When it is, it becomes an obsession. So his book is about everything, including God and the universe, because the sexual factor is itself a part of everything, including God and the universe. Much subsequent literature of sex, which has tended so often to regard the subject in clinical isolation, might well have benefited by recognition of this basic fact. But Geoffrey was before his time in this, as in other things.

His one and only novel *I Pronounce Them* sprang from one aspect of the same theme. He wrote it, he said, because he had to. And the reason for this inner compulsion lay in the many questionings which had sprung up in his mind regarding the whole nature of Christian marriage and the problems arising from its sometimes inevitable failures. "No one has really faced the problem of the 'innocent party'," he wrote, "until he has been faced with a man or woman whom he knows and loves, and been asked to decide what God's will is in their particular case . . . I have had to stand it many times, and been sick with doubt." So indeed have many other priests. So have many other men and women broken on the wheel of rigorism. The theme was a great one. Geoffrey felt passionately about it. But clearly the writing of novels was not his line. Robert Paterson, the respectable clergyman in a cathedral town which is a thinly disguised Worcester, and Jim Counihan, his friend and fellow parson who, with his "very large head, enormous dark eyes, and ugly face" is not even thinly disguised, do not as characters convince. And the plot, with its problem-demonstrating situations; Counihan's wife asking for divorce; his own desire to re-marry, and the presentation of similar problems in other characters on other levels result in a tract rather than a novel. Even so, it has its moments. The argument over the ethics of contraception in the vicarage study, with the doctor and the social worker looking with affectionate bewilderment upon a troubled parson opposing, because he feels the Church requires him to, the establishment of a family-planning clinic in his parish, faithfully reflects the process by which the

Church over the years has been brought, if reluctantly, to a sensible and humane view of this matter.

But what chiefly impresses about this honest, rather groping tale told, as Geoffrey said, "by a fool striving to help his fellow fools, and to guide their sorely wounded feet into the way of peace;" is at once its modernity and its courage. With its frank — a word not then as prostituted as now — revelation of problems still at that time by custom concealed; adultery, abortion, illicit love often truer than licit, the basic dishonesty of many social attitudes towards sex and marriage, it was far ahead of its time. It was something, after all, to put a foot through one of the windows which for so long, as in the sick-room of a Victorian consumptive, had been keeping fresh air from an unhealthy sector of society. *I Pronounce Them,* bad novel as it may have been, did just that. It was very popular, even reaching the stage in an adaptation at the Everyman Theatre.

Such, then, were the books of these years, written in snatches any time, anywhere, as the train trundled him about the country. He grew increasingly exhausted, increasingly indifferent to the many warnings that he was killing himself. "I took him to poverty-stricken Abertillery," wrote one who encountered him during a South Wales crusade, "there I left him, after he had walked through a crowded hall, mounted the platform, looked at his audience, and began: 'Are you afraid of poverty?' Ninety minutes later, when I returned from another meeting to collect him, he still held the gathering entranced. He had had no evening meal, and it was getting late. He glanced at a message I sent to the stage to say I was ready to take him to his lodging, and continued. I sent another message. When he finished, some thirty minutes later, I strode to the platform. He was surrounded with people getting his autograph.

"I took him, another day, to a mountain-side to address a huge open-air meeting. Without amplifying aids he spoke to the multitude. For two hours he got down to the root of things, in a district heading for Communism. On the way back, I tried to stop a man from forcing his way into the car. S.K. needed the opportunity for quiet. S.K. invited him in — and they talked all the way . . ."

"Wandering like Satan among the sons of men," he wrote in the Visitor's Book of the Toc H hostel where, gasping with asthma, he spent the ensuing night.

And what did it all amount to? The question can be asked about any human endeavour, and a disparaging reply is always possible. That is particularly the case, perhaps, in this whole matter of the Christian conscience and the economic order. "It is difficult, looking back — and casting aside the martyrs' crowns that have been posthumously awarded — to think that the Church's social protest in the inter-war years was anything more than the product of a sense of personal shame and financial guilt."[1]

A martyr's crown? Such a thing, as Geoffrey might well have said with one of his grins, would have looked most peculiar on his oversize head. In any event the social protest of the Church was always a periphery activity of that body, however hard William Temple might strive to move it nearer the centre. And always there was the vast, circumambient indifference of the world to contend with. Geoffrey knew, as few have known, what that meant, because he had the prophet's eyes to see. This is what he wrote of it, in a poem which, summing up the experience of these closing years of his life, beyond all others, catches the profound and mysterious sadness lying for him at the heart of things. At Golgotha, he says, men at least crucified Christ. But:

> When Jesus came to Birmingham they simply passed him by,
> They never hurt a hair of him, they simply let him die;
> For men had grown more tender, and they would not give
>   him pain,
> They only just passed down the street, and left him in the
>   rain.
> Still Jesus cried, "Forgive them, for they know not what they
>   do",
> And still it rained the wintry rain that drenched him through
>   and through;

[1] Anthony Howard — in *The Baldwin Age*. Eyre & Spottiswoode. 1960.

The crowds went home and left the streets without a soul
to see,
And Jesus crouched against a wall and cried for Calvary.

Did Geoffrey sometimes cry for his own? There were many
among those who encountered him towards the end of the
twenties who had the impression of him as of a man who would
welcome release, when it came, from the burden of life which
had become too heavy, too exacting, too saddened by the insights
of a prophet, by the constant wear and tear of an uprooted,
hard-driven, anxious existence which would have tried to the
limit a physique far stronger than Geoffrey's ever was. However,
as it happened, release was very close, by the winter of 1928.

CHAPTER IX

'That's All'

ONE morning early in the March of 1929 Geoffrey came out of his house in Worcester, *en route* for the station and a train for Liverpool. At the gate he hesitated, then re-entered the house. His wife and the children were all down with 'flu. He was ill himself; weary to the bone, stricken with the asthma which had dogged him through the years. And now he was nagged by the anxiety of leaving the family sick. He went upstairs; looked down at his wife, asking her if she could manage; if he should go. Half reassured, a moment later he left the house, and this time did not turn back. He had begun his last journey. A few days later, in the early hours of Friday, March 8th, in a bedroom at St. Catherine's Vicarage, Abercromby Square, Liverpool, he died.

Of course, he should not have set out. But then, there were many things he should not have done, for years past, if ever he were to know fullness of days. Yet for him any self-saving, anything other than an utter self-giving, was out of character. He had to burn out, like one of the Verey lights of the old front, in the old war. And now his light was arcing down in the last moments of its trajectory, before being swallowed up forever in the darkness. He had for some time past been well aware he was nearing his limits. "Worn out; but not worked out" was how he described himself. And speaking at Wallasey for the last time from a public platform, he had ended with the words:

> Christ, though my hands be bleeding,
> Fierce though my flesh be pleading,
> Still let me see thee leading,
> Let me build on!

He had gone to Liverpool to give a series of Lenten addresses at Liverpool Parish Church, but soon had to take to his bed. By the Thursday, although very ill, he was holding on. But then, quite suddenly, the tired heart finally gave in. Mrs. Studdert Kennedy, summoned from Worcester, travelled through the night only to find him unconscious at her arrival. By dawn he had gone. The press of Saturday, March 9th, reflected a sorrow quite extraordinary in its intensity.

One thing became immediately apparent. Geoffrey had been a national figure to a degree which would probably have astonished him more than anyone else. The fact was soon made plain — touchingly, surprisingly so. A decent regret usually attends the passing of the captains and the kings of this world. The right, the expected things are said, the dignities of a formal mourning are observed from afar by the passing crowds. Only occasionally does a death seem to draw from those crowds themselves some special reaction, expressed in simple emotional acts.

The obsequies of Geoffrey, which were elaborate and prolonged, gave rise to many instances of such.

They began in Liverpool itself, when his body was taken from the vicarage to St. Catherine's church to lie before the altar. Throughout that Friday some two thousand people of all sorts and conditions, including a coloured man wearing his war-medals, passed through the church. The following morning two hundred were at the early celebration. Afterwards, at the removal of the coffin for its journey to Worcester, some man unknown stepped forward to lay a packet of Woodbines on it, and passengers on the ferry by which it was taken across the river were moved to take part in a short service before the boat set out. At Worcester the body was taken to St. Paul's in Geoffrey's old parish, where the streets were packed to receive it, and where, among those who kept continuous watch by the coffin through night as well as day, were many of those drawn from the characteristic army of the period — the unemployed. A detachment of these, mustered at the Labour Exchange, marched in the enormous funeral procession which left the Cathedral, whither Geoffrey's body had in the meanwhile been taken, on the following Tuesday.

That was a funeral long remembered in Worcester; the silent streets, the shuttered shops, the crowds lining the route all the two miles to the cemetery; the wreaths with the sentimental notes: 'To a fallen comrade'; 'To Woodbine Willie'; 'To a man'. There were hundreds of them. And perhaps these, for all their crudity, were nearer the true nature of the man to whom they sought to pay tribute than the royal telegram which expressed the King's sympathy. The same could be said of the memorial services. There was a distinguished one at St. Martin in the Fields, another at Liverpool Cathedral, another at Bristol, another at Manchester. There was also one held, for some reason or other, maybe because of some warm memory he had left there, at Risca, in a South Wales deep in the depression. There was a parade on that occasion of a scout troop; 'Woodbine Willie's Own', and it is possible to feel that this among them all would most have appealed to Geoffrey.

But the world had not quite finished with him yet. After the funeral, after the memorial services, there was still some clearing-up to be done. The family, for one thing, was left in a difficult situation. There were two younger sons still to be educated and, though Geoffrey from his writings had in his final years made a fair income, he had given most of it away. This habit had never ceased. When at St. Edmunds he had been given a cheque for £200 as an Easter gift, he gave it immediately, somewhat to the indignation of the donors, to the Miners' Distress fund then in operation. Such property as he did possess he left, in a will written on the torn-off page of a field service notebook, to his wife. But he had at least been rich in friends, some of whom, including Temple of York, Davidson of Lambeth, and Kirk of the Industrial Christian Fellowship, launched a memorial fund appeal. They asked for £7,000; they received more, and one of the first to respond was the King. After that, here and there, memorial tablets appeared. That in Worcester Cathedral says all there is to say:

"Geoffrey Anketell Studdert Kennedy, M.C., a poet; a prophet, a passionate seeker after truth; an ardent advocate of Christian fellowship, Chaplain to H.M. King George V, Chaplain to the

Forces, Rector of St. Edmunds King and Martyr in the City of London, sometime Vicar of St. Paul's in this city. Born 27 June 1883, died March 8, 1929."

Meanwhile, there had been appearing in the press at home and abroad a great number of appreciations of Geoffrey. Most of them were endeavours to approach somewhere near the truth of what his essential nature had been, and it is clear that many of the writers found the undertaking difficult. The problem was to find points of comparison. Thus the Bishop of Kensington, preaching at the memorial service at St. Martin's: "He was quite unlike anyone else. He combined in his personality so many striking elements that there was in him something entirely original . . ."

What was it? That is the basic question, and it has never been answered. Perhaps it never can be answered, even though it is a matter of import, even fascination, since here was one who somehow seemed able, without for a moment getting his feet off the ground, to testify to the absolute reality and the absolute relevance of God. Partly, maybe, the answer lay in his insight into the truth that sacred and secular are one, so that no one in fact lives on the one side or the other of a fence dividing one from the other. There is no fence. So he was able, to a rare degree, to see God in all things, to see the divine, revealed in the common things of life, giving to all a dignity and significance.

But thus to define one of his master ideas — which in any event was not peculiar to him — is not to draw much nearer that absolute originality of which the Bishop of Kensington spoke. Certainly, he fitted into no ecclesiastical mould. "He was much more than a great Churchman," said *The Daily News*, "if indeed he really was that at all: he was a great Christian." And *The Scots Observer* well expressed the difficulties of tying any labels on him when it said: "To many of his friends he was a constant enigma. They disliked much of the freedom which he took with language and ideas; but the love which bubbled over from his heart they could not but love in return." Even so, there were revealing things written of him. Kirk, Dick Sheppard, F. R. Barry, and J. K. Mozley, each had something to contribute to the task of trying to form an overall picture of him. Kirk especially, spoke of two aspects of Geoffrey's character which seemed so oddly contrasted; the pugnacity which made him relish putting plain truths into plain words without fear of the often considerable consequences, and a "Franciscan simplicity, a wedding to purity, a kinship with all created things which endeared him to all who knew him as the same qualities endeared the Saint of Assisi to his friends." Kirk wrote as one who had loved Geoffrey greatly, so some partiality may be allowed. But the article does contain one very significant quotation from the last article Geoffrey had written for the I.C.F. journal — a passage which gives some indication of the price in mental and spiritual tension which had to be paid, which had for years been paid by him, in the ceaseless attempt to measure his faith against the facts of life as he saw them. "Every man, whether Christian or not, must sooner or later stand in the last ditch face to face with the final doubt. I know that last ditch well. I have stood in it many a time; and I know that before I die I shall stand there again — and again."

Both Barry and Mozley stressed the element of the prophet in Geoffrey, and perhaps it is here that the true source of his originality is to be found. The true prophet, as Mozley said, is a student of life who penetrates to its meaning in the light of the knowledge of God. The definition fitted Geoffrey exactly. But there was more to it than that. "The true prophet." Mozley added, "is one who sees life truly and does not speak smooth things to obscure the truth. He of whom we are thinking saw most truly one of the profoundest facts of life — its continual tension in all human relations, which inevitably involves the presence of suffering ... He gave no easy message; his sympathy for all sufferers cost him dear; but he never suggested that there was any means of evading the tension, conflict and suffering of life ... Geoffrey Studdert Kennedy did not spare himself. He bore the pain of his unflinching, open-eyed struggle to penetrate to the heart of things ... His sole concern was with facts as they are, and against them he sought no protection."

It was true also that his message seemed to come upon him from 'outside'. Many commentators made this point. Often he seemed possessed, used as an instrument by a force which he shrank from because it exhausted him so utterly. His friends dreaded the effects of these visitations upon him. However, as Barry said, "When God raises up a prophet for us, we do not stone him or persecute him; we either ignore him or kill him with overwork." And Geoffrey was never ignored. "Too little has been written," was Dick Sheppard's conclusion to a moving appreciation in *The Times*, "about this great and good man who could fill the largest hall in England. Those who went to hear him would never have come away saying merely 'what an orator!' They would have been conscious of having heard a voice that spoke to their very souls and said 'Thou art the man'."

But what was Geoffrey's message? What did the voice say? Characteristically, it was Temple who in aftertimes, when the emotion aroused by Geoffrey's death had long calmed down, set himself the task of sorting out into lucid order the main elements of it. There were, Temple considered, three such elements. They concerned Geoffrey's ideas of Society, of the Church, and of God. But before outlining any of them Temple made two important points. In the early twenties, Geoffrey's attraction was that of an oddity living on a wartime reputation. It generally required, however, only a very short contact with him to find, behind the eccentricity, behind what a later age would have called his gimmicks — and these diminished with time — a hunger and thirst after righteousness which compelled respect. Geoffrey was also, Temple considered, a student and thinker who knew what he was talking about, and took immense pains to know.

As to his ideas of society, it was inevitable, given the conditions of the twenties, to look first for the road to social justice through changes in the economic order. This might be called, perhaps, the political phase of his thinking. He never entirely abandoned it. The whole shape of the West's acquisitive society he was condemning long before it had become fashionable, not to say safe, to do so on Christian grounds. His voice inveighing against 'your dirthy money' and its power, or stating that the only grounds for any sense of social superiority — if indeed such existed—lay in the fact of superior services to the community; He loathed our acquisitive society; he feared it; found repulsive to live with all those status-symbols based on inequalities of possession, whether of goods or power, which most of us accept as part of the natural order. He could be anguished at being called 'sir' and having his bag carried, not because he deserved the title or was incapable of carrying the bag, but because he may-be for once looked good for a tip. Such sensitivity can appear absurd. Maybe it is absurd. But it is part of the price, part of the process, of seeing things as they are, and life as it is from the uncomfortable standpoint of divine justice.

Such, then, was the first stage in the development of his philosophy of society. But as time passed its economic and political emphasis merged into something much deeper as he came to feel that society could never be changed until the men making it were changed. The operative word here is 'feel'. Many have maintained the basic premise—that inner change must precede outward reform. The difference here was the intensity of personal realisation with which the truth gripped Geoffrey as the numbers increased of the men and women who came to him, to show him their sores and to seek, never in vain, his comfort and advice. Thus it was his ministry to countless individuals which saved him from the fate of the doctrinaire, which is too often to theorise without first-hand knowledge of the instruments by which, and by which alone, the theories may be turned into practice.

So Geoffrey's great brown eyes grew sadder as the years passed, and the full truth about human-nature seemed to stand revealed. Any just order of society would, it seemed, be a long time a-coming, even if it ever arrived at all, if its architects and subsequent inhabitants had to be these extraordinary, unpredict-able, neurosis-ridden, vicious, dangerous, loving and pathetic creatures, men and women, with their inconvenient habits of hating and loving each other, of sinking to surprising depths and rising to astonishing heights. Inevitably it becomes difficult, as Geoffrey discovered, to build too many hopes on any blue-print for human society, which leave out of account the guilt-ridden, the sexually deranged, the power-hungry, the alcoholic, the chronically lonely, the incurably ill, the snob, the poseur, the man with a criminal record and bright smile – in other words the whole lamentable, heart-breaking yet strangely heart-warming procession of suffering humanity.

Thus the emphasis of Geoffrey's interests passed from the outer to the inner condition of man as realisation came to him that, while, to quote Temple: "Economic conditions are among the forces moulding the moral tendencies of those who are subjected to them; far more deeply true is it that those conditions themselves are rooted in a moral state and outlook, which must therefore be the first object of attack."[1]

That last word is perhaps unfortunate as suggestive of some brisk frontal assault upon the difficulties arising from human nature's nature. Such was for Geoffrey's thinking. Like many another, he came to see that, while human relationships were critical to any human future, their problems were not really soluble on the human level. The only destination for the procession of humanity, carrying its halt and its lame, was the foot of the Cross. So the Church came to be for Geoffrey, with all its faults and monstrous inadequacies, the hope of the world because it was the repository and the guardian of a faith which, he came more and more to feel, alone seemed to make any sense of life.

So the Church was for him the place where sacred and secular were mysteriously intermingled. If all material phenomena were for Geoffrey expressions of spirit, he was equally suspicious of anything spiritual which appeared to have no material counterpart. Temple was especially illuminating at this point. Thus, writing of Geoffrey's Eucharistic teaching: "He held the full catholic doctrine – real Presence, Sacrifice, Communion, We take the Bread (so he taught us) and offer it, that it may be to us the very Body of Love. But while most catholic doctrine lays its stress on what the Bread becomes to us, he laid equal stress on what it was to begin with, which enables it to become that other and greater thing. Bread is the common food of men; but it is

[1] G. A. *Studdert Kennedy: By His Friends.*

220

first the fruit of man's labour ... So the Eucharist is the focus, the gathering into a single spiritual act, of all the meaning of human life, all the aspiration towards the perfected civilisation."[1]

As was noted earlier, this aspect of Geoffrey's teaching seemed to have particular appeal for Temple, and is re-echoed in certain of his own. It was at any rate representative of Geoffrey's thinking upon the Church, upon the whole sacramental view of things, not indeed as they are, but as they could be. The Church, in short, was a society in which love was at work, and with love comes understanding and forgiveness. As to the Church on its human level, as it appears from outside in the here and now, Geoffrey never seemed as concerned as some of his contemporaries about its inadequacies. True, he played his part in *Life and Liberty*; but there is no equivalent in his writing of Sheppard's *Impatience of a Parson*. He was concerned with larger, more fundamental concepts. The organisation of the body whereby those concepts had to be mediated to the world was not a primary concern of his at any time. Always a great christian, necessarily a churchman, he was never an ecclesiastic.

Last of all, because basic to all, was his conception of God. A great stretch of experience separated the Geoffrey who died in that Liverpool vicarage from the ingenuous, newly-posted padre who had once been moved to such furious thought by the simple question of a wounded man in an Amiens hospital; 'what is God like?' He never really ceased from developing his answer. Nor, let it be said, did he shrink from the possibility that God did not exist. This was, in fact, the last ditch which he knew so well, where he had stood often. It was the place where the appalling possibility loomed up, like some strongpoint in the old war, in the grey dawn of a scrupulously honest facing of facts, before the rum-ration of wishful thinking had got around, that the whole concept was a man-made myth. Geoffrey's very extensive psychological studies—he had been occupied with them as long ago as his teaching days—brought him nought,

[1] *Ibid.*

or at any rate little enough, for his comfort here. So he had written:

> Suppose it is not true,
> And Jesus never lived—

What he did was to pledge the whole of himself to the proposition that in fact it was true. Faith, he was never tired of saying, was a gamble. He bet his life, as he said, upon one side in life's great war. How could he be proved right? How could God be 'proved'? He must often and often have been asked this—the stock question from the crowd. The very manner of his reply, in one of the best of his verses, *Faith,* echoes the give and take of the street-corner stand,

> It isn't proved, you fool, it can't be proved.
> How can you prove a victory before
> It's won? How can you prove a man who leads
> To be a leader worth the following,
> Unless you follow to the death?

And that, of course, was exactly what he did. It follows, that such ideas as he developed of the nature of God are worthy of respect because they were fought for so hard, and tested so rigorously. It further follows that those strange evidences, conveyed in many different ways which many noted—that he walked very close—too close for comfort—to a living Christ, are all the more moving. The outsize compassion, the soul-shaking sorrows, the natural affinity with the poor and the dispossessed, the anger with the money-changers, the fascination of him for certain intellectuals who from time to time, like Nicodemus, felt constrained to find out what this odd bird had to say, even his death, worn out and despairing, all had, and have, a peculiar look about them.

'The great illumination', as Temple calls it, which came to Geoffrey in his search for an answer to the question put to him in the hospital at Amiens, was that God is personally involved with the sufferings of mankind. That was his master-theme always. And if that has not been made clear already in these pages then they have failed badly to tell their tale. He was groping for it in his discussions with Mozley when a young man. He worked his way to it through the war and afterwards. God was transcendent, certainly; he was indeed 'the kingdom, the power, and the glory', the towers of York and Bach's *Mass in B Minor*! But he was not remote. No vague 'one above' he was not indifferent to the fate of his creation. He was immanent, pervading all things, involved in all things. And his self-identification with suffering invested that suffering with a mysterious dignity and significance. So the Cross, with an empty tomb and a risen Christ beyond, was the centre of things for Geoffrey, at the end, as at the beginning.

That end, all things considered, with its weariness and sense of failure, was a highly suitable one. It is difficult not to feel that if Geoffrey had gone on to be in any sense a 'success', as the world understands that word; the holder of dignity and position, it would somehow have done violence to that feeling about him which so many treasured so much — that he was so oddly like the Master whom he tried to serve. That being so, it would have been a pity if he had marred the picture by appearing to climb any particular ladder, or becoming respected, or comfortable.

But it was all right. All these dangers he successfully avoided. Perhaps that was his only success. Certainly, he thought of himself as a monumental failure as he looked back over the way he had come. And this sense of failure, a little while before he died, he allowed to spill over into verse. They were among his last written words. Let them be so in this story:

> It is not finished, Lord.
> There is not one thing done,
> There is no battle of my life,
> That I have really won.
> And now I come to tell thee
> How I fought to fail,
> My human, all too human, tale
> Of weakness and futility . . .

I cannot read this writing of the years,
My eyes are full of tears,
It gets all blurred, and won't make sense,
It's full of contradictions
Like the scribblings of a child . . .
I can but hand it in, and hope
That thy great mind, which reads
The writings of so many lives,
Will understand this scrawl
And what it strives
To say—but leaves unsaid.

I cannot write it over,
The stars are coming out,
My body needs its bed.
I have no strength for more,
So it must stand or fall, dear Lord
    That's all.